Trailer Park *to* White House

Credit for Book Design Cover – Rupa Limbu

~ Trailer Park to White House ~

I want to thank God for this hard, but amazing life He blessed me with. God gave me this book title 4+ years ago so I began writing, stopped writing when I was told my writing was horrible, started completely over, wrote on the weekends and weeknights, and poured my heart into this book a little at a time. I never stopped pursuing this endeavor even when I was afraid of what others would think or when I became unsure of myself. It's been difficult to finish because this book is making me vulnerable to people's opinions and criticisms; and being vulnerable is scary, which is why so few people do it. But, I stayed with the task and have finally bloomed after growing through a whole lot of dirt.

I want to thank Major Padgett for editing my life story. Major Padgett made my words readable. He organized my thoughts into something that made sense. Major Padgett encouraged me and consistently held me accountable. Thank you for the many conversations and for helping my words turn into form. I want to thank Jason Stebbins for being my ghost reader. He made my words become clear and relevant for civilians. He's kind beyond words and encouraged me to keep going when I wanted to stop. I asked many people for help, but they were the only two people that actually did help. A THANK YOU would never be enough. Your kindness made my book come to life! Thank you for helping in making my dream become reality.

I want to thank Christian for sticking with me and supporting me in all the dreams I chase. You've been with me since this book vision started and I'm so thankful for you. You love me and I love you. You're my best friend. It's just us!

Last but not least, I want to thank the United States Air Force for giving me a life worth living, giving me a military family, and allowing me to wear the uniform. It's an honor!

I chose the pseudonym "Asher Shannon" because I am serving in the military and have many years left to wear the great uniform. Also, the name "Asher" in the Bible means "Happy" and I thought Happy Shannon was fitting for a name.

If this book can help at least one person then it was worth the time, sacrifice, and tears. My hope is that you learn from the pain I endured and from the mistakes I made, and then be able to apply my lessons learned to your life. As a result, you would be able to possibly overcome one or the many issues you could be dealing with.

Remember, I'm not a writer so please be kind with the criticism, negative opinions, and judgement.

Table of Contents

Trailer Park

Introduction - Hi!
1 - Unwanted, Unloved
2 - Homeless and Hopeless
3 - Sperm Donor
4 - Mother Dearest
5 - Sticks and Stones
6 - Glimpse of Kindness
7 - People Will Not Like You, Shocker!
8 - A Thorn Among Roses
9 - Innocence Stolen
10 - Life Sucks….Embrace It
11 - Surface Deep
12 - Everyone gets a Trophy
13 - Turning Point
14 - I had no one, but me
15 - Defeat is Fuel
16 - Jesus
17 - You'll never amount to anything
18 - Victim or Victor
19 - Relationships are Tough
20 - Jail or Air Force
21 - Coward
22 - Not a Doormat
23 - You're Fat!
24 - Beautiful Disaster
25 - Goodbye
Transition - Mess to Message

White House

1 - Sink or Swim
2 - Managers Solve Problems…Leaders Change Lives
3 - Three Times a Charm
4 - Rescued
5 - My Person
6 - Lott of Lessons
7 - I'm Not Good Enough
8 - Jealousy
9 - Difficult is Remembered
10 - Gunshot to the Chest - Suicide
11 - Pain is Real
12 - Pentagon and Congress
13 - Courage
14 - White House
15 - Frenemy
16 - President and First Lady
17 - Love
18 - Air Force Kicked Me Out
19 - Who am I?
20 - Less is More
21 - Not everyone is a Superstar
22 - Biggest Winner
23 - Life Coach
24 - Major Debacle
25 - Fear
Closing - Not done yet!

Introduction – Hi!

Trailer Park to White House is a self-help autobiography based on the first 40-years of my life. I divided my story into two parts. The first part covers the struggles in my childhood. I had to dig deep within to overcome thinking I would never be worthy or good enough. My damaged thinking was ingrained into my DNA until finally leaving for the Air Force's basic military training when I was seventeen. It wasn't until I left the unhealthy environment I grew up in that I began to understand how the hardships had molded me into a resilient and unique person. Although I endured much heartache in my childhood, I know 'now' each tear made me wiser, kinder, better, and stronger.

The second half of this book is very different because I show how I took the stumbling blocks of my past and turned them into the building blocks of my future. They show the growth I undoubtedly gained within my character, maturity, moral compass, and humanity. Together, both parts of this book give the reader insight into how I transformed every struggle in my life into a lesson learned. I humbly believe if my life lessons can help at least one person then I've fulfilled my destiny. All I want to do is help others achieve their highest potential. For every person feeling they have nothing, I hope after reading this book they know they can become whatever they choose to be.

My story is to *inspire* you to dream, to dream big, and to go after your dreams. Let nothing stand in the way of your destiny. Never take "no" for an answer unless you have exhausted all your options. However, continue to seek more ways and to try again for the sake of your dreams.

My story is about *hope*. I came from nothing and ended up working at the White House. Anything is possible. You must work hard, never settle, always do your best, keep pushing through the peaks and valleys, have a vision, know your worth and believe it, leave the past and negatives behind, trust in your ability, use your talents and gifts (you were given them after all) for the betterment of mankind, share the knowledge you learn with others, find your inner strength and persevere through any hardship, understand what you are capable of, play fair always, respect others, treat others as you want to be treated, and to always try your very best no matter the circumstance. Always have hope. And if you're presently down, please know that better days will come, I promise.

My story is for you to *never settle* for good when you can have great. Personally, I never want to live in a trailer park again. It's not that I am embarrassed of where I came from anymore. It's about wanting to have better for myself. In fact, I want to give my daughter what I never had growing up. I don't want her to experience what it's like wondering what you or your family will eat or how the bills will be paid. When you settle for mediocrity, you lose. Instead of fulfilling your fullest potential, you could squander your time chasing the elusive life of ease and comfort. Friend, it's not good enough to *live* life when you can <u>*thrive*</u> in life.

My story is for you to know you *can ask for help* and not be ashamed. When you have nothing, you must let pride fall and be willing to seek assistance. Be open to receiving help from others. Don't be ashamed or embarrassed by your situation. One day you may be able to return the favor. Life throws us lemons all the time because life is hard, unfair, and people can be mean. When lemons are thrown, learn how to make lemonade. One note of caution: please don't abuse assistance because that's when it could turn into selfishness.

My story is about a person crawling from the lowest social class and being able to stand saying, "*I did it*" in a proud, but humble manner. I worked hard, harder than anyone I know. For you, know what you want, go after it, earn it, and make no excuses so you can say, "I did it!" You can do it! The struggle to get to the end of the rainbow is worth the pot of gold!

My story is about *generosity*. With no family to push me or help me, I had to learn the value of generosity through strangers. I've had specks of kindness shine throughout my life, which touched my heart and made me a better person. I'm forever grateful. When you have nothing, your eyes are opened to poverty and it emboldens you to help everyone. I want to give back just like those who gave to me.

My story is about *strength*. You find out who you are when faced with adversity. You roll up your sleeves, wake up early, and fight your way through each day. When you only have yourself to depend on, you know what needs to be done and you do it. What I learned, sadly, is people rarely care about you or your future. They're too busy caring about themselves. Therefore, you must take life by the horns, climb over the walls (or break through them), and apply your own strengths. You can do anything if you put your mind to it. Self-esteem is the key to success in any endeavor. So stop living small, smile more, and believe in yourself because you're awesome! When you live large, your self-esteem grows and you ultimately become a forest of strength.

My story is about *adventure* and unexpected events. You never know how Mother Nature's going to get your attention, how opportunities will present themselves, or what's behind doors 1, 2, or 3. It's life. Therefore, don't get stuck in a Groundhog Day scenario repeatedly doing the same thing day-in and day-out. It gets old. Instead, find joy in unexpected events as they are the spice of life. Adventure, happiness, and soul-pleasure can be found in these unexpected events as they occur each day. Try to see them as the best moments of your life, or at least the most memorable.

My story is about *learning* from poor decision-making. Yes, I've made mistakes, plenty! Haven't we all? But, did we learn from them and not repeat them? I didn't. I've been a repeat offender many times. Now at the age that I am, I have learned the importance of good decision making. I ask how, why, what's the reason, what will be the outcome, who is affected, and how will this play a role in my short-term and long-term goals? Yes, I made a lot of mistakes, but 'now' I truly understand the importance of weighing all of the pros and cons before making a big decision. It matters, believe me.

My story is about *love*. No matter what happens in life, things can turn out wrong, people may hurt you, your job may suffocate you, people may lie, things you believe to be good may not be, and dreams may crumble for some unknown reason. No matter the circumstance, you must always start by loving yourself. If all else fails it will be the one thing that keeps you going. Loving yourself when tides are storming in, when people let you down, when you get fired, or when your loved one irreparably breaks your heart is extremely vital to overcoming whatever is thrown your way. When you love yourself, everything is possible. Self-love is the root of your strength to carry you through the storm, even when there is nowhere to go or no one to turn to. Your love for yourself maybe all you ever really have.

My story is about things working out better than one could ever *imagine* or dream of. I never thought I would make it to where I am, experienced the things I've done, or accomplish my unrealistic dreams. I've discovered the peak you're about to reach on the mountain you're climbing usually has another peak after it hidden from view. I've learned to keep climbing until you can't climb anymore. *The world is your Mt. Everest.* Dreams do come true! **Climb and conquer!**

It is my hope that you would trust in these life lessons, adopt them as your own, and build on them. In life, don't we all build on each other anyway? If not, we really should!

Remember every day is a fresh start, a new beginning. Every day is a new opportunity to become what we desire. Regardless of how filthy your past has been, your future is still spotless. Don't start your day with the broken pieces of yesterday. This is your life and you've got to fight for it. Fight for what's right. Fight for what you believe in. Fight for what's important to you. Fight for the people you love (and please don't forget to tell them how much they mean to you).

Put your hand over your heart, do you feel it? You still have a purpose and time. Realize how blessed you are because you still have a chance to do something because you're still here. Stop for a moment and think. Whatever you still need to do, start doing it today. There are only so many tomorrows and tomorrow is not even guaranteed.

You are more powerful than you know. Take back your mental, emotional, and spiritual power by saying, "I will survive. I will thrive. I am forging ahead because giving up is not who I am. I will stay the course and persist until I succeed." Repeat this to yourself daily. Speak it from deep within your spirit and your soul. You might have to do this while down on your knees, praying, crying, or screaming at the top of your lungs. Nonetheless, look at yourself in the mirror every single day and say, "I love you" and promise to act like it. It's important to be nice to others, but it's even more important to be nice to yourself. When you act as your own best friend, you allow yourself to be happy. When you are happy, you become a better friend, a better family member, and you inspire others around you to be better too.

Resist the feeling of being overwhelmed, powerless, or being a victim. Choose to proclaim victory instead!

Life may take you over some bumps, cause some bruises, drop you into potholes, or hang you over cliffs, but don't let it clip your wings, scare you into submission, or eradicate the power you have in making your dreams become reality.

Believe you can make a difference…right here...right now…with your voice and your story! Believing in yourself is key to life and it can open a door to a brighter future. Remember that self-doubt is the barrier you place in front of the door and it can be removed with a positive mindset thus making it possible for you to laugh, love, and live again. Most important of all, remember when you walk out the door into the dark world that You Matter.

Everyone will write your story if you let them. Instead pick up the pen and write your own story. You are in charge of your present and your future. What happens going forward is because you have allowed it. Choose wisely…your future life depends on the choices you make today.

~ ~ ~

So, now it's time for the first part of my story. I experienced many emotions while writing this book and if you're like me, be ready to laugh, cry, cheer, yell, etc. Emotions get you to think because they make you exposed.

So here we go! Let your guard down and be vulnerable with me.

While reading, think about your situation and how you could try to apply the lessons learned in your life. Some of my testimony may help you in resolving, avoiding, or bettering what you may be going through or potentially go through.

Hugs to you, my dear friend, for taking this journey with me.

I. Trailer Park

Chapter 1 – Unwanted, Unloved

Wow....Where do I begin? It was a lifetime ago, but worth every detail because I believe it's important for us to remember where and how we began in life. We must know where we've been, what has happened, and how it is all relative to where we are now and where we want to end up.

I was brought into this world to save my parents' marriage. My mother was so emphatically determined with saving their marriage that she stood on her head after intercourse to get pregnant with me. Can you visualize a woman standing on her head immediately after intercourse? It was somewhat unorthodox, but after a few tries of head standing it worked! Yes, it's true so laugh away. Okay, let's stop visualizing now. My parents already had my 3-year old sister when I was born along with my father's other kids. However, my mother was desperate and thought I would be the answer to her prayers. Contrary to her initial belief, I turned out to be a disappointment to her and to my family.

When my parents initially met, my father swept my mother off her feet and convinced her to leave Arkansas and move to Louisiana to be with him. After the move, my parents began to have a volatile marriage consisting of mental, physical, and emotional abuse. According to my mother, their fighting was because of my father being older and thinking he knew everything. In retrospect, I see that as control and manipulation. To note, I never got my father's side of the story so it's all I ever really knew about their relationship. My mother was tired of being under my father's heavy fist and verbal attack, not to mention his cheating on her. I was supposed to be the answer to hope, happiness, and health in their marriage and ultimately restore peace, but it didn't work out that way.

The divorce was inevitable because my father beat my mother so severely while she was pregnant with me, she had to be hospitalized. I believe this was the turning point in their marriage that led to its demise. Instead of my birth saving their marriage, I played a big role in them splitting up. The fortunate part of it for me was my mother standing on her head and me being born. The unfortunate part was within two weeks after giving birth my parents divorced, which portrayed a role in my abandonment struggles.

I'm proud of my mother for having the guts to leave my father. She was faced with leaving the security of a house and taking a 3-year old and a brand new baby to begin a new life. It was also stupid because she left us vulnerable and anything could have happened. But what do you tell a scared 23-year old woman with two small children to make her feel everything was going to be okay…nothing! She didn't have any family to help. It was just her and us. Our first home after she divorced was in her car. If you ponder her situation for a moment, it's actually quite amazing to see the strength she had at a time of total uncertainty. Of course I only know my mother's side of the story because my father wasn't a part of our lives after I was born and when he did come around the past was never mentioned.

We eventually moved into our new home, a trailer, and my father and half-siblings would occasionally come to visit. Sadly they rarely interacted with me. At that time I was yearning for attention from anyone, but never received it. I suspect it may have been due to my circumstances of being born disabled. At birth my hands were trigger-thumbed to where my thumbs were attached to the insides of my hands.

Imagine waving at someone or even trying to hold a baby bottle….it's difficult or awkward without the use of thumbs. Imagine trying to use a computer mouse. Thank goodness we didn't have computers when I was born. I digress, sorry.

I ended up having surgery later to correct my disability, but even still, never received the love and attention I needed or wanted. I would have given my thumbs just to be held. Don't get me wrong, the surgery was great, but the love would have been better. I don't believe my family could have fathomed what a hug or holding me would have done for my self-worth? It's heartbreaking. I've learned some people with a good family take it for granted while we, on the other hand, could only hope for one.

My birth was not one to be celebrated. I was born into a family where I wasn't wanted (father), where I was only wanted to save a marriage (mother), where I infiltrated a family (half-siblings), labeled the cause of the divorce (sister), and into a world where living day-to-day was extremely tough (yay me). Talk about distress. I realize that none of it was my fault, but dealing with being despised from birth sure makes for a rocky start in life and a complex one at that. My family labeled me the black sheep and treated me as such. It was painful. I just wanted to be loved, but instead found myself confused by not knowing why the most important people in my life treated me so poorly. It took years to overcome most of it; and I would be lying if I didn't tell you that sometimes I still struggle with abandonment thinking. I'm a Work-In-Progress (WIP).

I may have been too young to understand all of that back then, but looking back at it I would say it was probably hard being a baby, living in a car right after I was born, having a mother recovering from a beating, and having a 3-year old sibling despise me. Even though my birth created hardship back then, I am thankful for how I started out in the world. I grew up with less than a silver spoon in my mouth and because of it I discovered the true meaning of an earned life.

The hardships I endured helped me gain my independence and strength while loneliness taught me the love I have for myself can be enough. These attributes carried me throughout my life, which resulted in *perseverance* during struggle, *hopefulness* during heartache, and *generosity* towards others when having hardly anything to spare.

Moral of the Story – If you have a kid, do it for love. You must be sure it is what you want and it's not for selfish reasons. It is a decision you're making for the rest of your life, not just for yourself, but for another person. Having a kid isn't for saving your marriage or your life…you're an adult…you do that on your own. If you're having kids for any other reason than love, it is truly not fair to the innocent child. The world is bad enough as it is without bringing innocent kids into the mix to save you. You must save yourself.

If you are not feeling wanted or loved by your family, know it isn't your fault. If you haven't done anything wrong, you must realize it's their problem, not yours. Keep being you. If they end up loving you, great! If not, let it go because you can't do anything about it anyway. You will only doubt yourself and you will constantly analyze why they didn't love you. You must come to terms with it and simply accept what is. <u>Your love for yourself is enough</u>.

I'm being brutally honest with my words because sugar-coating anything won't help you heal from the abandonment. Please know I'm only trying to help those of us who feel unloved. As someone who has always wanted love, I can relate to the pain of feeling abandoned and unloved. It may seem like the pain you deeply feel will never go away, but once you accept what is, you will eventually heal. However, until you come to terms with everything, I am sending you a big hug. My heart cries out to you and for you because I was at the point where you are now. Time does heal all wounds.

Please know that no matter what has happened, you were made for a reason. You are amazing. You are here for a purpose. You have talents and strengths no one else has. You have something to offer. You are loveable. You are good. **You are a gift,** a very precious gift.

You are here for a reason, alive and astonishing. You really do have the courage and strength required to make your life count despite how your life started, and the poor decisions once made. Your ending is your new story.

Once you turn 18-years old, you can no longer blame anyone (your parents, teachers, friends, family, relationships, etc.) for how your adult life ends up because the decisions you make are the ones you choose. There can't be a blame game because when you point a finger at others, you have 3 fingers pointing back at you. You're an adult; therefore, it's time for you to take accountability and responsibility. This is tough love.

Bottom line - You can spend your entire life blaming the world, but your successes and failures are entirely your own responsibility.

Friend, it doesn't matter how your life starts, it only matters how it ends.

Chapter 2 – Homeless and Hopeless

When you're two weeks old you don't recall much, let alone living in a car. Yes, my mother, sister, and I lived in my mother's car after I was born. For how long, I'm not sure, but either way I know it was a small living space for a car. I don't know what the weather at that time was like, but it probably wasn't comfortable, especially while living in the humidity of the south. I don't know how my mother and sister used the bathroom, cleaned themselves, brushed their teeth, washed their hands, or performed any other daily ritual, but I imagine it wasn't pretty. Suffice it to say, living in a car is a last resort to living on the street when you have nothing else to your name.

I was a newborn with a car seat for a bed, at least I hope. I can't fathom how my mother felt with having two small kids to tend to, let alone herself, and with no one to help. I imagine she was scared, embarrassed, hungry, or maybe even in pain, but thankfully it was shelter and any protection is better than living on the street. We were a family, destitute and alone. We didn't want to be in the position we were in, but had no other choice. It was extremely humbling and taught me over the years to appreciate everything I have. One distinct lesson I took away was when you pass someone living on the street, don't laugh at them or pass judgement; instead open your heart and extend a hand. Give them the benefit of the doubt, they may have had no other choice.

As for our family living in that car, we were finally saved, so to speak. Some hero, unbeknownst to me, rescued us from our dreaded abode and moved us into a trailer. I'm not sure who it was, but I wish I knew so I could thank him or her. To this day they are definitely an angel in my book who saved us from a world of darkness and pain. For me personally, this person's giving heart will always be remembered in a good light. Further, it's one of the reasons why I try to give as much as I can. There will always be people who need help and I implore you to help when you see people in need. *You can't take anything with you*, but you can leave a good name and reputation behind. Plus, your stroke of kindness may trigger a chain reaction within other people that could potentially reverberate compassion throughout the world. It's something to ponder. I digressed for a moment, sorry.

After our family's penance of living in a car and eventually moving into the sanctuary of a trailer, the rest of my childhood up through adolescence was spent living in trailers. At seventeen when I left, I vowed to never live in a trailer again. I have nothing against trailers, they just remind me of the pain I endured for so many years. The pain motivated me to work my bottom off to ensure I would never have to return to the pain I left. In hindsight, it made me realize the car we had to live in gave us temporary shelter and the trailer served as a more permanent one, but each in itself was just a shelter. It taught me that it's the people who live in them that make them feel like a home. Growing up, I never had a home.

Another joyful (tongue-in cheek) aspect of my home life was my mother's smoking. Imagine a trailer with the constant reek of smoke. To skip the pleasantries, the ceilings and walls were stained brown and everything smelled, including my bedroom. I had the smallest bedroom because I was the youngest and when people think small, they have no clue as to how small this one was. Let's just say I had a closet. I don't think anyone could grasp what living in a trailer is like unless they've actually lived in one. Unless you've lived in such a small space with someone who chain smokes, it's hard to comprehend the angst you experience from constantly smelling like it. If you think the trailer sounds bad, imagine what the car smelled and looked like. Aye-Kurumba!

From my experience, living in trailer parks were horrifying as a child. I had no mentors or people to look up to; nor did I have someone to give me the push I needed in life. I would have never made it out of that existence if it weren't for the choice I made in the beginning of my senior year of high school. I probably would have become a transplant into another dead-end trailer park never knowing what a promising life would have been like.

I was on the path to a life of drugs, alcohol, substandard living, no education, no goals, no dreams, and becoming just another stupid kid following in her mother's bad footsteps. I can't imagine that life anymore nor do I ever want to. I disliked the first seventeen years of my life. I felt like I was nothing. I was told I would never amount to anything and I believed it. **I felt unloved, unwanted, and hopeless**. I found when you lack hope you are lost, but having hope is sometimes all you need to move forward in life.

On a lighter note, my mother did want my sister and me and she never gave up on us even when life was hard. I used to ask her why she didn't give us a better life and adopt us out to parents that could afford us. She would always reply, "I couldn't. You both were all I had." I wouldn't be who I am today, after leaving home of course, if I didn't go through the hardship of living in a car and trailers growing up. It was a valuable lesson. It was my staunch reality. I wasn't given a silver spoon or parents who had money. I was given a life of poverty, poor-beyond-poor, and had to experience what it was like to just survive. When faced with survival, you find a way to claw, scratch, pound your way through, and do whatever it takes to live. My mother taught me how to survive in the worst of conditions and taught me the meaning of perseverance.

Being homeless and hopeless set the course of my life, but will not be how my life ends. I yearn to help every person get off the street because no one should be living in those dire conditions. I yearn to help every person know their worth, to have hope, and to trust that life can get better. Hope is a healing word and a life-giving mindset.

Moral of the Story – When you experience what it's like to have nothing, you give more freely and strive to become a selfless person. You want to help people who feel helpless. You want to give people food because you've experienced hunger. You want to educate yourself because you know what it's like to be around uneducated people. You want to pursue goals and dreams because you know what it's like to go through life aimlessly. You want financial success because you know poverty. You want to work your butt off every day because you know what it's like to live in fear, or experience the adversity of living in a car. You want to protect your kids from the negative experiences you had and vow to do anything to spare them a life of despair. You vehemently discourage smoking because you remember smelling like an ashtray. You avoid stagnant people because you know there are those out there who will push you towards your dreams. You want to persevere and thrive because you know idleness. You want to become a role model for those who never had one. You want to love people because you know what it feels like to not be loved. You want to stay away from drugs and alcohol abuse because you know how it destroys a person's life.

I know these things because of what I saw and experienced early on in my life. I would never want those things to happen to you. I only want the best for you because you deserve it. You should never have to experience the emptiness of having nothing and feeling like a nobody. People should never have to live a negative lifestyle or in an environment that deprives them of their own vitality. We are the United States of America; the world's greatest nation where no one should have to live on the street, be hungry, or go without.

Please reach for the moon and even if you don't make it, at least you will land on the stars. You only have one chance in life so make it count. You are a person of great significance so never feel hopeless. You will overcome whatever it is you are going through. Have hope with confidence for positive outcomes!

Your past should never define your future.

You got this – I believe in you!

Chapter 3 – Sperm Donor

Growing up I never got to know my father. I probably saw him a total of twenty times throughout my life. He left my sister and me when we were young babies, when I was brand new to the world. He didn't fight for us and rarely came to visit. He gave little child support money for us to live on and chose his new wife and her family over us. He never said "I love you" once to me nor called to say "hi." He never came to any of my sports events or spelling bee contest. He never read me a story, said bedtime prayers, held my hand, or gave me a real hug. He never asked me if I was okay, taught me about boys, or walked me down the aisle. He never laughed or talked with me. He did buy my sister a car, but never did anything for me. From my personal standpoint, he was never there for me and treated all of his other kids better than he treated me. With all of that said, he did contribute (well, I hope) to bringing me into the world and for that I'm grateful.

In light of all of my father's selfishness, there are a few things he did do for us. I remember him telling us a lot of jokes albeit most of them were dirty, taking us clothes shopping every once in a while, taking us to the movies and then sneaking us into a second one (not a good impression on a five-year old), and afterwards taking us to eat at Wendy's. That's about all I can recall. There was never any expression of love. It felt like a superficial office engagement.

As a young adult when I talked to God, I asked, "Why couldn't I have had a normal family? Why couldn't I have had a dad?" It's saddens me because I never knew what it was like to sit on his lap, feel protected by him, or be called a daddy's girl. I didn't know what it was like to get his opinion or thoughts on a particular subject. I always dreamed of having a dad in my life, but figured it wasn't in my cards. I always wondered why he chose to be in the jewelry business instead of the father business.

I concluded with one sad fact that I was never wanted. I used to question why, but I don't anymore. I've grown to believe that some people aren't capable of loving or being a parent and have their own reasons for not getting involved. It's not for me to wonder about anymore. I choose to believe my father had his own reasons for being good to his other kids and my older sister, yet not to me. He was their dad who bought them stuff, spent time with them, talked with them, and helped them in times of need. With me, it was like he saw a foreign object that sat curiously in the corner which he chose to ignore. He would purposely stay away, avoid getting close, or be alone with me. I was nothing to him. I felt it then, I feel it now, and will presumably feel it for the rest of my life.

One has to wonder why her parents would get divorced when she's only two-weeks old. I came up with my own hypothesis. You see, my father and my mother both have O-positive blood (universal recipient) and I have O-negative blood (universal donor). In science class, we were taught that two positives don't make a negative and since I am a negative blood type, I question if he really is my biological father? This could be the reason as to why he never treated me like his child. Who would expect a father to take care of a child who he wasn't directly responsible for? Only Saints do that!

Now that we've determined I possibly defied science to come into the world, I would like to point out there was a man who treated me like gold. I'm tearing up just thinking about him. His name was Jimmy. Jimmy thought highly of my mother and gave her odd jobs to help us out with our finances. I remember him treating me better than anyone else while I was growing up.

I never thought writing about my childhood memories would make me dig so deep emotionally. This is good therapy if anyone needs it. Just start writing about something that made a deep emotional impact in your life. It will get you to raise critical questions about your past, which in turn may lead you to the answers you've been searching for all along. Sorry for digressing, back to Jimmy.

Jimmy is the one man whom I felt shared my enthusiasm for me being born. He would hug me, buy me the biggest burger and fries, and made me feel like I was special. For once, it wasn't my sister or my father's kids being treated this way, it was just me. Looking back, Jimmy was the type of person a kid would want for a dad. He was a father figure in my life for a few years and made a tremendous and lasting impact. I will never know why he treated me so well. Maybe he felt sorry for me because he saw how my real dad never showed an ounce of compassion, love, or joy. Nonetheless, Jimmy was a kind-hearted man who showed love to a young impressionable girl that (maybe) wasn't his own. He is a testimony to what makes America so wonderful. He was the epitome of people who have big hearts and try to be there for others no matter what their circumstances are.

In my opinion, children who grow up in fatherless homes have a much greater risk of major challenges in adulthood than those who grow up with a father in the home. Children with involved fathers do better across every measure of child well-being than their peers in father-absent homes. The growing epidemic of fatherless families has taken a grave toll on children, both young and old, in the form of emotional, social, spiritual, academic, physical, criminal, and suicidal issues later on in life. That's the bottom line-- kids need to have a father who is involved. I know I needed one and still do. Tear. This should make any person pause and think about bringing kids into the world.

Being a parent is one of the greatest gifts in the world, a part of you is born and will continue living even when you take your last breath. This could become your greatest legacy. Meaning your legacy could be remembered great or rotten…it's up to you to determine what it will be.

Moral of the Story – If you had a father involved in your life growing up or even now, you are fortunate and blessed. Many kids grow up without a father figure in their life, which profoundly affects their childhood development. They don't have the role model to provide a male point of view, teach them about the world, or to guide them into adulthood.

A father is important to the family, to both sons and daughters. A father in the home is the bedrock of the family. He teaches his son how a man should look and behave; and teaches his daughter how she should be loved and cherished. Granted, this only works if the father has a good heart. We have plenty of fathers with ill intent out there doing things they know are wrong. Sorry, but it's true.

<u>Kids need their fathers</u>! If a father isn't man enough to step up and take his role seriously then he should move out of the way for a man who will or simply choose to not have kids in the first place. Fathers, please help steer your kids in the right direction; a direction that allows for goodness to prosper. Be that role model, please! Kids, along with me, are yearning for you to answer your calling.

Chapter 4 – Mother Dearest

Imagine raising two kids ages three and younger when you're 23-years old and have no one to help you. Then add the fact you only have a high-school education with no professional or vocational skills. "Difficult" would be a conservative word to use. Instead of giving up or allowing someone else to raise her two kids, my mother worked three jobs and provided for us the best she could. Sure there were countless babysitters and a 3-year old taking care of an infant, but she got it done. My mother would wake up at 3 a.m., work a full day, come home to check on us, leave again for another job, come back to check on us again, and finally go to her third job. She did this for years. She was skinny as a rail and malnourished because she usually only ate the equivalent of two bologna sandwiches (with no cheese) a day. To add to her difficulties, she lacked ample rest. Sleeping on our couch most of the time didn't help. Though we were barely making it, she always worked so we could have a place to live. We didn't have much (hardly anything), but we did have a roof over our heads.

As far as food was concerned, while I was growing up our usual diet consisted of red beans and rice every Monday, hot dogs, chips, TV dinners, soda, cookies, sweet tea, and every other imaginable cheaply processed food that came in a package the rest of the week. Thinking back, I can't believe I wasn't 200 pounds and suffering from heart disease. I never saw vegetables or fruit and didn't really discover those naturally rich foods until I was about to leave home at 17. Our eating lacked nutrients, but our thought was at least we had something to eat and our stomachs had stopped growling. My favorite thing was getting a slice of bread, smothering it with barbecue sauce, slapping on a piece of cheese and baking it in the oven. I ate a lot of it.

There were also chores to be done and because my mother wasn't home a lot, I was the designated cleaner. I kept the house spotless including my room, which became my childhood sanctuary. My kitchen duties consisted of taking everything out of the freezer and refrigerator once a month and performing a thorough cleaning, which my mother taught me. I would dust, vacuum, and do laundry once a week. I knew how to do all of this by the age of five. Nowadays, it's disheartening to know most children, teenagers, or young adults are lazy to hard work and chores. They waste their time with electronic gadgets, disconnecting themselves from the reality of human connection, and are clueless when it comes to dealing with the tough things in life. Also, there are some people who are handed everything with no sense of appreciation, let alone understanding what it's like to earn a living or to clean a refrigerator.

Like my mother, I believe in hard work. Since she worked all of the time while growing up, I never saw my mother actually get a good night's rest. This may have contributed to her always being angry. She lacked that calm, nurturing spirit one would hope to find in a mom. I think she loved us, but I figure it was tough for her to show it while working so hard to provide monetarily. Strangely she was nice to my sister, but didn't seem to have the energy or patience for me. To her chagrin, I was an extremely energetic kid, moving fast, and going ninety miles per hour with no brakes. I believe I got my energy from my mother, but she never saw it that way. She saw me as an overly rambunctious kid in contrast to my sister's relaxed, easy going spirit.

Though I hated not having a dad, it was even harder not really having my mother around. I never knew what it was like to be tucked in, woken up, or have fresh baked cookies out of the oven. I never had anyone help me with my homework, talk to me about the birds and the bees, brush my hair, take me to church, teach me how to be a lady, or just cuddle with me. Disappointed, I spent most of my time alone in my room. I was a loner, but also a survivor. It's a shame because all I wanted was to be loved and to be shown what love really was. It would have made it easier for me to know how to give love in return as I've grown into an adult.

My mother did find the time for men interestingly enough. The men in her relationships were either married or became her husband or boyfriend. I had five step-dads, not including all of her boyfriends. I'm not sure how she had time for them, but they were always around. Imagine the impression it made on us kids. I always thought she had a man in her life for one of four reasons. First, she was lonely and just wanted male companionship. Second, she needed someone to help pay the bills. Third, she needed someone to make her feel good about herself. Finally, she simply wanted to have sex. The free time she did have should have been spent loving on her kids and preparing them for life as adults. The fact of the matter is stable and healthy relationships are good. It's when they are routinely unstable they're more of a detriment than a benefit. I will never know the true reason as to why my mother chose her way of life, but I know she regrets those decisions now.

If a woman has to be in a relationship and can't stand to be alone, there's a potential problem stirring. They're also more likely to connect with bad company if no one else is around because they lower their standards. It's sad, but true.

Bad company is waiting for some vulnerable, unsuspecting soul to latch onto. Speaking as a woman, a woman should know she doesn't need a man to complete her; she needs to find the strength that can come from first completing herself. A woman needs to learn how to take care of herself before relying solely on another person for support. A woman doesn't need a man to make her happy because she should first learn to find things that foster happiness within herself. A woman should never use a man for anything. A woman should not use people, period. Note: This paragraph goes for both man and woman.

With all those men moving in and out of my mother's life, she still managed to make work a priority. She worked herself to the bone to provide for us and through it all taught me the value of hard work. I learned how to roll up my sleeves, show up early, stay late, get my hands dirty, be loyal, and work my tail off. I don't shy away from hard work; I gravitate towards it. Being a part of a team, helping others, providing for your family and yourself, doing more than expected, and trying to make yourself better is tough, but the payoff is worth it. Whatever goal it is you're striving for, give it your all to the end just like I try to do daily.

Hard work won't kill you - it will make you better. We all may have regrets in the end, but a life of hard work shouldn't be one of them.

Moral of the Story – Hard work is what this country was founded on, but the glory days are gone. In today's society, people are getting paid millions to sing music, act, or play sports while ordinary people are barely cutting it to make minimal wage or finding they have to work several jobs to make ends meet. It just doesn't make sense. Our middle-class is rapidly vanishing while the rich are getting richer and the poor are getting poorer. We have illegal immigrants working the blue-collar jobs while legitimate citizens steer away from that type of work because they feel it's beneath them. As a result, some U.S. citizens have lost the understanding of what their country was built on. They're becoming dependent on illegal citizens and allowing them to hold up the United States' very foundation.

When people are faced with the undesirable circumstances that force them to take the less than desirable jobs, they shouldn't have a choice but to work hard. The upside is they will become a better person because of it. Working hard is a core attribute we need in order to build great things. Doing your best, striving to accomplish your dreams, and being a positive example to your family, friends, neighbors, and colleagues are all a part of that foundation required to build a stable and prosperous future.

Every person should work hard, and perform excellence in all they do. Being able to look at yourself in the mirror at the end of the day is the paycheck that can't be taken away. *You earned it!*

As for mother's, life is already hard and raising children takes a commitment. It's like getting a tattoo on your face…it's a forever thing. Therefore if you choose to be a mother, make sure you love your kids and show them so they will know it. Kids need their mother's love more than anything in this world. And if you can't show love, be selfless and let another mother have the role or simply choose to not have kids in the first place. A mother's role is crucial to a child. And as a child matures into an adult, please know they will always need their mother's love. Mother's, please go hug your children and never stop praying for their well-being.

Chapter 5 – Sticks and Stones

Dealing with a broken, dysfunctional family and having a mother that was scarce took its toll on me while growing up. I wet the bed almost every night until I was about 8-years old. It wasn't that I was lazy or didn't want to wake up to go to the bathroom, I was a sound sleeper with a weak bladder. I found out about my weak bladder after (finally) going to the doctor. The doctor was a saving grace to me in so many ways.

I went to school smelling like urine in my early childhood years. My mother wasn't home in the mornings to help me with a bath so I would simply wake up, change my clothes, and go to school. My issues didn't go unnoticed. Kids would call me names and tell me I smelled, but it never really occurred to me that I actually did. I got used to it. I know…too much information, but there is a point to this. These experiences became a driving force that actually served as a benefit later to me in life.

Now add gross to already disgusting, imagine this. I would get home from school, go out to play, and get hot and sweaty, which would add to my rich aromatic fragrance. I don't remember how often I bathed, but I do remember just rinsing off with water in the bathtub and never obliging to use soap. Downright gross!

When I finally did go see the doctor, he prescribed 'bladder therapy' for me. In therapy, they taught me how to perform Kegel exercises. The exercises taught me how to strengthen my bladder muscles and they pretty much did the trick. I stopped peeing the bed, except for some rare occurrences. The worst part was over. Unfortunately my bed still smelled and the option to get a replacement didn't exist so I decided to sleep on the floor. I was guilty of occasional accidents while sleeping on the floor, but didn't want my mother to know. My solution was pouring bleach over the pee spot to get rid of the evidence. With the floor becoming saturated with bleach, a white circle began to form, but I still slept on top of it. Over a month or so of doing this, I began to itch and developed a severe rash on my rear-end, but I didn't understand why. It eventually hurt to even sit down so I finally showed my mother and she was baffled as to what could be causing it. The rash became so bad that my skin started to blister. One day my mother happened to go into my room and noticed the bleach spot on the carpet. Scared out of my wits, I finally had to confess to what I was doing. Thankfully my mother decided not to add any more blisters to my bottom and told me to stop. Whew! The downside is, I had to return to sleeping on my wretched, smelly bed. The blisters and redness eventually went away, but sleeping on my bed reminded me nightly of the bladder problem that I thought I had put behind me (pun intended).

The problem I had with my bladder was a legitimate physical disability. The reality of physical disabilities, such as mine, isn't always apparent to the causal onlooker. People treat us with contempt when the truth of the matter is our lives are in a state of turmoil and we don't have the means or know-how to overcome it. We become stigmatized by a judging society, which leads us to believing we're unworthy. The misfortune in many cases is that individuals can't afford to go to the doctor for their uncommon, but normal condition and are unjustly branded as outcasts. My heart goes out to them. They are my kindred spirits needing reassurance.

This brings me back to my days in grade school. The kids were really mean. They would attempt to hurt my feelings, but fortunately I was naïve to it. Nowadays, kids are so incredibly cruel to the point of driving others to kill themselves. Even with campaigns to eradicate it, bullying is at an all-time high.

Bullying is usually intense or continuous aggression by means of physical, verbal, emotional, or mental abuse. The intent is negative, malicious, and there is frequently a power imbalance between the parties involved. The impact on a bully's target can be substantial, resulting in negative emotional, physical, and/or mental hardship.

Students have the right to go to school and have the right to feel safe, valued, and respected. For many young people, school has become a dreaded place because of the actions of a few students who bully. **I was bullied, and it was mean, but do people even understand what the word "mean" means anymore?** Sadly, it doesn't mean much.

There is also cyber-bullying, thanks to technology. Cyber-bullying is carried out through the use of electronic devices, such as our cell phones, computers, video gaming systems, and the Internet. The ways in which youth and adults communicate through these devices have changed dramatically. Technology has brought bullying to a new level by invading the homes and mobile devices of children and adults, 24 hours a day, 7 days a week.

As a result of bullying and cyberbullying, kids are killing other kids or killing themselves. Suicides among our youth are tragically high and rising each year. The youth see no way out and just want the cruelty to stop. What is going on? Where is the love, respect, and kindness to help others? My heart is for those who are hurting deeply because of name-calling and other slander and don't have the parents at home who would help their children see their worth or serve as a refuge in their child's corner. I am here for you. I know how it feels. You are in my heart and prayers. Please be strong. It might hurt right now, but you will make it through this. It will pass, I promise. And guess what, just to put a smile on your amazing face, ironically, those bullies might be working for you one day. I survived and so will you.

Moral of the Story – For anyone that has a disability or ever had one, it's real. Your problems and struggles merit respect. I validate you. If you can't afford medical care, research your symptoms through the Internet. If you don't have access to a computer, go to the library where access is free. There are ways for you to get help. If you need it, contact me personally and I will help as best I can. You deserve it.

For the kids that are struggling due to name-calling or any other type of bullying, I am lifting you up in prayer. Words hurt. Words can hurt even more than physical abuse. Bruises fade, but words have the power to destroy our minds, if we let them. Know you are stronger than those who bully. Bullying is a sign of weakness and is inflicted by others to make them feel better about themselves. Surprisingly, you should feel sorry for the bully because they are the pathetic one who acts out of insecurity. If you see someone being bullied, be there for him or her and try to intervene.

Please know this dear friend, time will pass and you will eventually be freed from the verbal or physical abuse. I promise you that you will make it; I did. I am praying for you. I'm your biggest advocate.

How people treat you says nothing about you, but it says everything about them!

Chapter 6 – Glimpse of Kindness

Even though the first seventeen years of my life were tumultuous and wishfully forgettable in some respects, I do have a handful of good memories. I loved school as a young girl even while being hungry and stinky a portion of the time. It was a place for me to run, laugh, play, and have plain ole fun. To add to it, both my kindergarten teacher and the school bus driver made it all the more special.

On my way to school every morning, I would stand behind the bus driver (unsafe, but worth it) and peer over his head while he drove the bus. He was a patient old grandpa and his name unfortunately escapes me. He would let me operate the handle to open and close the door, which to me was the perfect start to my day. I was his appointed helper and he made me feel like I was the luckiest kid in the world. He would bring me crackers to eat and always smile his big grandpa smile. He would ask me about my day at school while taking us back home in the afternoon and actually took the time to listen to me. He lovingly told me every day to do my homework and always checked back the next morning to make sure I did. It was the first time in my life I felt like someone took a sincere interest in me.

To add icing on the cake, my kindergarten teacher loved me to pieces. She offered rewards to our class for good behavior. I won little prizes for taking the best nap and was singled out for a solo singing part in my kindergarten graduation. She held my hand as we walked and would braid my hair for me. She taught me how to read and as a result later on I qualified for the 3rd grade advanced reading program and have been a stellar reader ever since. She always hugged me, allowed me to be the first in line to eat breakfast and lunch, and even gave me extra snacks. I would get to sit on her lap and she showered me with attention. I think she was this way with all of the kids, but either way she made me feel loved. Sadly I've forgotten her name as well, but I will never forget how she and "Grandpa" made me feel. I was the happiest, luckiest, most important kid in the world. I was fed, cared for, asked about, and hugged. They made me feel like I mattered.

This grade school experience was my first glimpse of human kindness. It was genuine kindness where I couldn't do anything for them, yet they did something for me. I will never forget how those two people, an old man and a young woman, made me feel. *They touched my heart so deeply* yet will never know the profound imprint their acts of kindness left on my heart and soul.

This chapter is short, but reflects the powerful impact people had on my life due to kindness. It makes me realize that people are hurting everywhere and no one knows their story. Wouldn't we have a better world if everyone was kind and showed they care about one another? Kindness ends wars, heals pain, fills voids, stops people from self-destructing, prevents unnecessary heartache, and eases struggles. It can make people feel like they matter and touch them so deeply that they remember a kind act nearly 35 years later. Yes, kindness is powerful, needed, and wonderful, yet has been slightly condemned because of a few deceptive individuals who taint it with their ulterior motives. We should take a stand and bring kindness back in both word and deed. We should begin by winning individuals over through selfless gestures of kindness, leaving no room for doubt that our gestures are genuine. It could do so much for someone and is so desperately needed. I experienced those precious gifts of kindness and because of what people did for me I've chosen to pay it forward unto others for the rest of my life.

Moral of the Story – Kindness is powerful. When was the last time you were affected by someone's genuine kindness to help you, to make you better, to push you towards your dreams, to surprise you with a present, to speak words of hope into your life, to love you when you don't feel loved, to help you in times of need, to offer prayer, or to take an interest and really listen to you? When was the last time someone was there for you no matter what, treated you with respect and dignity, held you accountable, offered a shoulder to cry on, spoke words of wisdom, lifted you up when you were down, or was there for you when you had no one else?

Kindness - a beautiful long-lost treasure, which needs to be rediscovered and given plentifully to all. There's nothing else in the world with such a powerful force as kindness, other than love. But if you have love, genuine love for others, then kindness will follow. There's never too much kindness and it is always appreciated, especially when we know we are unworthy of its blessing.

Kindness is offering a smile, extending a hand, feeding the hungry, offering a cup of cool water on a hot day, opening a door, giving loving words, lifting others up, making a homemade gift, writing a handwritten card, giving a foot or shoulder massage, or high-fiving a stranger. Kindness comes in many forms. Just find which form is easiest for you and start spreading it today.

Kindness…it's sweet, like honeycomb to the lips. More importantly, <u>you will never regret being kind</u> and neither will the other person you blessed. Looks may fade, but a kind heart never does nor does it ever go out of style.

Chapter 7 – People Will Not Like You, Shocker!

Imagine someone hating or disliking you for no reason, and you not knowing why? It hurts, doesn't it?

I didn't do anything to my sister, yet she hated me. Maybe, hate is too strong of a word so let's say she disliked me. I have no idea why! She was the favorite and I only know that because my mother said it out loud once in front of both of us. We were sitting in the living room while my mother and sister were arguing. I was sitting on the floor minding my own business, watching television when my mother said to my sister, "You were always my favorite." They both looked at me for a moment and then turned back towards each other. I will remember that day, that moment, and those words for as long as I live. Those words hurt me then and haunt me now.

My sister was burdened with watching me when she was only 3-years old. Such a huge responsibility would be tough on any kid by having to watch your baby sister at a young age. I must admit, I peed on her while sometimes sleeping with her in the same bed when I was scared at night, which could result in loathing someone's presence. However, even after I stopped wetting the bed and no longer peeing on her, my sister's dislike for me continued. As I got older, I gave my sister the space she wanted, stayed out of her hair, and carefully avoided bothering her. Nonetheless, it felt like she insisted on disliking me from the moment I was born.

She was robbed of her childhood and never really bounced back after our parents' divorce. Our father was her daddy and she loved him. As the story goes, when I was born, her world came crashing down and she redirected her wide range of negative emotional distress on me. I couldn't blame her because I too believed I had broken up our parents' marriage. I had ruined her happy little family and was the cause of her anger and sadness.

My sister's contempt for me began with little instances. She would do something wrong and when our mother got mad, she would say to me, "Just tell mom you did it because she will spank you softer." Gullibly I would confess to the crime I didn't commit and get my butt handed to me. She never did confess. I took the beatings for her misdeeds. I was her fall guy and I fell for it every time. I realize I did it out of hope that she would like me one day.

There were times when she played with me, which was nice. I can count those days on two hands. When she was nice to me, it felt like it was the best moments in the world. During my 8th grade year, she took me shopping to get a dress, shoes, and earrings for a banquet, but I found out later she stole them. We were chronically poor, but it still didn't make it right. There's more to come on that. She would buy me Taco Bell sometimes…it was heaven. She gave me pizza money once in a while for school lunch…it was heaven. She let me drive her car when I was in high school to go see my friends…it was heaven. She curled my hair for my senior prom and made me feel pretty…it was heaven. There were glimpses of love here and there and I loved her during those times. I even loved her when she disliked me. Admittedly, I have always held onto the idea of having a strong sister bond relationship.

Over the years I grew to despise my home life and longed to get away from both my mother and sister. Sometimes I would sneak out of the house to go hang out with my friends, but my sister would manage to hunt me down (always mother's savior). She was my prison guard out to appease our mother, the warden, by capturing me so she could put me back in my trailer cell of misery.

She got the spoils growing up, the bigger room, new clothes, friends, and a car, while I got the smaller room, hand-me-downs, and no car. I was okay with it because I found joy in playing sports, reading, or playing Barbie's. I accepted being a loner because I knew I was a bother to my sister.

I remember once when she started her period, everyone made a big deal out of it. My mother and a few family friends taught her how to use a female toiletry for the first time while we were all at a waterpark. They praised her and welcomed her into womanhood. They also talked with her, did her hair, and made her feel special. I was happy for her and couldn't wait to have mine so I could be celebrated too. When my moment finally arrived, at least I thought had arrived, I was in the bathtub. I jumped out of the tub, dripping wet, screaming, "I got my period, I got my period." Indifferent, all they said was, "where are your clothes, come show me?" I looked down and pointed at a little red dot around my private area. Needless to say, it wasn't the 'period' I had hoped for. It was a false alarm. I was oblivious as to what a period really was. So to my dismay, I felt like the biggest loser on earth and it didn't help that my family laughed at my expense. I eventually did get my period, but with no fanfare. It was just another uneventful day, my mother and sister didn't even get off the couch to come to the bathroom with me. I had pink stained undies and had no idea why!

A day with my sister seemed to be filled with disrespect. When she drove me to school in her car, she would banish me to the backseat. She would call me names and make me feel like dirt. She put me down in front of people. She even held me down to pee on me to make up for all the times I peed on her. The mental abuse she inflicted on me far outweighed her physical abuse. Her disdain for me started when I was young and instead of waning over the years, it gradually grew worse.

While in high school, my sister began having health problems. She started gaining weight and became insecure. She stopped playing sports and fell for the first guy that gave her attention. After she graduated from high school, they got married. Shortly after they married, my sister's husband made some bad decisions and wound up back in jail. With nowhere else to turn, my sister decided to move back in with us. I was sad that she moved back in because I had to move out of her big bedroom back into my little closet bedroom in the trailer. Plus my mother showered her with attention and I became the 'nobody' again.

She stayed with her husband and would drive every other weekend for four hours each way to go see him in jail. I would ride along with her just to get out of the trailer. Ironically, it was freeing for me even though we were visiting a prison. After arriving to the prison, I would stay in the car and eat a burger my sister bought me while she would go in and visit her locked-up husband. I felt bad for her. She told me she didn't leave her husband because they were in love. But, I feel she stayed because she didn't love herself. **Insecurity...the greatest form of prison to damage a mindset.**

He did eventually get out of prison and they got back together. Not learning from past choices, my sister and her husband were both sent to prison. I believe my sister's problems began when she began gaining weight. At that time she began to slide down a slippery slope of self-esteem despair. She became insecure, which gradually led to unhappiness and losing her self-worth. She yearned for love and attention to the point of sacrificing her own well-being. Eventually she and her husband were released from prison just in time for him to go back to prison again. This time, they finally divorced and still my sister's cycle of heartache continued. She met a new man, got married, and she, again, went back to prison. It's heartbreaking to know that her lack of self-worth destroyed her life in a sense. Consequently, she turned even more hateful towards me as the years passed. I never did anything to her, but help her emotionally, financially, and mentally. And to this day I still try to love her because I know it was her deep-rooted issues, her demons that kept us from being sisters. I dream of the bond we could have had together.

Moral of the Story – It's a fact of life, people will dislike or hate other people. Period. Maybe because they dislike themselves? It could be from their emotional and mental demons playing around in their minds that creates so much hardship and pain for them. One will never know.

It's tragic for someone else to have to deal with being hated by another person for any reason. Hate simply serves no purpose. People acting out in hate need help and prayer or they will continue to isolate themselves from the world, only amplifying their downward spiral to complete darkness.

If you're dealing with a situation like this, know it's not you; it's them. Unless, of course, you did something illegal, immoral, unkind, or unethical, than you are the problem. Let's not go there with this lesson.

Don't allow someone's cruelty to rule over your life. It's not healthy nor is it justified. Instead, establish boundaries by identifying what you will and will not tolerate from someone else. If individuals cross your boundaries, be prepared to remove yourself from their toxic environment. Your health and sanity matter more than theirs.

The adage, "It's them, not you" is true, but I know from personal experience it's difficult to not be hurt by what others do and say. Therefore, knowing they're the problem and you're not is half the battle. During trials such as these, know 'you matter' and someone else's hateful attitude shouldn't be allowed to keep you down or hold you back from being your best. **Let go of their anchor!**

I plead with you, let hateful people deal with their problems while you do what you can to never hurt anyone like they have hurt you. Make this your biggest milestone in life!

You can also surround yourself with the sort of people that give your life meaning. It's a great choice to make! Choose life-giving people!

Most importantly, how others treat people says more about them and their character than about you. All you can do is treat people the way you want to be treated. Remember….the *Golden Rule*.

As for my sister, I pray for her to love herself fully, realize her potential, and make her life count for something so she can one day feel great joy in her life. I wish that same thing for you. If you have someone in your family who has hit hard times, either accidentally or purposefully, pray for them and try to be a role model of hope, hard work, and forgiveness. Help them navigate to a better place, a healthy and safe place. **Never look down on someone unless you're helping them up.**

Chapter 8 – A Thorn Among Roses

In fourth grade, I got the fluke chance of spending the night at a classmate's house. I have no idea as to why it happened, but I remember feeling privileged. I never went anywhere and was excited to stay overnight at someone's house. I don't remember what she and I did that night, but what I do remember is the next morning and how it changed my life. That morning made a lasting memory.

It was the morning before school, we got up, and all went into the kitchen. My friend's mom was making breakfast, her siblings were sitting at the breakfast table, and her dad was eating while holding one of the kids and talking to us. Her mom made us homemade English muffins with eggs, cheese, and ham…just like McDonald's, only better! While sitting there eating my breakfast sandwich, I was thinking, "Is this real, am I dreaming?" I even pinched my arm to reassure myself it was real. It was my first impression of what a real family looked like. Here was a mom cooking in the kitchen, interacting with her kids, and even asking them about their homework. It was the first time I saw a dad actually sit with his family and love on them. I remember chuckling because one of the kids had egg dripping from his lips while talking about math. It was so much fun. We were sitting at the table, sharing stories, and eating. I noticed my friend staring at me probably wondering why I was being quiet. I was soaking it all in, not to mention eating two of the best breakfast sandwiches of my life. This wasn't a movie scene. It was the real thing. Here was a family with the last name Thorn, living in their happy home not realizing, ironically, they were actually a family of roses embracing a thorn, me. They profoundly changed my way of thinking about family. Family could be a beautiful thing.

It was at that exact moment I woke up to the sad, stark reality that something huge was missing from my life. I wanted what my friend had because it made me feel alive and happy. I wanted a real breakfast sandwich every morning. I wanted a dad to hold me on his lap and talk with me. I wanted a mom to ask me about my homework. I wanted a sibling that actually liked me. I wanted it, but I couldn't have it. What I did get was the realization that not all kids get to grow up in a loving, nurturing home. It was a bittersweet moment because it made me smile and get teary-eyed. I was happy for those kids while sad for myself.

I lost touch with my friend after my stay over. She moved away, but left me with a lifelong memory of how a family could enjoy each other in a loving home. I wish I could thank them for showing me how a real dad and mom takes care of their kids, loves them, and teaches them the importance of being a family.

As a result from the breakfast experience, I try to cook-up my own memories with my family. At dinner, we sit at the table with no technology and talk about the best and worst parts of our day. It is a way for us to stay connected and to show our love for one another. Even though I lack the intimacy that comes with a strong family upbringing, I do my best with my own family by sharing quality time with them and that's what matters.

In today's era, I feel if more families broke bread together instead of breaking out the iPad, iPhone, or laptop than we'd have less entitlement, less violence, and less emotionally unhealthy people. <u>When interaction and intimacy converge, real relationships are created.</u> These relationships help people learn how to **compromise**, **communicate**, and **connect**. These characteristics help children grow into emotionally healthy adults. It's time to fellowship with our families, a real connection, instead of a virtual facade.

Moral of the Story – A family can be the best part of your life or the worst. We weren't made to be alone. A family should be a safe haven where we grow with each other, love, fight, eat, and are simply connected with each other, forever.

A gathering around the dining room table isn't just about consuming food to nourish your body, it's about spending time with others, which nourishes your heart and soul. Talk about anything…your day, school work, friends, favorite television show, favorite book, favorite sports team, favorite singer, favorite color, favorite memory, scariest moment, your 'whatever'…just talk. Don't sit idly in front of the TV or have the music blaring and not talk. Don't sit in silence or have the phones out. Connect with each other. Just do something…together! What a beautiful concept of an indescribable bond of connection.

We are not meant to be sad if we're alone so stop feeling sorry for yourselves. Instead, brighten someone's day by inviting others to join your dinner table, volunteer at a homeless shelter and share a meal with someone not as fortunate, go to Starbuck's, grab an empty table, and strike up conversation, or drop by an American Legion and talk with a Veteran. No matter what you attempt, try to connect with other people. It will leave a lasting *impression of hope*.

You never know what others are going through or what they have to share about themselves so connect with others and get real. We can learn from every single person, but we must be open to the idea and be willing. A chance encounter of connection could change someone else's world, or yours.

There are a lot of thorns in the world so be a rose to someone.

Chapter 9 – Innocence Stolen

There was a time when the hair on the back of my neck stood up, my stomach hurt, and I knew something was wrong, but I couldn't put a finger on it. It was when my mother's boyfriend, Raphael, was around. I think all girls recognize this fear, but don't actually understand it, especially if they are naïve and have never experienced this type of uneasy situation before. My mother had been seeing Raphael for a while and his presence made me feel weird and uncomfortable. It was the way he looked at me. When I was playing outside, eating at the table, riding my bike, or sitting in a canoe, I noticed he was always looking at me. If someone else saw him looking my way, they probably didn't think anything of it, but it bothered me tremendously. He never touched me other than hugs, but the look in his eyes was eerie. I would tell my mother about my discomfort and how I felt, but she would blow me off and say I was overreacting.

The overwhelming feeling and weirdness I was experiencing only grew more intense over time. It left me feeling threatened and I wanted to hide instead of play. I hated when he came over and I hated when we went over to his house. He had a nice home and a lot of money, which would lead people to believe he wasn't a threat, but when he was around my stomach was unsettled. I came up with excuses to avoid being around whenever I knew he was coming over to visit. It was effective because I didn't see him as much. The uneasiness finally stopped once he was no longer in my view or I wasn't under his watchful eyes. I felt happy, free again, and could laugh out loud without having to feel guarded. Life was simple and joyful again for a young kid.

Then it happened. One night I was home alone and Raphael stopped by to see my mother. He came into the trailer and made small talk with me. Uneasy, I said I had to go outside to meet my friends. He stood up to leave and then walked over to me. He embraced me for a hug, put his two hands on the sides of my face, and kissed me. It wasn't a friendly peck, it was a deep-on-the-lips kiss. One of his hands went down to my rear and he pulled me into him. I was so shocked and scared. I didn't know what to do. Paralyzed, he pulled me closer. I couldn't breathe. I didn't know what to think. Out of desperation I put my hands up and pushed him away. I don't know how much time had passed, but I knew I was shaking. I was on the verge of tears. He let go, looked at me, said goodbye, and as he headed for the door asked me to tell my mother he stopped by.

As soon as he left, I locked all of the doors and ran into the shower feeling the urge to throw up. I felt dirty and used. I felt like trash. I was dazed and confused. Why did he do that? Why did he touch me when he was my mother's boyfriend? How dare he? He took what wasn't his. The nagging feeling in my stomach when he always looked at me didn't compare to the feeling I had at this point. I stayed in the shower for so long that I turned into a prune. When I eventually did get out, I went into my room and hid under my bed. I was around ten years old and felt like the grossest girl in the world. I wanted to die and to add to my suffering I knew my mother would hate me or not believe me. I cried for hours.

When my mother finally did get home, I told her everything that had happened. As I anticipated, she didn't believe me. She flat out called me a liar and said I was making up stories. Instead of wanting to protect me, she attacked me. On that day my life was never the same. Instead of my mother confronting Raphael to seek the truth, she kept seeing him.

Fortunately, I never had to go with her again to his house and eventually she and Raphael broke up. I'm not sure if it was because of me not coming around anymore or something else. All I know is I never saw him again.

What bothered me most about my encounter with Raphael was my mother not believing me nor trying to protect me from that sick man. Deep down inside she may have suspected I was telling the truth, but didn't want to jeopardize their relationship. Therefore she chose him over me. It was at that moment when I stopped loving my mother and realized she never loved me like she should. If she did, she would have chosen to believe me or at least sought out the truth. One thing is for certain, it hurt from the physical wounds he inflicted then and it still hurts from the emotional scars from my mother now.

I wonder if he is still alive because if he was and I had the chance, I wouldn't think twice about kicking him in the balls. He harmed me, hurt me, and emotionally devastated me. I was forced against my will to indulge in his twisted fantasies. Too shocked to do anything, I stood there helplessly having to deal with something I should have never had to experience. He stole my innocence and my right to gracefully blossom into a respectable young woman. Because of his selfish act, I became afraid of guys, being looked at, being touched, and even being kissed.

Fast forward, I vowed to never be like my mother so I taught my daughter how to yell, scream, kick, fight, be aware of her surroundings, follow her gut instinct, and keep her eyes open for Situational Awareness (SA). Also, I would believe her!

For you specifically, when the hairs stand up on the back of your neck, know there is a reason for it. Don't ignore the signs that your conscious is warning you of. Be prepared to protect yourself. Kick the creep where the sun doesn't shine.

Moral of the Story – Kids are wrongfully touched everyday by people they know even in their very own homes. Kids don't ask to be born. Their parents brought them into this world and it's a parent's duty to keep their children safe. It is the parent's obligation to listen to them and heed what they say happened. It's a parent's job to protect their kids and to kick butt if someone wrongfully hurts them. Kids are precious. They don't ask to be touched, raped, hurt, or destroyed to accommodate someone else's selfish, lustful desires. If a kid is hurt, than it's the parent who let the child down and failed to protect him or her from harm. More importantly, listen to kids when they tell you something. Bottom Line - Be up in your child's business to protect them.

If you've ever been a victim, know it wasn't your fault. Know you didn't do anything wrong. Whether you were a kid or otherwise, know it was their fault, their sickness. You are the innocent one in all of this. BELIEVE IT. Let yourself heal, love yourself, and search for a way to come to terms with what happened.

If you were a victim of someone's horrible selfishness, I prayerfully ask you to share your painful message to help others understand the dangers lurking so they may avoid the same heartache. Your message could be the reason why others may never have to go through what you did. Know you are an Overcomer! You are **Goliath strong** by going through what you have and taking the stance that you won't let the innocence taken from you be an anchor holding you down in life. I'm proud of you for all you have overcome.

Chapter 10 – Life Sucks…Embrace It

Let me speak some truth. Every single one of us will face a situation one time or another in our lives that makes us want to run away. For me, I wanted to run away constantly as a kid, but couldn't. So instead, I ran away in my mind. Growing up the way I did was tough so I remained alone most of the time. I was embarrassed of my life, which caused me to avoid being around people.

My mother was married 5 times in addition to all of her boyfriends. That being said, there were a lot of visitors at our house while I was growing up and many of them even lived with us. It was why I chose to isolate myself in my little bedroom. I found books to be an escape and would close myself in and read for hours. I found myself getting lost in books, imagining I was somewhere else in the world. The stories I read had happy endings. They were about love, family gatherings, barbecues, laughter, and real bonds between families. I did read suspense novels, but preferred the day-to-day life stories about families because to me it was what a true life story should be like. The books allowed me to escape from the world that surrounded me. My imagination allowed me to become a part of the story and I would lose myself in them. Yes I would get lost, consumed, taken away, and those were the moments when I found the most joy growing up. There was nothing better than reading a book and getting consumed by it that all my cares and pain disappeared, making the world feel like everything was good.

The stories filled my mind and heart with the things I was missing most in the real world. In them I had a daddy that played games, let me sit on his lap, talked with me, played ball with me, taught me right from wrong, protected me from the bad guys, and loved on me. I was happy…if only it weren't make-believe. Don't get me started about books I read with mothers.

Books were my escape, my outlet. The books enhanced my life and I became better because of them. My vocabulary improved and my pronunciation began overriding my Cajun slang. Not to mention the spelling I gleaned from it wound up helping me become the fourth grade Spelling Bee Champion. Books became my saving grace and without the glimpse of hope they instilled in me, I'm not sure I would be where I am today.

The books I read came from the school and public libraries. I didn't have money to purchase books when I was younger so my treasures were found in the shelves-of-the-generous. I have no idea how public libraries came about, but I am forever grateful to whoever had the vision to create them. As a kid, libraries were the equivalent to rich kids getting to shop at the mall, Hollywood kids going to Disneyland, or traveling to another country. Their airplane ride in the sky had nothing on my airplane rides to make-believe land. A big THANK YOU to the public libraries will never be enough. The beauty of technology has allowed libraries to grow beyond the Dewey Decimal System into a rich, affordable resource for all to enjoy. It's a place for people that don't have much to experience a whole other world. It gives me goosebumps.

As a friendly reminder – "**The man that doesn't read is no better than the man that doesn't know how to read**."

Back in the day, it wasn't just about reading books; it was also about Barbie's.

I would spend hours playing with them. They were all I wanted for Christmas and my birthday. Any chance I got to make a wish, it was for Barbie's! I would play with the Barbie's hair, dress them up, drive them around in their car, happily live in Barbie's mansion, and let them kiss on Ken. In those times, I was Barbie and I had everything…a beautiful house, a cute guy, nice clothes, and awesome hair. I was the 'bomb.com.' That's what I wanted in life…all the things everyone else had. In reality, I was the hand-me-downs, the ugly duckling, chubby legs and cheeks, the ugly smelling house, smelly body, and ugly car. And that's why I played with Barbie's so much. They allowed me to dream of what I could have and become in real life.

Reading books and playing with Barbie's allowed me to escape my horrible home life. This escape made my mother's 'unwelcome boyfriends' vanish from our house. It made me momentarily forget about how one of my mother's boyfriends would be looking through my panty drawer, while another would be saying rude and disparaging remarks, and another boyfriend would be 'rocking' the trailer. I hated the boyfriends! They all sucked with one exception, Jack.

Jack was my fondest memory of all of my mother's boyfriends. Once I was sick and staying with my mother at Jack's house and I was up coughing all night. I couldn't stop. I think it was a cold. I remember vividly hearing Jack say to my mom, "Maybe you should give her some cough medicine and check on her." By his prompting, my mother got up and actually gave me some cough medicine. If only for a minute I could believe her kind gesture was because she loved me, life would have been grand. Jack's few seconds of concern and compassion for a sick, coughing kid was forever imprinted on my heart. People will always remember how you make them feel.

Another boyfriend who lived with us for a few years was 'Pops.' Pops had a temper with a full head of curly hair to go with it. One good thing Pops did was work at the mall, which allowed me to meet one of the, then famous, Huxtable kids, which was a really big deal. Also, he took our family to Virginia and Washington D.C. once. I'm not sure why we went, but I do remember so many people running around the memorials. Those were the only two things Pops was good for. He was mean, never cooked, yelled at us, and told on me whenever I did anything wrong. I couldn't go outside for ten minutes without him whining to my mother about how bad I was. Man, I got whipped a lot because of him.

One time when Pops was around something happened that I'll never forget. My dad came to see us with his new wife, Brenda. My mother wouldn't let me go outside to see him, and made me sit next to her on the couch, while my sister was able to go outside and be loved on by him. Looking back, my mother always kept me from him. That day we had a trailer full of people and I heard my mother calling Brenda names and saying how she was a good-for-nothing, just mooching off of my dad. I was dying to see my dad and angry with my mother for putting him and Brenda down. In response to her good-for-nothing comment, I said, "What's the difference between Brenda and Pops?" My mother immediately backhanded me in the face in front of everyone. I didn't cry even though I had a huge handprint welt on my cheek. I will never forget how Pops looked at me with nothing more than a big smile on his face. My only regret out of all of it was I didn't get to see my dad.

If only I could see Pops now. I would say a few uncomplimentary words to him that would make him angry, and I would have the satisfaction of knowing he couldn't go tell on me anymore. Even better, my mother wouldn't be able to slap me for it.

In a nutshell, my mother's husbands and boyfriends sucked. They were there for "adult time" and a place to stay, instead of being there for love and having a real family. I got spanked, abused, and had my most private possessions snooped through and those were the reasons why I read books and played with Barbie's. To escape life.

What I learned is anyone could escape life, it's for the easy. But embracing a sucky life makes a person strong, resilient, and courageous. *When I spoke up that day and got slapped in the face, it was then that I embraced my sucky life!* It was powerful!

Moral of the Story – Books and toys provide an imagination that can't be bought. The creativity within our minds that comes from reading and pretend playing allows us to escape reality and seek what it is we want out of life. It provides a glimpse of what can be or maybe should be.

A valuable principle I learned as a child is for adults to consider the people coming in and out of your lives. **Quality matters!** I learned some people are unaware and don't know how to treat others appropriately. They make others succumb to their life of misery and stagnation. The men my mother surrounded me with didn't attempt to create a better life for themselves or for me. Their lives weren't pleasant and they ensured the people around them had sucky lives too. I implore you to never allow someone else to drag you down (or your children). Instead, give other people a life preserver and encourage them to do better. We need more people to be selfless in pushing others to become their very best.

An opportunity to escape is what many people desire during life's biggest challenges. For me, it was books and Barbie's. They gave me hope by allowing me to pretend I could escape to another world if only for a little while. It was a better world, especially when life sucked the most. These opportunities to escape are what made my life bearable and are what provided wisdom of what I could become.

For you, I challenge you to embrace a healthy escape, if you don't already have something. If you are escaping with alcohol, drugs, gambling, cutting, or other harmful activities, I ask you stop. Seek help and eliminate the dangerous escape route. Extinguish it. Instead, try an alternative method to escape the hardships of life. Exercise, journaling, praying, reading, bubble baths, serving in the community, or trying a new hobby are ways to embrace the hardships of life.

Lastly, if you ever want to escape life by suicide, <u>I ask you contact me immediately. I will help you</u>. *One life lost is too many and you are way too important to me.* Life is never that hard for you to end your life. That's for weak people and you are not weak! Here me clearly – YOU ARE NOT WEAK! Put your hand over your heart and feel that sucker pumping…you are STRONG enough to make it through anything that holds you anchor to despair, sadness, and heartache.

There are ways to escape hurt in a healthy way. They will help you 'eventually' overcome the sorrow you feel. Please know you are brave enough to cope through the pain and be able to let go of the anchors holding you down…I promise.

Chapter 11 – Surface Deep

I've never had a poker face; therefore, people know exactly what I am feeling. I wear my emotions on my sleeves. I might have appeared to be strong on the outside, like an M&M, but man I have always been a softie on the inside. In fact, my emotional responses were either misinterpreted or taken out of context because I react too quickly with my mouth or my facial expressions. Break/Break: I am a very passionate person and am working on my poker face and tact, especially in this politically correct world we live in today! Laser beam days are long gone!

As for my passionate personality, I was written off as the bad kid and my sister was made the trophy in our house. If we had a fireplace, she would have been displayed on the mantle for all to see. She couldn't do anything wrong. She got the good grades, had a job, took care of me, played sports, said the right things, and was the child everyone loved. The injustice was that no one saw her true colors and no one really saw mine. People usually tend to see things as skin deep.

Many times my sister would do something wrong and ask me to cover for her. She would break things, lie, steal, and she even slept in a cemetery once with my cousins. Everyone loved her…it felt like the episode on the Brady Bunch where Jan repeatedly said, "Marsha, Marsha, Marsha!" I don't know why everyone loved her so much, but it was unmistakable. It may have been due to her being a good actress and I wasn't. Nonetheless, everyone called her an "angel" including our family and friends. I was called the "little devil" and I still have no idea why to this day. I wasn't malicious, mean, or bad. In fact, my sister would do bad things and never received punishment for it, thanks to me. She would play the, "Shannon, you won't get spanked as hard because you're smaller. Mom will take it easy on you." card. Like a lamb to the slaughter, I would go back and tell my mother I did it, get spanked hard, and endure the pain while my sister sat there and watched. This happened so many times with me getting spanked and crying and her knowing she was the reason. But she never spoke up, she just watched as I cried.

To solidify the contempt my family and sister had for me, we would get postcards while growing up with two little girls drawn on the back. One of the girls had a halo while the other had horns. Guess who got the horns? It gave me a complex.

It was all about her growing up, which made her into a self-centered and hurtful human being. If you didn't accommodate her wants and desires, everything would be miserable and fireworks would explode. You had to stay quiet and not speak your true thoughts around her so everything would remain as calm waters. There would be no attempt to shine light into her darkness as it would have been a futile attempt anyway. I just wanted to be kind and to have a kind sister.

Sadly, my sister's darkness eventually caught up with her and reality prevailed. She should have known she couldn't play 'Jekyll and Hyde' forever. The law saw through her disguise and compensated her with multiple trips in and out of prison. Her sense of invincibility took its toll. She has had a rough life, but it's from her own doing. Sure it might have started out poorly, but it ended poorly because of the choices she made. Every Saint was once a Sinner and every Sinner can become a Saint.

For me, being referred to as the "little devil" was irony at its best. I was actually pretty compliant and only had a few bumps along the way. I took the hits I earned while I also covered for others. I had a soft heart for my sister and took the beatings for her out of love. Have you ever met someone who took the fall for someone they loved? That was me, the 'little devil' all the time. I followed the rules with the exception of my normal teenage years, but in all I was a person that loved the feeling of 'being good.' I was the girl with a smile on her face for others even though I endured much pain within my heart.

It was my goodness that made me 'bad.' For example, one day while riding in the car with my mother, sister, and aunt, we were pulled over by a cop. The cop got out of his car, came up to our driver's side door and as soon as my mom rolled down her window, I screamed, "Suey….suey, suey, sueyyyyyyyyy." My aunt prompted me to do it by saying the cop would like it. Unbeknownst to me, my mother did get a ticket and to add icing on the cake, my aunt and sister kept laughing about it. Because of my antics, the cop nastily looked at me and I got a spanking in the end. I was gullible and trusting out of wanting to please my aunt. I didn't want to think about anything else other than to see her smile. I was your typical 'People Pleaser' and still am to some extent.

There are many people who are not what they seem. Although they appear to be wonderful, loving, and good, we find out they are like the main character in the movie, "Single White Female" - a fake trying to be liked for the wrong reasons. These types of people aren't true to themselves and end up harming others because they're role-playing instead of revealing their true identity. Eventually their true identity is exposed and they could leave us as fools. In the end, we can't be blamed for their falsehood because we didn't force them into being someone they're not. They are accountable for who they are, as we must be for ourselves.

Some people appear to be an angel, but are a devil in disguise…or vice versa. A 'little devil' might be thought of as a bad person, but in reality might be filled with goodness, love, positivity, and the desire to sacrifice for others at the expense of themselves. Allow yourself to find the goodness in people. You'd be surprised, when things get tough, who comes to your side and who is the first to abandon you.

"Be courteous to all, but intimate with few, and let those few be well tried before you give them your confidence." George Washington

Moral of the Story – Never judge a book by its cover. The person you think is good, may not be. So never think someone is good until they have proven themselves. You can never fully know a person's intentions, but by observing their actions you can determine if their actions align with their words. It can be difficult to find people who demonstrate integrity or strong moral character in their lives. *Be more surprised by the people who show solid character than those who don't live up to what they preach.*

For the people that judge a book by a cover and don't guard their mouths from hurting others, well this is for you. The old nursery rhyme, "Sticks and stones will break my bones, but words will never hurt me" is a bunch of bologna. Words hurt. Physical wounds hurt, but mental sabotage stays with those you hurt forever. It's better to build up a child than to repair an adult. Don't judge others by their appearance or call them names. Get to know them for who they really are. Being called the "Little Devil" was not appealing nor is any name calling appealing to anyone.

People should change/grow/evolve for the better over time. If you know someone who is the same person they were five years ago then they are not growing. We shouldn't want to be around stagnant people because we are meant to learn from our mistakes (wisdom), learn from our experiences (knowledge), and learn from ourselves and other people (awareness). Evolving into our purpose and discovering our deepest desires are a beautiful thing! Yes, be like a tree and grow!

Walk your talk! *Be a life-giver instead of a death-maker.*

Look past the cover of the book. There's more than meets the eye.

Please never call anyone names because it's not kind nor is it right. If you're ever tempted, please remember how name calling made you feel….it hurt the very essence of who you are…and sometimes, you will never overcome the abusive and hurtful words spoken to you.

The times when you're angry or upset are when you're more capable of making the worst speech of your life. Take a pause before you react in unkind and harsh words or simply walk away to take a time-out. Adults need time-outs too and probably should use them.

Words can be life or death…<u>always choose to speak life</u> to people even if you don't like them or they hurt you. Why? Because you will be the more noble person by not stooping down to their cold-hearted level.

Chapter 12 – Everyone gets a Trophy

'Hard Work' is what our country's founding fathers stated would be necessary to realize the American Dream. Hard work is exactly as it refers, hard. This is why so very few people do it. It's easy to stay at home and get a free handout, but why don't people feel guilty for taking something they didn't earn?

My hard working years started in a water bottling plant when I was very young. Well, *technically*, I didn't work there, but my mother did and I was alongside her with my sister every other Saturday for two years of my life.

Being so young I didn't know what to expect when I first stepped into the building, but I was amazed. It was a small warehouse filled with machinery, boxes, pallets, forklifts, and a lot of water bottles. It was magical. My mother got a job there because of Jimmie (the nice man, maybe even my father?). I think she was paid under-the-table, while my sister and I were paid with lunch.

Our goal on those days I was there were to fill 2500 cases with 6 bottles in each case, which equaled to 15,000 gallons of bottled water by the end of the day. So what did we do to produce those gallon jugs of water? Glad you asked. We would carry in tons of cardboard flats, fold them into boxes, tape the bottoms, line the gallon jugs up, cap them once the jugs were finished filling from the water filler, put them into the boxes, tape the boxes shut, stick coded labels on them, and stack them. We didn't get to drive the forklifts to move and load them, we just did the dirty work. The fun part of the job was stacking the gallon jugs on the assembly line, placing the stickers on them, watching them work their way down the track to get filled, and then capping them. We would have to refill the lids, refill the labels, ensure nothing would get stuck, fix it if it did, and ensure the water filler always worked.

The work was constant with no breaks other than lunch and there was no time to use the bathroom without my mother, sister, or I having to cover for one another. The gallon jugs were always timely placed in line, their labels quality checked, filled with water, capped, and loaded into boxes. It was a turn-key system, with no room for error, and an all-day function.

Imagine producing 2500 cases of bottled water in a day. It was all-day standing and repetitive work. I would whistle sometimes and try to sing to help pass the time, but it was never enough. My mind was focused on the machine, the water, the labels, the boxes, and the constant flow of it all. I guess that's where my love of water came from, along with my sense of goal accomplishing, only accepting excellence, and a hard work ethic. This job also instilled my desire for checking off items on a checklist.

It was fun to see a huge number of flat boxes dwindle as they were transformed into ready-to-ship cases of bottled water throughout the day. There was no better feeling than the end of the day when everything was done. Completing the job was extremely satisfying. Yes I was exhausted, but the inner feeling of successfully completing this enormous task outweighed my exhaustion.

The lunch breaks were the best…it's what I lived for. We didn't have a lot of money so when we were able to eat out, it was a treat. We would go to the same place for lunch in the little city of Abita Springs, Louisiana. It was a little dive of a diner that was the equivalent of filet mignon to me. I would get a burger and fries. It was an amazing burger and the steak fries were delicious. Ahhh…thinking of it now makes me salivate. We would stay there for a good hour and relish the taste of the food and the great customer service. I loved the waitresses. They were snappy, funny, and nice. Plus, they would give me extra ketchup and a refilled drink without asking. It was hamburgers in paradise.

Okay so back to the manual labor. I learned what real work was as a kid. Most kids, at the age I was back then, never get to experience hard work. A lot of kids aren't even placed in an environment to see it firsthand. I witnessed what my mother had to endure to make ends-meet and I was proud of her during those times. She always gave it everything she had, probably because she didn't have any choice or have someone else to help her. It was then when I admired her the most.

During the working hours we barely talked because we were so busy and had to focus. One small mistake and we had contaminated water to deal with, which would delay its delivery to the people in the Parish. Speaking of contamination, one time we had to shut the plant down for a few hours and it was because of me. This is personal, but honest. I don't know what I ate, but I had the worst gas ever. I kept pooting and the air was filled with the smelly aroma and it wouldn't dissipate because we were in an enclosed room. We were laughing about it at first, but then couldn't breathe because it was so bad. That day turned into night because the work had to be done. The only fortunate thing we got out of it was a break for our bodies and for my stomach.

The water bottling experience was tough for a kid my age, let alone an older woman. There's much debate nowadays if people would be willing to do that type of work for the pay we received and the amount of work we had to do. We would be sore for days. But the decision was easy for us, we needed money to live on and money to buy food so we could eat.

The experience taught me how to roll up my sleeves and not shy away from getting my hands dirty. I think those times were some of the best days of my childhood because although I wasn't using my mind much, I was strengthening my arms, legs, and body. It also made me mentally strong. I became a strong kid and appreciated the amount of trust given to me to help with such a huge responsibility. I learned the value of hard work, which some consider a lost trade these days.

Moral of the Story – In this day and age many kids don't understand the true essence of hard work. Nowadays, some give into the sedentary life of sitting back with their computers, iPhone, Play Stations and video games, and have to be coaxed into going outside. You ask them to help out and some throw a fit. To make things worse, many parents allow it. We are giving kids (and our adult kids) everything they want without the true gift of earning a hard day's wages.

Kids love to experience new things. If they and their parents could only recognize how technology interferes with their opportunities to do so. Parents should instill the value of hard work within their kids and curb their inflated expectations of getting whatever they want in life. Parents should teach their kids not to quit when things get tough, start things and finish them, to have goals in place, and to experience successful completion.

Kids are missing out. It's up to all of us, including parents, to not hand kids everything without them making an effort and sacrificing something to get it. Let them experience as many things as possible for themselves. Let them work for it, earn it, and to appreciate it.

My vent: My heart doesn't cry out for the kids that have to work for what they want or to help their families. My heart cries out for the kids that don't know what hard work is. As a result, a lack of work ethic could turn into laziness as adults. This leads to looking for a handout instead of earning what they work for. We have more adults between the ages of 18 to 35 living with their parents than we ever have before. We have more grandparents raising their grandkids because the parents refused to or can't. We have more people wanting entitlements than actually wanting to work. We need to stop giving everyone a trophy just because they participated and give trophies to people who actually earn them. Vent over.

Working hard my entire life is all I've ever known. And because of it, I am a self-sufficient individual that pays my bills on time, doesn't require anyone to take care of me, and can function effectively and responsibly as an adult. The proof is in the pudding. A strong work ethic doesn't just benefit you. <u>A strong work ethic benefits others as well</u>.

Are you earning your lot in life or collecting hand-outs? Are you proud of the hard work you're doing or just doing enough to get by? Are you teaching your kids the meaning of what our country was founded on or are you giving them everything just to appease their complaining?

Hard work needs to brought back into style….just saying!

Chapter 13 – Turning Point

There comes a time in a young girl's life when things begin to dramatically change. Things start getting bigger, hair begins to grow in places, and things don't make sense anymore. You have no clue how things got from A-to-B and are left to figure it out because you don't want to ask anyone. Then you go to the mirror and start examining everything, and I mean everything.

Fourth grade was a turning point in my life. I was the multiplication queen, fourth grade spelling bee champ, running the school recess games, and at the same time getting little boobies, and hair on my legs. Granted, I didn't start my period until later on, but I started developing much sooner than that, which I didn't want nor did I understand. Who likes hair on their private parts, on their legs, or under their arms? Not me, especially when you're a kid! I didn't know what was going on. I wanted it to stop, rewind the clock, hide under the bed, and keep living the glory days of my pre-pubescent school life. It wasn't fair. Girls don't want to go through these changes, but they do want boobies. Everyone likes boobies.

After I started changing, boys started to notice me a little more. I was still the poor girl, but the girl with little boobies. I couldn't hang on the monkey bars by my ankles any longer due to the fear of my shirt sliding down. What made it even more challenging was I didn't wear a bra. We were poor and I wasn't big enough for a bra yet, a training bra maybe, but not a bra.

I was noticing boys more too and one boy in particular was beautiful, like California beautiful. He had blonde hair, blue eyes, tan skin, and a dynamite fantastic look. I chased that boy everywhere and wanted him to be mine. He flirted with me and I was head-over-heels with my first school crush. Then it all changed. Fourth grade ended and we moved onto junior high school. **California Boy became Mr. Stud while all I got was a muffin top.** My California Blonde let me go in terms of friendship, flirting, and recess play. He was interested in the pretty girls, not us homely ones. That hurt more than life could imagine at that age. When you're not wanted by the one you want, life sucks, you get depressed, you begin questioning your worth, and you start criticizing everything about yourself. And this was fifth grade stress. Imagine what high school stress would be like…aye-yae-yae!

When leaving the familiar and comfortable elementary school life, I collided with the other kids. I was no longer the spelling bee champ or recess leader. I became the girl that stood out for being poor, smelly, and weird. I didn't know how to alter who I was nor become the young adult I was supposed to grow into. I still wanted to be the innocent kid. I wanted to play and not have to put on makeup. I wanted to wake up late and head straight to school without bathing or brushing my teeth. It didn't help that I had no one there to tell me what to do. I was lost in transition. I was stuck at this turning point in my life.

Not only was I ignored by my crush, I was also being bullied by a red head. This girl was beautiful on the outside, yet mean on the inside. She would make fun of me, call me names, and just be outright rude to me. I had no idea why I was the target of her bullying and criticism, but I desperately wanted her to stop. She was good at hiding the torment she caused me. Everyone thought I was whining or making it up. Because of people like her, I realized that not only was

I lost in life and without the crush, but also lost with friendship. Then it all changed one day when a heartfelt person came along and befriended me. That person was Chasity.

Chasity was a girl who lived in the same trailer park as me. She was my first real friend. We dreamed together, played together, talked about our bullies, and ate at the uncool table in the cafeteria. We laughed, sang, and sat by each other on the bus. Chasity was my best friend, the one who got me through the rough times, and rescued me from heartache. She was there to walk home with me when I broke my ankle. She was there to save me when I got locked in the closet at school. She was always there when I needed someone. Our friendship was the turning point I needed in order to face the unwelcomed changes that had arrived. The transition from elementary to junior high school was still tough, but I wasn't alone anymore. Sure, I wasn't the big girl on campus, but I wasn't alone and that's what mattered. Chasity made my life better. She taught me that I didn't need a lot of friends; I just needed one. Because of her, I made it through one of the biggest trials of my childhood. Thanks Chaz for being a real friend to me for 30+ years.

It's better to have four quarters than a hundred pennies. Meaning quality matters more than quantity.

Moral of the Story – Moments in life seem uneventful when everything is going well, but then there are the moments when complete chaos breaks out and nothing seems to make sense anymore. You lose your friends, relationships end, are lost and can't seem to find your way, get bullied and harassed, and then out of nowhere comes the silver lining. There's hope in your life again. There's a light that makes the darkness less dark. Things come together and all is well again in the world. Those are the moments when we need to stop and smell the roses, appreciate the still waters, and be thankful for the calming moment.

Things might seem bad now, but the sun will eventually shine again, and life will get better. Hope comes in the morning. Have patience. There will be a turning point, I promise.

As for the Bully! Please know we are not responsible for someone else's actions. When other people choose to be mean to us for no reason, please know they are the insufficient ones. When the bully starts picking on you and inflicting pain, know they are the people that need help because they are insecure, sad, and dealing with their own trials. It's easier for them to point a finger and take their sadness out on you rather than look at the three fingers pointing back at them.

Know you can handle whatever comes your way. In the meantime, have one friend or willing person to help you through the rough times. If you don't have anyone, please contact me and I will be your friend or help you find one.

Friend, the rough seas will come, but those times are what makes a skilled sailor. Therefore, *to be skilled you must be tested.*

We can't know peace unless we know trouble. You got this!

Chapter 14 – I had no one, but me

As seventh grade ended I excitedly headed into the summer before 8th grade began. Seventh grade ended on a good note with Chaz, sports, and grades, but I decided to set my sights on something great, my first real goal. I wanted to be editor of our junior high yearbook and to be considered for the position, the winning candidate had to sell the most sponsored ads. I didn't know how to sell ads so I instinctively opened the phone book and began calling businesses. To my dismay, I barely got through the letter 'A' and realized my initial approach wasn't going to work. After racking my brains for days the light bulb went off and I had an 'ah-ha' moment. I decided to look at last year's yearbook ads to see who bought them and then categorized the ads into big, medium, and small businesses. I called every single business ad on my list and wouldn't you know it, I had sold five ads. But I knew in my heart it wasn't enough to win.

First of all, I knew Kirby, the other 'wannabe editor' would be hot on my trail and I knew he was a lot smarter than me. I had to do something to make sure I would sell more ads than him. I anxiously grabbed a pen and paper and dove into my first ever salesperson's brainstorming session. I wrote everything down I could think of and the thoughts began to rapidly fire off one-by-one. It didn't matter to me how stupid they sounded. I just wrote whatever came to mind. After getting all of my thoughts down on paper I started making more phone calls based on my brainstorming ideas and low-and-behold I sold more ads.

My next big "ah-ha" moment came while I was searching through the Yellow Pages (do young kids even know what that means?) a second time, but this time calling the companies that listed the 'Big Ads.' Wouldn't you know it I sold another five ads. Elated and determined to keep the ball rolling, I sat there pondering what to do next and came up with the idea of calling the other students' parents. Not just any parents, but the parents with businesses. It occurred to me they could create a caption in their ads for their sons or daughters. I sold more ads! The ads kept rising in number as I watched my goal get closer and closer.

After twenty ads were piled into my bucket, I again went back to the Yellow Pages and started calling even more businesses. I took up my entire summer pursuing all of the sponsors I could find for our yearbook. I called company after company. I experienced my first lessons in perseverance, thinking creatively on how to sell and market, which routes to take, when to stop if things weren't working out, and how to reframe my thinking if the brain-well went dry. My brainstorming was revealing physical and mental energy within me I never knew I had until that summer. I found effort and determination were developing my character and, at the same time, a new and more efficient way of creative thinking.

The challenge I faced was tough. I had no one to help me brainstorm or call the companies in the Yellow Pages; it was just me. It was my goal, mine alone. If I wanted it, I had to work for it. I had to dig deep inside myself and decide if I was good enough. *Could I do it…alone? Was I capable?* Was I smart enough to contact these companies and talk to their management being only 12 years old? I had many lingering questions with no answers. But I forged ahead. I experienced many defeats, many setbacks, many tears, much heartache, and many people telling me, "No" to my requests, but I kept on going. I had to muster the courage every day to prove what I was made of. As I battled through, I became a person of true perseverance.

I didn't quit. Even when times were tough, when I wanted to do other things, or when I was alone, I never gave up. When feeling discouraged with so many "No's," I didn't complain (out loud). It was the best feeling in the world to trudge through my mire of suffering and to come out triumphant on the other side.

I put off my own wants and desires to succeed. While my friends were having sleepovers, I was outlining ads. While they were sunbathing at the pool, I was scratching off names and adding design covers. While they went to the movies, I stayed home and called company after company. Not having money to go to the movies did make it a little easier though.

I gave up my summer break to tackle something bigger than myself and can look back and say I have no regrets. That summer taught me a lot about myself. I discovered who I was, what I wanted to become, how to think, how to organize, how to achieve, how to brainstorm, what it felt like to have a purpose, and, most importantly, what it felt like to accomplish a goal.

When school started that next fall, (I can see it now if I close my eyes), we assembled in the classroom on the first day, and our teacher and her staff member stood up to announce the winning candidate for the yearbook staff editor. Let me first say, a person's name matters. They called my name! I won by selling the most ads, more than anyone else. I accomplished my goal! I became a Rebel Yearbook Editor. I can hardly put into words the feelings I had when my name was called. I was filled with the joy of accomplishment and utter bliss. The hard work and amazing amount of success was a gift that couldn't be bought and only earned. Yes I was only 12-years old, but never experienced such a feeling of grandeur. It was beyond anything I could imagine. I had done it.

The most valuable lesson I learned that summer was the importance of setting goals. I never really understood what goal setting entailed before that summer. Interestingly enough, I profoundly discovered the goal I set for myself was all I craved. After that revelation, I found myself waking up and going to bed thinking about becoming an editor. That's when I learned if you **want** something bad enough, you will find a *way* and if you **don't** want it bad enough, you will find an *excuse*. Setting a goal provided a clear image of what I wanted and it felt great checking off my milestones while I accomplished them. I realized if you don't set a goal, you are marching through life aimlessly, searching for something to achieve, minus the fun of course. If you aren't growing, learning, and achieving, you are basically standing still in life with no purpose or direction. *If we were meant to stand still, we wouldn't have been given feet.*

I learned how determined I could be when I wanted to achieve something. Never in my life had I really achieved anything. I was just going through the motions of attending school or playing outside with no desire to do anything else. Looking back, I can say it was a life without purpose.

Realizing the possibility of becoming an editor opened up something new inside of me. That was the first time I decided I wanted to become someone in life. I didn't want to be the poor trailer trash girl any longer nor did I want to grow up with that stereotype or association. It was the first time I wanted something more meaningful. The thought of doing something with my life made me happy and feel alive inside. I had the taste of success, a purpose, and a new goal. The new goal was simply to make something of myself by always having something to strive for.

What are your goals in life? What are you striving for or to become? Are you evolving into someone better or are you the same person you were 5-years ago? Once you're through learning and growing, you're through.

Never let your past dictate your future. You are capable, you just have to get prepared. Stop thinking less of your worth and start thinking more of your worthiness.

Moral of the Story – That summer I worked grueling hours for something I believed in even though I was plagued with doubt by telling myself, "I'm not good enough" or "I'm just a girl from the trailer park." Only when my name was called, did I stop and consider myself worthy and realize I had the ability to be someone. I realized at that moment how anyone could accomplish anything they set their mind to, become who they want, do what they want, and believe they are worthy. To overcome doubt, a person must work hard, earnestly try, give up their excuses, and prioritize their life desires. It may demand considerable effort, but it's worth it because nothing good ever comes easy.

Your mind can play horrible tricks on you. Please don't give in to the mind games of your past. Instead, determine who you are, what you are capable of, and go for it. Anything is possible. **The sky is the limit.**

If you fail, get up, brush yourself off, learn from it, and try again. It takes time to achieve something worthy and it doesn't happen overnight. Be patient. Enjoy the journey because it's the part of the goal that teaches you the most.

The destination (goal achievement) is the personal reward, but how you achieve it is the real lesson.

If you don't have a goal, set one. You need it. Goals help you identify your values, which helps to establish discipline in your life. Goals give you something to strive for. They give you purpose. Purpose gives you passion. Passion gives your life meaning and a life filled with meaning gives you a legacy.

Please use your mind and feet and move. Go after your goals. Don't quit until you reach your destination!

I ask when you feel defeated with your goal progress, go look in the mirror so you can see how capable you are because guess what, you're standing. So, turn the frown upside down and keep putting one foot in front of the other. Just take one step at a time.

Life is a marathon, not a sprint.

Remember this - Quitters never win and winners never quit. Winners also never make excuses, but non-winners are full of them. Something to ponder…

Chapter 15 – Defeat is Fuel

Growing up I was always outside playing, running, throwing, hitting, tossing, moving, or jumping. As a result of being naturally athletic, playing sports came easy to me. I didn't think about how to play, I just played. Sports have always been a distinctive part of who I am, but playing them in school changed my life.

It all started with softball tryouts. I tried out for the girls' softball team and was astonished when I found out I didn't make the team. How could this happen? It was my staple sport, the best sport I played, but I didn't make the team! I was standing on the sidelines watching some of the girls moving to the left while I moved to the right. I wasn't sure what was going on until the coach said, "Kids to the right, you're out. Thanks for trying out." That was the first time I experienced such a crushing blow of defeat. I was heartbroken. I was usually the kid picked first, the fastest kid in my class, a naturally strong female, but it didn't matter as I was cut from the team. I sat there in disbelief.

On that day I vowed to try my best in everything I would do going forward in order to avoid ever experiencing that dreadful feeling again. My training started the next day. I went out to the softball field with a friend and had her teach me how to throw a softball the right way. It was evident I had the speed and power, but my accuracy was off. Isn't that what life is like sometimes? You're going full throttle, feeling like everything is great, heading in the right direction, but end up in the wrong place. It was like that for me. So to restart my softball legacy, my friend and I started throwing the ball back and forth as she taught me about foot placement and how to accurately throw. Within weeks I was throwing like a Major League Baseball player, minus the team. The lesson I gained from not making the team was to never give up, especially if you want something badly enough. I might have been cut, but I wasn't a quitter nor was I going to let defeat define me.

Next on the horizon was volleyball. I began the same ritual of attempting to perfect or get better at the sport. I now understood firsthand how practice makes champions or at least enables people to make the team. I learned how to serve, set, and bump, and because I was short I decided to forego spiking the ball and leave it up to the people who had height. After a month of preparation, I attended the tryouts and I made the team. My strategy worked! It was thrilling to be a part of something official, a real team. We played, lost, laughed, cried, and became a single cohesive unit. Yes, playing a sport not only changed me for the better, but also transformed me from being a lone hard worker into one who cared about the welfare of others. It wasn't just about me, but about several people that comprised the team. I adopted the spirit of, "A solo player just plays, but a team wins, loses, and plays together. It's a family!"

Next on the agenda was basketball. I became a consistent 3-point shooter and was fast on the court. I could pass, swish, steal, and had an overall love for the game. I practiced tirelessly day after day and the hard work paid off because I made the team!

Basketball was great, but it was my coach who changed my life in a positive way. For some reason, he decided to call me "Scooter" and though it seemed like a friendly gesture by a coach, he still yelled at me, but not in a bad way. He encouraged me, taught me how to be a better player, challenged me, and most importantly believed in me. He brought out a "spark" in my life. Coach Selzer was a man who had the biggest heart for us kids and made sure we improved our game every day. He was always ready to critique and challenged us to think. He confronted us when he knew we could do better and encouraged us when we didn't believe in ourselves.

When I did something good, Coach Selzer would scream, "Good Pass, Scooter" and the feeling gave me an uplifting boost. On the other hand, he was quick to take me out of the game if I didn't follow directions. He wouldn't sugar coat things and knew how to show us tough love.

One time we were playing at an away game and I was playing Point Guard when I made a 3-point shot. To my surprise, instead of congratulating me, Coach Selzer took me out of the game immediately and said, "You can shoot all day long and make it, but if you don't follow the plays than you're only helping yourself." He benched me for the rest of the game. It was a hard lesson. I learned even if I was a good individual player, basketball was a team sport and I had to play as part of the team. More than anything, Coach Selzer taught me the value of teamwork.

My teammates also taught me valuable lessons, such as kindness and sisterhood. One challenge I faced on the court that I couldn't overcome was being poor. I had to play basketball wearing ratty shoes. I would slide all over the floor and sometimes slip while slowing down. One day while at a game, my teammate, Kasey, noticed my pathetic shoes and shocked me by taking off her shoes and handing them to me. She looked at me and said, "I have an extra pair and you need them." These shoes weren't just your run-of-the-mill kind, but top of the line red Nikes! At first I thought, "I'm so lucky!" but humbly realized there are real MVPs out there who share more than luck, they selflessly share their blessings. The one in my life that day was Kasey. She demonstrated to me how real MVPs are the ones who think of others more than they think of themselves. She blessed me and that's what an MVP does!

To break in my 'new' super-shoes, we were playing against a formidable team and as I played I was no longer sliding all over the court. The improved control those shoes gave me helped me lead our team to a victory. Because of her, I was running better-than-ever, stealing passes, and grinning from ear-to-ear like I had just won the lottery. Well thanks to her, I kind of did. Kasey's loving act taught me about the power of selflessness and kindness.

That day Kasey shaped my thoughts about other people. From her giving heart, I gained a new respect for the needs of others. She didn't blink-an-eye in giving me her shoes nor expect anything in return. As a result, I never forgot the sacrifice she made for me and have used her generosity as a reminder to pay it forward when others need a helping hand. Thinking about it, aren't we all teammates? Isn't this why we're all here; to be loved, accepted for who we are, and to be help one another? We all should be willing to help one another when our paths cross, especially in times of need.

Back to Coach Selzer. Not only did he change my life on the court, but he also changed it in the classroom. Have you ever met anyone you wanted to be your best for? Well in junior high school, it was Coach Selzer for me. He was also my history teacher and he was fascinating to listen to when he taught. He motivated me to learn and even made me want to do my homework. For his class, I studied vigorously, listened intently, and even made flash cards to ensure I got an "A" for the class. But even with all of that, I still teetered on the line between an "A" and a "B" for my final grade.

One day during practice, Coach Selzer gave us all a wager. He said, "Whoever scores 100 points on the final exam in history class will get an "A" as their final grade." Not wanting his challenge to go unanswered, I began studying before our games, before each practice, and studied even more when I got home. Test day finally came. I had prepared painstakingly for it and was confident I could get the elusive '100' points. When the tests were passed out, I quickly went through its entirety, certain my answers were right until one question had me stuck. It had two possible answers and I started to sweat. I was at a loss looking up and down searching for the answer in my head and my stomach started to hurt knowing the perfect score was within my grasp. I couldn't decide. In the last minute before 'pencils down' was called I went with my gut and circled my answer.

I sat in anticipation for minutes waiting for the results of our tests, but it felt more like hours. Finally Coach Selzer came back into the room with the announcement that one person had gotten a '100' on the test. Another classmate was looking at me smiling because he knew I had studied just as hard for the test as he did because he also wanted the '100' score. We waited and waited while Coach Selzer called out each person's score. When he reached my name he said, "Shannon, your grade was good and I know how hard you studied and I'm sorry to tell you…but you will be getting an 'A' for the class…since you got a '100' on the exam." I literally jumped out of my desk and screamed. Everyone looked at me like I had two heads, but I didn't care. I got a '100' and I made Coach Selzer proud of me. Another example of how hard work pays off.

By Coach Selzer caring about me as a person, he made me want to better myself. He may have given me the tools, but he allowed me to use them in the manner that was best for me. He was a coach that changed many lives, not just mine. He taught us that life isn't about money, the things you buy, or the stuff you accumulate. It's about who you touch, who you help, and how compassionate you are towards others, which are the most important factors in life. It's about inspiring, motivating, encouraging, and giving people the opportunity to become their best. It's about living every moment, cherishing the greatness around you, and appreciating everything that is good within you. It's about giving to those less fortunate than you by humbly sacrificing your time and talent and voluntarily investing in helpful causes.

He taught me how if you want something, you will prepare yourself for the task and practice. Practice helps you get better than who you were the day before. If you're not getting better as the days pass than you must ask yourself one question, "What are you doing in life?"

For us all, a person must know they can truly change the world. All it takes is one kind act, one person, one gift, one pair of shoes, one practice, or one basketball game at a time.

Moral of the Story – If you fail at something, don't give up. Fall seven times and stand up eight. Not making the softball team crushed me, but the failure didn't define me nor did it stop me. Instead, the defeat fueled me to work harder and to try again. That defeat is what connected me to Coach Selzer and Kasey.

Coach Selzer taught me about working hard, to hold myself accountable, to be a part of something bigger than myself, to have fun, and to be fully committed to everything I do. He challenged me to become my best, give my best, and never settle for less. He taught me the basketball court may not be a part of my life forever, but my education and character would. He taught me to work just as hard on those two things as I did with dribbling the basketball. The biggest lesson he taught me was the importance of teamwork. Teamwork showed me how we, as a society, can accomplish great things together. Let's all be a Coach Selzer.

One person can make a difference in the lives of many. People can teach you, but you have to be willing to learn and be receptive to their teachings. A person can help you become your best and offer feedback, but it's up to you to do something with it. They can give you feedback in a way that you accept or deny, but it's up to you to recognize when it's constructive. A person can give you the tools, but it's up to you to use them.

Kasey taught me the power of selflessness. She gave up something and expected nothing in return. Her kindness for someone less fortunate was never forgotten and appreciated to the heart's core. Let's all be a Kasey in someone's life.

Every 'person' has the power to influence someone's life for the better. <u>That 'person' is us</u>. We should strive to teach others how to be grateful for life when the opportunity arises. We can uplift, encourage, inspire, and brighten the lives of those around us by offering a helping hand. We can bring smiles to someone's face by expressing love, offering hope, and celebrating in joy. We can create laughter and display playfulness, which could become a person's favorite memory of the day. If people leave our presence with a smile and feel better off than we have done our best.

Be a life-giver and a change agent for good! *The world needs kind life-giving people like you.*

Chapter 16 – Jesus

The summer before my freshman year of high school I was extremely blessed to have spent it with my grandparents in Arkansas. It was the first time I had ever left home and did something like this and I have no rationale as to why I went for the summer. Maybe it was because my mother couldn't afford a babysitter and my sister was working. Not sure, but the logical solution was to send me away. Or the more obvious conclusion was my mother didn't trust me to be at home alone and my sister didn't want me there. Either way, I left for Arkansas and it radically changed my life. A few other benefits were being able to meet a few of my (heavenly) friends, getting to know my grandparents, and my first teen crush.

Let's start with my grandparents. The life of my grandparents was simple due to them living on a farm. For me, it was exciting being around horses, cows, chickens, and skipping rocks on the running creek while exploring the hills of the countryside. For them, to add spice in their lives they did volunteer work in the community. My grandfather drove the church bus every Sunday to pick up the kids that couldn't get a ride to church, while my grandmother taught Sunday school. This type of down-to-earth lifestyle was a new experience for me and I loved every single minute!

While visiting that summer I became close friends with three people. Making friends with them was a dream, but keeping them as forever friends became reality. We shared something that could not be understood unless you go through something similar. More to come on their story.

I should also mention my first teen crush. It started on my grandpa's bus. He and I would sit together and I would act awkward by telling weird jokes. (Ummm…don't judge…this was odd for me because I never had a boyfriend before. But somehow my attempt at joke telling had worked and he held my hand. Sigh! Jump up and down! Happy Dance!) Every girl liked him because he was a James Dean look-a-like, but he chose me. Even though he was just my summer crush, it was a pivotal time in my life because I was also becoming a young woman. He made me feel special and no longer invisible as the poor, chubby girl. With all the happy memories of hand holding and acceptance, this is where the story about him ends and the real story begins.

There was a summer camp everyone my age was attending for an entire week, but I couldn't afford the fifty dollars to go. To my surprise, someone in the church graciously paid my way. Next thing I know, I was setting off on a bus heading to camp and along the way found myself riding beside two other girls. We arrived at camp and the two girls and I decided to hang out together. We became instant friends. We laughed, swam, played games, and went to church at night. I never went to church before my visit to Arkansas, but found the messages interesting even though I didn't understand most of what they were saying. It was the first time I heard the name "Jesus" in my life and I was almost fourteen years old.

Side note: One of my new friend's boyfriend also attended church camp with us. Unbeknownst to me, they prayed for me, which I had no idea they were doing until the last night of camp.

Everything was going great and I was learning a lot, but the last night stopped one of my new friends and me cold in our tracks. We were standing in a big living room with a fireplace and singing church songs. We stopped singing to allow someone to preach a message and then we started singing again. I don't know what came over me, but all of a sudden it seemed like everything stopped and there was silence. A calming stillness came over me and it was a beautiful feeling. I had never experienced such a thing in my life and I had never felt so much peace. I had never felt so much love before, like someone really loved me and wanted me. My friend found the same peace that night and we both accepted Jesus Christ as our Lord and Savior. She and I started crying and our tears became reflections of joy. We spent the next few hours in the bathroom together discerning on what just happened, talking about our past sins and behaviors, and letting our new-found peace wash over us. We were new, we were whole, we were loved, and we were forgiven! We cried everything out in our hearts and were about to embark on a new journey. We hugged and smiled knowing it was a brand new beginning for both us.

When we left the bathroom, our other friend and her boyfriend prayed with us and cried with us. That's when they told us they had been praying for our salvation the entire week and how their prayers were answered. It was unbelievable. I had never been prayed for before and to have people pray for you was indescribable. We left holding hands and thanking God.

The next day was filled with sunshine and a beautiful sky that illustrated how my life was a new beginning. We had breakfast, cleaned up our cabins, and began making our way back to reality. I was scared. I didn't know if it would last, or if I had it in me to be in His will. I didn't even know what to do next.

When I got home I told my grandparents what happened. They were overjoyed while we hugged and cried together.

That following Sunday I was baptized in my grandparent's church with my grandparents and the entire congregation roared with applause.

The rest of the summer went by in a flash, but the feeling of God never left me. He stayed with me, in my prayers, and in my heart. I had a Father for the first time in my life. I had someone love me more than I could have ever imagined! I had a brand-new start in life. I had died so that I may live.

When I left to go home when the summer ended, I still had my overwhelming feeling of peace and being loved, and it was humbling to know Jesus died on the cross for me even though I was a sinner and didn't deserve His precious gift. His precious gift was my salvation.

Even though I'm not worthy of His priceless offering in my eyes, I am forever grateful knowing He performed the most selfless act of love, which is to die for another person. Jesus did that for me…and for you.

In His eyes, I am worthy…You are worthy!

Moral of the Story – Things will happen in life that we can't explain. At one point, we are on a path of what we deem as good until something explodes in our face and wakes us up to the fact that we are lost and we're not good. But before it's too late, by fate, we find our way to goodness again. My fate was God.

Serendipity - I was meant to find God that summer and to experience His love. I was never meant to be lost and without His direction. It can be heartfelt to reflect on a time in life that was never supposed to happen, but does. God set me on my path to find Him by sending me to my grandparents' house that summer.

When we look past ourselves, we will see people struggling or some who do not have purpose. If you witness someone like this, help them. It's what life's about. We're all in this together, just trying to survive. To help someone find their purpose, consider sponsoring a kid to go to church camp, taking a homeless person to get a meal, or striking up a conversation with a random person. You never know what someone is going through unless you become vulnerable enough to open up to them. It means you have a caring heart and we need more people with those.

The bottom line is by you reaching out and showing you care is sometimes all the other person needs to jumpstart them again in life and potentially struggle a little less. It may kickstart their purpose in life too.

Life is too short to live without meaning. You are capable and have so much to give. I believe in you, just like my grandparents and praying friends believed in me. Their belief allowed me to know God and resulted in the most love I have ever felt. I want this for you.

Heaven and Hell are real places and it would be a detriment to find out where you'll go after you take your last breath. Acts don't save you, only Jesus does. If you don't know if you'll go to either Heaven or Hell when you die, please contact me and let me help you know for certainty.

God loves you! Period. Exclamation Point!

Chapter 17 – You'll never amount to anything

My freshman year of high school turned out to be a special time even though I didn't continue going to church upon returning home from the summer I spent with my grandparents. My mom wasn't into that "stuff" as she proclaimed so I kept myself busy with sports and school to pass the time. I had a great year playing sports while my mom was falling in love with her fourth husband. However later in the year, I fell into a bad crowd and started sneaking out at night. Since I was new in my walk, I wasn't knowledgeable about Jesus and I didn't have anyone teaching me right from wrong. Plus, I didn't even have a Bible. As a result, I lost my way with Jesus. Even with being lost, everything was going okay (if you could declare that) for me as I was starting my sophomore year of high school.

A few months into playing the best volleyball I could, unexpectedly my life turned upside down. My volleyball coach called me and informed me that since I had been failing school I was disqualified from playing basketball. I became devastated. Then to amplify my problems, I kept hanging out with my wild child friend who exposed me to more bad sights and bad people. I was staying up late, sneaking out, and lacking good nutrition. My diet consisted of chips, cheese dip, and all other processed junk foods.

I became a loner at school. No one would hang out with me and my one friend had dropped out of school. My sister was in jail and I was failing at all levels of my life. I had no one to take care of me, no one telling me to do homework, no one feeding me, and no one to love me. When people spoke to me, their words were full of negativity and despair. I was heading down a road of destruction and to a life where nothing good would come out of it. Even though I was surrounded by the kids at school, many of them I had known since third grade, they saw me as a face of isolation and sadness. I felt like no one cared. Then it got even worse. I thought my life was over because of a decision I made out of pure desperation.

One night before school I didn't eat dinner because we didn't have anything to eat nor did I eat breakfast the next day. I was starving and desperate to find something to eat, but no one was willing to give me money or share their food with me as I painfully watched them eat. I found when you're hungry, you will do anything to survive. The desperation that sets in makes your mind reason that at all costs you must eat and even be willing to do something you're not proud of, especially when it appears you have no choice. My stomach was growling. I couldn't focus and I was hungry, very hungry. If you have never experienced the feeling of dire hunger before, you are blessed.

At lunch I stepped into the food line hoping someone would be willing to buy me some food, but had no luck. The man who collected the money allowed me to get in line. As I was walking beside some people, the pizza called my name. I don't know why I did it, but I did. I grabbed a slice of pizza and I tried to hide it as I began to walk out, but the money man caught me. He slammed down his moneybox and yelled at me to stop while grabbing my shirt. Everyone was looking at me and laughing. I was humiliated, but still overcome by my growling stomach and sheer starvation. The next thing I knew, the money man was taking me down to the Principal's office.

We got to the Principal's office and the money man told him what happened, and the Principal actually began yelling at me, calling me names, and told me, "**I was a loser and I**

would never amount to anything." Then he kicked me out of his office. I had to sit outside and wait for my mother to arrive. They had already called her because they were suspending me for stealing.

Stealing the pizza was wrong, but what hurt more was how it was handled. The Principal could have asked, "Why did you steal? Why did you take the pizza? Why did you go in line?" I would have told him the truth if he had asked, but I wasn't allowed to speak while in his office. *Getting disciplined while you're literally starving is something I don't wish on my worst enemy.*

The Principal's comments were seared into me and are still with me today, sadly. It's a horrible feeling when someone tells you how worthless you are and how you will never amount to anything like the Principal said to me that day. His comments hurt. They tore me apart. They made me doubt who I was and for the first time in my life I didn't want to be me. All because I didn't want to be hungry, humiliated, or called names anymore. I had a worthless identity, alone, and friendless. I wanted the hurting to stop.

When people speak words that impact your life, they can either help you or hurt you. The Principal at my school didn't just verbally crush me, he stole the very essence of what made me want to live. I had never felt as worthless as I did at that moment in my life. There had been numerous times while growing up when I felt really bad about myself, but not to the point of worthlessness.

My mother arrived and I got in trouble. As a result of the suspension, within a few weeks out of the blue my mother moved us to a town fifteen miles away called Picayune where we started a new life with my fourth stepdad.

Everyone I knew looked at me like I was horrible and had ruined their lives. It was a bad feeling being weakened by hunger to the point of compromising morals to steal food, but it's even worse when you're alone and no one wants to associate with you.

Due to our move to Picayune, I began attending a new school. I was nervous and alone. On my first day there, I wore the best outfit I had that was given to me by my friend who dropped out of school. I wanted to fit in. No one knew how bad my heart was aching or how sad I was. Lonely people wear masks to hide and I wore one perfectly. By the end of the day everyone knew the new girl, but had no clue as to the pain looming inside of me. When school got out, I went home and joined step-dad #4 to eat the dinner he made. The day was uneventful and became the norm for the rest of my sophomore year.

The year sailed by and even though I felt better about my circumstances, I could still hear the Principal's voice. His words haunted me daily and eventually became the catalyst in my life that would transform me into everything I am today. His words made me want to prove him and everyone else wrong. I wanted to show people, a kid from nothing can become something if they try hard enough. So I dug deep inside and discovered I had far more than what meets the eye. Today, I'm thankful because one man's ugliness helped me make my life beautiful. <u>I did this for me!</u>

Moral of the Story – Words hurt. People can speak life or death into your heart and soul. The words we speak can tragically change someone forever even to the point of death.

Please breathe life into people when you speak to them. The world is bad enough so why make it worse? People have many reasons for doing the things they do, but don't assume you know them until you've walked in their footsteps. We have a natural tendency to fatefully judge books by their covers and draw the wrong conclusions based on the biases we form from the world around us.

The masks we wear only hinder us from a life of being accepted for who we truly are. It's understandable why we choose to wear masks. They allow us to protect ourselves from pain. They serve as a cloak to hide our sacred vulnerabilities from others. However, we should really help remove the layers and get to a person's core. In doing so, we can encourage others to own their real identity as there is only one of them in the world anyway.

Please speak life into people. Look for their masks and encourage others to reveal who they truly are. When they reveal themselves for who they are, encourage them to own their greatness and to help them shine their light into the darkness that may obscure their world.

More than anything, if you see a person in need, help them. If you see a person struggling from hunger, give them food. If they're parched with thirst, give them water. If they're downcast, offer a kind word. Open a door for a stranger. Buy someone a cup of coffee. Donate clothes to charity. Volunteer to be a Big Brother or Big Sister. Donate to or serve at your local Food Bank. Be a giver and serve everyone you meet. Many people need help, but may be too embarrassed to ask. These are always opportunities to help.

And for the loving sake of goodness, never assume anything about anyone. Instead, ask them why they do the things they do. *There is always a reason why.* **The problem is only a few of us care to know** and that is very sad.

Chapter 18 – Victim or Victor

Have you ever experienced heartache that hurt you so much it was hard to breathe? Were you ever told you were not good enough? Have you ever felt like a failure or a loser? Did it stop you from trying again? Did you give up or did you put on your big girl or big boy undies and give it everything you had to succeed? When it was over, did you realize the journey was as important as reaching the destination? All of these questions I experienced and the answers progressively shaped my life because I did not give up when faced with adversity. Instead, I experienced great joy by overcoming the obstacles that were potentially blocking my success.

Playing sports is something I love so I decided to try-out again for softball. Being cut the last time I tried out had me on pins and needles, but I vowed to give it a throw (pun intended). I wasn't a quitter and wasn't sure how it would play out, but what I feared most was the uncertainty of never knowing. I had already experienced what it felt like to not be selected and I didn't die. And I knew I might experience the same gut wrenching heartache of failure again, but I would rather live with that awful feeling than live with regret. The stumbling block from my previous experience didn't stop me from trying again so it became a building block instead. I put feelings of failure behind me. I knew in my heart if I would be cut it wouldn't be the death of me and it would only make me stronger. After the last try-outs, I had decided to persevere through any storm in my life, give it all I have, and strive for success.

On the day of try-outs, I remember the coach hitting balls to us three times and having to throw to first base. All of my throws were hard, but a little off. I knew my throws were harder than most and I could bat so I felt like I was a potential selectee for the team. I knew how far I had come from the first time I didn't make the team so I kept a positive attitude throughout the entire tryout. And this time I made the team. It was anti-climactic. None of the other kids said anything about making the team nor did they make a big deal about it. We packed up our gear and left that afternoon from try-outs. It may not have been a big deal to them, but it was a gigantic deal for me. When I made the team this time, I knew my journey was just starting. I stayed grounded and paid close attention when the coach spoke and how he treated us. I promised myself I wasn't going to let making the team get in the way of learning and becoming my best. Because that is what mattered…**being a winner in life is celebrating small victories, never stagnating, and becoming the very best person you can be.**

Then boom! Just when everything was going right, it all came to a screeching halt. I was playing basketball in my trailer park court and hit a 3-pointer, but when I came down I landed half on the cement and half on soft ground. My foot immediately swelled and turned purple and blue. Barely able to walk, my friend helped me to her trailer where her uncle and aunt looked my ankle over and realized it was broken. I hobbled down to my house to find my mom and gave her the bad news. We didn't have health insurance so I ended up having to limp around for almost two weeks until my mother finally took me to the doctor. Sure enough, they placed my foot in a cast and restricted me to crutches. All sports were off limits including track, which I was also competing in. My accident cost me a year. Softball and track were my lifeline to staying fit and engaged with teammates. All I had to look forward to now was not tripping with the crutches.

With my down time, I had the opportunity to better my grades. The grades portion was relatively easy. It's ironic how studying and doing your homework would get you A's. I made the Principal's Honor Roll List, which gave me back some of my confidence. It felt good to be called on in class and know the answer. It felt good when some of my classmates asked me to help them with their classwork. The famous quote, "If you are the smartest person in your group, you need a new group" proved to be a profound quote because I began seeking out new, smarter friends and paying close attention to how they studied. I was reading more, which improved my vocabulary and I even started tutoring other students. I fell absolutely in love with learning. Yes, I finally found my place in school. I discovered a lifelong passion for learning. I became a Nerd.

Since the Nerd in me awakened, minus the pens in my pocket, my yearning to play sports was reborn when my ankle finally healed. I decided to try out again for softball. I had missed the window for basketball and my new school didn't have volleyball so it left me with two options: softball and track. Since both sports were previous failures because of not making the team or breaking my ankle, I wanted to make the team and actually play ball and run.

The day of tryouts arrived and I was nervous. I had been down this path before, but for some reason my palms were sweating, my heart was racing, and I had to use the bathroom every five minutes. I knew I had improved, but now it was do or die. I was playing shortstop and the first ball the coach hit to me took a bad bounce and it screamed passed. I faced forward and asked him to try again. The second ball was a grounder. I scooped it up and perfectly threw it to first, very hard actually. The first baseman winced and yelled, "Good

Throw." My confidence returned and we did the same routine about four more times without a hitch. This time, the coach didn't tell me to go left or right to cut the players, he just said, "Next." After tryouts concluded, we found out that every person made the team.

The practices were electrifying and our team bonded quickly. I found new friends who were uplifting and focused, with one girl in particular. She played outfield and, interestingly, we looked like each other. We started hanging out and I would even spend nights sleeping over at her house. We became inseparable, on and off the field. We became best friends.

We had a very successful year of softball and we decided to try out together the next year. When the next season came, we all made the team again. On our way to our first tournament, our coach named two captains for the team. He chose the second baseman and me. That year we went to state and many of us were named All District Players. I never gave up on my dream of playing softball and persevered by practicing to be my best. I never expected to get the results I did and never dreamed of the determined person I would become, but I did realize that if I tried anything was possible.

While on a high note, I tried out for track again. I made the team and was a fast sprinter, but an accident occurred. A classmate accidentally bumped into me causing me to fall down a couple of stairs thus reinjuring my weakened ankle. It wasn't broken, but was very sore. I had my first track meet the next day and decided to go ahead and compete in the meet anyway. I ran poorly and finished last. I couldn't believe it. Even though a compromised ankle was the culprit, I began to doubt I was cut out for the track team.

While talking to my coach about it, he helped me ice my ankle and reassured me that everything would be okay and told me to let my ankle rest for a week. After a week, I began practices again and sure enough I was running at full-speed. As a result, instead of quitting track as I was tempted to do, I placed first in many races including the team sprint competitions and winning the district long jump championship.

As I reflect on the obstacles I endured during my softball and track experiences, I was plagued with doubt and was ready to give up because of a few setbacks. Out of determination and dedication, I didn't give up. Instead, I practiced incessantly and overcame my fears. Eventually my hard work paid off and I accomplished what I set out to do. Not only did I learn from my failures, but I also didn't let them define me. I learned the mental aspect of playing sports is just as important, if not more, as the physical aspect. It's good to be physically healthy, but even better to be mentally healthy. Will power will get you further in life than shooting 3-pointers or hitting grand slams. A mental aptitude is forever, while an aptitude for sports could be temporary.

Mental sabotage is real…and I allowed it to hold me back too many times. If this resonates with you, please eradicate the negative thoughts holding you back. You and I only have one life and *a life filled with regrets should not be in our Bucket List.*

Moral of the Story – Never give up! You might face hardship, failure, loss, heartache, or hurt, but it doesn't have to define who you are or who you will become. Failure could be due to lack of planning, lack of understanding, lack of trying, lack of preparation, lack of skills, and that's alright. No one is perfect. Not everyone can be an All-Star. No one can be the best at everything. But a person can learn, overcome, try, get better, and can become their best self. It just depends on how bad they want things in life.

Are you the type of person that stays down because of failure or rises up to the challenge? Are you the type of person that can envision what it looks like to really put effort into something you want to earn? Are you the type of person that is willing to do whatever is necessary to overcome what you had previously failed at? Nothing worthy comes easy. It takes days, if not months, or even years to better yourself. It's not an overnight process, but a commitment to work hard even through struggle. Remember pain is temporary, but achievement and perseverance through pain becomes permanent. It's up to you in the outcome you receive.

Friend, have no regrets, work hard for what you want in life, and never give up trying to achieve it. Your dream is around the corner, but you must work to get there. Staying down is easy, getting up takes work!

Don't play the victim card. Instead become a victor!

One thing to understand is my victor lesson was based in sports. But the lesson can be applied to anything. Singing, acting, parenting, teaching, leading, music, friendship, relationships. It's anything that sets your heart on fire with passion. *Improvement takes work and if it were easy, everyone would be an achiever.*

On your journey to success, you will face frustration, setbacks, and obstacles, but you must remain undaunted, focused, patient, and faith driven.

Your day when you proclaim victory will come!

Chapter 19 – Relationships are Tough

Everyone remembers their first real relationship, well at least I hope.

I only had crushes and never had a boyfriend prior to moving to my new high school. Probably because I was a little heavy (even though I was athletic) and I was ragged looking with disheveled hair. I didn't have anyone to teach me how to apply make-up, perform proper personal hygiene, teach me the importance of daily bathing, or how to dress. I had a disadvantage compared to other girls. It also didn't help that kids were mean.

Sure I liked guys, but no one ever liked me. What is ironic about my first relationship is at my old school I was called a "slut" by the boys, but never even made it to second-base. I had only kissed before and I don't even know if I did that correctly. I had to accept their stupid cruelty. I knew the truth, but it still hurt being called horrible names. So you can imagine my amazement when a relationship finally blossomed at my new high school. This boy was dreamy by all accounts and to me he was Mr. Wonderful. He had dark hair, green eyes, and tanned skin.

Let me explain. One day this handsome guy came up to me and we started talking. I had plenty of confidence and started telling him stories that made him laugh and we discovered we had several things in common. It was fun to joke, flirt, and have someone take a real interest in me. This kept going on for about a month and then the day came…he asked me out! I was shocked, excited, nervous, happy, and probably changed my clothes a hundred times. Girls, you know what we do. We put on an outfit, go look in the mirror, change into something else, and repeat the process over and over and over. Eventually we settle on an outfit, usually the first one we tried on.

The big night finally arrived! He showed up to our trailer, knocked on the door, and step-dad #4 answered it. Step-dad invited him in, chitchatted for a few minutes, and we headed out. I had no idea how to act. Was I supposed to let him open the door (too presumptuous)? Do I open the door myself (too feministic)? Eventually I figured to just go with the flow. We ended up driving around town for a bit ('cruising' in my day) and settled on eating fast food. The night was perfect! To top it off, he asked me to be his girlfriend! (Happy Dance, Happy Dance!)

For the next five-months we were inseparable. We stayed together over the entire summer and into the new school year. I was beginning my junior year in high school and he was starting college. It was exciting to be together, but the newness of having a real boyfriend was beginning to wear off. Throughout the time we were together, our differences towards each other were starting to show and we began growing apart. Eventually our conflicting interest became too great and we ultimately broke up. I was okay with the breakup. I gained a lot of wisdom from it being my first relationship. I will always reflect on the things I learned, both good and bad. It taught me a lot about myself and the things that I can and cannot tolerate.

That relationship reinforced my belief that I was a good catch. Yes, I wasn't from a rich family and had a few extra pounds, but either way I was an okay gal. Being accepted and valued for who I was is what made me happy, really happy. My self-esteem improved because someone was genuinely attracted to me for the first time and it was more than just my homely appearance. He accepted me and what

I had to offer him was enough. *It was a liberating feeling!* I felt acceptance in every facet of who I was as a person. I learned being who you are wasn't about other people's image of you or your association with others. It's about being good with who you are as a person and not caving into other's false projections of who you should be.

The second thing my first relationship taught me is I don't like camping. We went camping a lot with his family. We either slept out in the open or in a tent. It was great being with him and his family, but sleeping in a bag with mosquitoes trying to suck your blood was not my cup of tea. Camping taught me how to compromise when graciously appeasing someone else. Yes we should try something new, but if we don't like it, we should limit the amount of times we're willing to do it. I'm up for making others happy, but there's a give-and-take limit when it comes to doing what your significant other loves to do. You can explore and find compromise with the things both of you like. It would be a true win-win for the relationship and it would keep it real.

The third thing it taught me is how society's view of women is skewed in many ways. First, I was carrying a few extra pounds back then, but that didn't make me fat. People called me fat and it was wrong. A woman doesn't have to appear anorexic to be considered beautiful. It's not the body that creates a poor body image for a woman, its society's ugly bias on what a body should look like. A beautiful body comes in all sorts of sizes and colors and it is made beautiful not by the size of a body, but by the goodness within it.

It's about the person having a heart filled with love, a positive mind, acting worthy, speaking goodness, having hands that deliver kindness, and feet that walk in compassion. I was always looking down on myself because of what others said, but I came to realize it was their reality that was different from mine and it was okay for me to be different. What is not okay is pushing your reality onto someone else and forcing them to believe it. People should accept what they look like on the outside and love everything about themselves, even if it's different from what others think is okay or acceptable.

The fourth and final thing I learned from having a serious relationship with my boyfriend is how to deal with conflicting interests and not settling. Even though I enjoyed being in the relationship and learning a lot about myself, it was the way it ended that taught me the most. My guy already had dark physical features, but he had an even deeper internal darkness. He started to experiment with smoking marijuana. As an athlete and having dreams of doing something with my life, I was scared and wisely avoided the stuff. Plus, my mother always told me drugs were bad. Ironically, I found marijuana in my mother's work bag one time. Even after finding her conflicting message, I still vowed to stay away from it.

Sure I was by him and told him that I didn't like what he was doing, but I still chose to stay with him instead of leaving. I wanted his attention and love so I set aside my morals just to be around him. His smoking became more frequent and he was in a stupor most of the time. It was like he was smiling at the clouds whenever he was awake. He lacked motivation and the camping all but stopped (one good thing). He just wanted to stay lit up. He began to crave it and felt like he needed it to exist. Our laughter stopped, cruising stopped, and we just hung out at his house. Our relationship went from my natural high to him being high all the time. The effect of the drug took its toll. He started getting bags under his eyes, gaining weight, and just wanted to play video games. His habit was destroying our relationship and brought us to a fork in the road. Should I give up my happiness for his aimless life? The question was tough, but the answer was obvious. I had to end it with Mr. Wonderful who was now Mr. Darkness. It hurt. It hurt like hell. He was my first boyfriend and I thought I was in love. But I knew it would hurt even more if I stayed with him. Crying, I said goodbye, wished him the best, and left.

People that want or need love from others more than they love themselves will never be happy. Love yourself first and then you open the door for others to genuinely love you in return. If you put others first, you end up putting yourself second and this will eventually lead to resentment.

It is sad to write this, but Mr. Wonderful was killed the year after I left for the Air Force. He was behind the wheel driving home when he got into an accident and died. I don't know what happened, but know his death was tragic and premature. My heart aches for his family knowing what he could have become. Rest in Peace, Dear Friend.

Moral of the Story – Relationships teach us a lot about ourselves and how we interact with others in an intimate setting. We learn what we like/dislike, accept/reject, love/hate, and what we're willing to live with, compromise on, or walk away from completely. *We must accept ourselves fully and love who we are completely.* We shouldn't do things we don't like just for someone to like us and we should never settle for another person's love when he or she is doing things that don't mesh with our future or our morals.

Our value is not dependent on what someone else thinks of us. It's what we think of ourselves that matters the most.

We should not buy-in to society's view of women and beauty. Looks fade, but a good heart never does. Beauty is more than skin deep. It's of substance, character, confidence, morals, principles, kindness, softness, and inner joy. If a person can look into a mirror and see their positive impacts more than their wrinkles, love handles, and cellulite, than that person is far more precious than a ruby. **Beauty is in your heart and it shines brighter and more radiantly than what the world thinks beauty is.**

Relationships are tough, which is why many don't last. Being able to put someone before ourselves is a hard thing to do because it requires us to be selfless. And we're naturally selfish people.

Relationships are tough, but they could also be a beautiful blessing in your life for a variety of reasons. Find your reason.

We're not meant to be alone, but it is better to be alone than to be with the wrong person. And if you're in a relationship and you feel lonely, please reevaluate your relationship.

Never compromise your morals just to be liked. It's better to be alone than to be with someone who doesn't value your beliefs. There's plenty of fish out there that would.

It's better to be loved and liked for who you are than to be loved or liked for who of you are not.

Chapter 20 – Jail or Air Force

Have you ever made a decision you whole-heartedly regretted? I have. Have you ever made a decision which seemed small and irrelevant, but ironically changed the course of your life? In fact, it may have even saved your life in a sense? I have! I wasn't thankful back then, but am forever grateful now. One day in a fluke situation I made a decision that changed the course of my life…forever!

In the beginning of my senior year of high school we were administered the Armed Services Vocational Aptitude Battery (ASVAB) test. The ASVAB measures your abilities and helps predict your potential academic and occupational success in the military. It's administered annually to more than one million applicants, high school and post-secondary students around the United States. I didn't have a second thought while taking the test, but afterwards I learned I did well enough to receive a phone call from a recruiter. The recruiter called and began talking to me about my future and a career in the military. We even talked about the possibility of me going to college. I was intrigued and excited to say the least. I didn't think I had a future beyond high school and now all of a sudden I had the hope of going to college.

Living in a trailer park and not having any direction in my life after high school was a little scary. I didn't have money to go to college nor did I have any chance of making it out of our trailer park. I was destined to work at the donut house, pizza joint, or wait tables like my mother and sister. My mother was poor, my sister was in and out of jail, and I had nothing going in my favor. As I spoke to the recruiter, I collected as much information as I could. I needed a ticket out of the life I was living and hoped this would be it.

The recruiter came to the house and gave me the Kool-Aid speech, which I drank up, if not guzzled. There was a chance I could learn a trade and leave the lackluster way of my current living situation. I wouldn't have to deal with my mother anymore either! More than anything I could go to college, the first in my family. Talk about a brand new life!

My current life sucked. My mother was mean, which resulted in me telling my mother, "Once I graduated high school I was leaving and never coming back." I hated it there, hated my circumstances, hated how poor I was, hated how my mother kissed my sister's butt and did everything for her and nothing for me, and I hated the thought of what I would become if I stayed. I hated it all while loving the delightful ideas of what the recruiter was promoting.

The recruiter said he would guarantee me a job in the medical field and I would become a different person, like the successful people I saw on television. He gave me all the specifics about military life, what was expected and required, and explained endless possibilities of my promising future. At that time, *I had no future so anything looked a million times better.*

After a week of pondering, I called the recruiter and told him I was in. There was one problem though. Because I had just turned seventeen I had to have my mother sign on my behalf. Reluctant, I asked her and she was actually eager to sign me away. Maybe she was fearful if I stayed in the trailer with her she would have to take care of me. So instead, she would gladly send me off into the wild blue yonder even if it meant going to war.

The recruiter came over the following day and we signed the paperwork. The next week I was sent to New Orleans, LA

Military Entrance Processing Station (MEPS) to get a military inprocessing physical. The physical was standard protocol with the doctor checking your vitals, heart, ears, eyes, chest, skin, hair, making you walk like a duck, and so many other things. The only weird part was being inspected head to toe, almost nude with only wearing a bra and underwear, standing there with twenty other girls. Yes, the military is not one for modesty.

Imagine standing there cold and shaking while being inspected by a doctor. I didn't know what to think other than this is crazy! It's one thing to be in the locker room with your teammates changing, but it's another thing to be almost nude with other people you don't know while being looked over by a person you just met. The military doesn't joke around. They embody the philosophy of team dependability, which means your team sees all of your flaws. They want to see your strengths and weaknesses just in case one day one of them may have to save your life or you may have to save theirs. Anyone that thinks the military isn't hard core, better think again. It doesn't start after you complete Basic Military Training (BMT); it starts when you're physically standing there with your fellow recruits walking like a duck.

I passed the military physical and was now on my way to sign the final stack of inprocessing paperwork. There was so much paperwork, which makes sense when you're about to commit your life to the military for the next four years. I was nervous, excited, and shedding tears of joy and fear. I signed the paperwork devoting my life to protect and defend the United States of America. After the physical was finished and paperwork signed, I was ushered into a room with a flag and was asked to raise my right hand to swear the

Enlistment Oath, which every enlisted member must do. All members repeat the Oath, which is the final step at MEPS.

The words you swear by are as follows, "I, (state your full name), do solemnly swear (or affirm) that I will support and defend the Constitution of the United States against all enemies, foreign and domestic; that I will bear true faith and allegiance to the same; and that I will obey the orders of the President of the United States and the orders of the officers appointed over me, according to regulations and the Uniform Code of Military Justice. So help me God." On 21 October 1993, I swore this Oath and officially joined the Delayed Enlistment Program, which meant I would have to wait for a departure date to begin Basic Military Training. The reason I was held up was because I needed to finish high school first. But upon graduation, I would be sent to Boot Camp for six long and arduous weeks.

Side note: One month later after graduating high school, I would depart to embark on a journey that would forever change the trajectory of my life. A small decision resulting in a radical result to a different life. This was truly a decision I would always be thankful for. Thank you, Air Force!

We have one life and if we live it to the fullest (rejoice from the good and learn from the bad), one life is all we really need. A life fully lived is a great life indeed!

It is never too late for a fresh start, a do-over…you're one decision from the rest of your life.

Moral of the Story – We must make choices in life. Some choices are life altering while others are barely noticeable. The day I committed my life to serve our country would undoubtedly be the second biggest and best decision I ever made. We may never know how much a single decision can shape our lives until many months, years, or decades later. I am thankful for deciding to join the military even now as I write this twenty-something years later.

Joining the military gave me more than a job. It gave me a family, a career, and taught me about things that are bigger than myself. It taught me about protecting and defending my fellow citizens of the United States of America at all costs, even in the face of death. It taught me about honor and sacrifice. I do not want to think of what I would have become if I didn't decide to join. I wouldn't have been able to reach my potential and grow into the person I am today.

Every decision we make, no matter how big or small it is, has the power to help, hurt, or change us. So we must think carefully before making a decision too quickly or to avoid making decisions for the wrong reasons. We must recognize and embrace the wisdom we gain from the accomplishments and failures of our decisions and consciously use that wisdom to make even better decisions for our future.

Let's be real. Some decisions we make can end up being the worst decision of our life. If that were to happen, embrace it, learn from it, and never make the same decision twice. None of us are perfect. Sometimes we choose well while other times we choose poorly. No matter what, it's our life and we must be okay with who we are, what we choose or not choose, what we have done or not done, and what we do to positively setup our lives in the future.

The choices you make today definitely impact your tomorrow and your life path years later. Please choose wisely.

Chapter 21 – Coward

Disclaimer – This chapter is of my opinion. My opinion does not dictate your opinion. It's okay to agree to disagree. Actually most people disagree with my opinion on this subject and its okay!

Drugs, illegal or legal, can be ruthless to your mind and body, if abused. This includes marijuana and alcohol. So if you disagree with my opinion that marijuana and alcohol are not problematic drugs, let's choose to agree to disagree. The fact is most drugs can damage brain cells and interfere with a person's neurology. Don't even get me started on opioids and pain killers. It's tragic and heartbreaking to see lives destroyed and the growing number of drug-related deaths.

In high school, marijuana was everywhere. Whether it was cruising the main boulevard, going to a party, or walking through the parking lot on my way to school it was there. People were smoking the green weed, rolling joints, or inhaling it from a bong. I had never seen people do these things before I entered high school. I was taught drugs were bad and to stay away from them. Even though I was surrounded by people who used drugs, I fortunately never had the urge to join them. Not to mention I had just enlisted in the Air Force; therefore, leaving my horrible home was my main focus and I wouldn't do anything to mess that up.

Not only was I fearful of drugs, I witnessed first-hand the affects they had on people. I witnessed people skip school, fail classes, miss out on sports and social engagements, and even choose to experiment with other drugs. It was a precarious situation they got themselves into and it was scary to me. I saw many friends lose their identities and ultimately their lives due to the influence of drugs. Their motivation declined, but their fallacious laughter increased. Something as simple as a yellow dot on the wall would make them laugh hysterically. They were unable to keep a steady job and became recluses with dazed eyes, staring into their future abyss.

The friends around me began doing drugs more frequently, even during the week instead of the occasional one or two times over the weekend. It seemed like they were addicted and wanted to alleviate some sort of pain they had to escape life's problems. It was sad because instead of them facing their problems, they were in essence running away from them. They were hiding behind a false wall of safety, believing it would keep them from harm indefinitely.

Drugs harm the body in different ways. When chemicals are introduced to the brain, the chemical messengers in the brain are altered, causing the brain to send a different set of signals to the body. Chemicals can cause individuals to see, think, and act differently than they normally would, which is why drug use affects individuals in various ways.

Drugs can also cause individuals to isolate themselves, which could lead to depression. Drugs can negatively impact the relationships drug users have with their loved ones. They may cause individuals to become aggressive or non-caring, making it difficult to make new friends or even keep existing ones. People using drugs may have a difficult time setting goals and may even lack confidence. Regularly using drugs may destroy motivation and drive, heighten feelings of anger and resentment toward others, drastically change eating and sleeping habits, remove the willpower to deal with personal problems, and can cause their lives to become worse. Drugs may create emotional instability, which may increase the desire to experiment with a variety of other drugs. Drugs may change who you are and can eventually cause harm to yourself and others.

Even though I never did drugs, I was a coward because I didn't talk with my friends and boyfriend about the impacts of using them. Instead, I stayed with them when they were stoned because they were all I had. If I truly cared about their well-being, I would have spoken up. But I was a young, naïve kid. I didn't know what to say or how to say it so I remained quiet. I saw some of my closest friends go down the path of destruction and I chose to say nothing. I have to live with that for the rest of my life and hopefully find a way to forgive myself for lacking the courage to speak up.

Some of my friends could have become something. Instead of wandering around in a routine of despair, their dark habits eradicated any chance of finding a light to their promising future. They quickly lost their innocence of living a care-free life and stumbled upon the abrupt roadblocks that come with the compromise of using drugs. They were happy in the now and never thought of the later.

Their compromises came with a cost. Most young adults at a certain age leave their parents' home and begin their path to adulthood. But most of my friends remained at home until they were finally kicked out of their parents' house. Once kicked out, they lived with other people, barely kept jobs, and depended on financial assistance from others. Sadly, they never gained their independence and continued down the 'high' road of destruction. It breaks my heart to think what they chose to endure.

I often wonder what would have happened if I would have tried to intervene with the choices they were making. Possibly nothing, but at least I wouldn't have regrets. I should have spoken up. I may have stood alone in my conviction, but I would have at least had the chance to extinguish the fire when it was just beginning to take hold of their lives.

Some of my friends did end up quitting their drug habit and making something of themselves, which is wonderful. But you have to wonder what they could have done with their lives if they never did drugs in the first place. Others weren't as lucky and my heart cries out for them. <u>Bottom Line</u> - *Don't be a coward like I was!* Speak up even if your voice shakes or even if you stand alone.

Moral of the Story – Overuse of drugs will destroy your mind, impair your judgment, weaken your decision-making, and kill your potential. When you have drugs in your system, they chemically disrupt your brain cells. They darken your glow in life and may become a gateway to using other drugs. Trying one drug weakens your thinking, making you vulnerable to the allure of using others. Nancy Regan had it right with her campaign, "Just Say No."

Above all, don't be a coward like I was. It's okay to intervene in a situation where you see people going down a wrong path. It's okay to stop them from destroying their lives. Join their parents, loved ones, and close friends in the objective to eradicate the irrepressible poor decisions they are making that could harm them…and their future forever.

I ask this of you - if you see your friends using drugs or just messing up, please be courageous and speak up. Help them by saying something because there's a higher probability they'll choose the right path and end up thanking you for it later. A small act of courage can lead to an enormous act of change. Encourage and help them kick their bad habits!

Chapter 22 – Not a Doormat

My senior year of high school sped by after I joined the Air Force delayed enlisted program. During the year, I stayed busy playing softball, hanging out with friends, studying hard and getting good grades, and running track. I found track to be utterly amazing. It made me feel empowered, strong, beautiful, fit, and healthy. I began to really fall in love with who I was and noticed the positive effect running had on my body and mind. I realized being skinny wasn't important anymore, but being strong was.

One day a friend asked me to go out with her and her boyfriend on a double date with someone I'd never met. I was always seen as average so I decided to get dolled up. I wore a cute little outfit, curled my hair, and did my make-up. When my friend and the guys showed up, my date was the most handsome and physically strong man I had ever seen. He was dark headed, tall, had muscles, was a few years older, and worked offshore. We immediately connected, began bantering, and flirted with each other. When he kissed me politely on the lips at the end of the night, I saw fireworks. He was pure yumminess.

We started spending time together. He would attend my track practices, take me to get some food after, and then take me home. We talked all the time. I had a boyfriend. When he left for his offshore work, he would leave me his car so I no longer had to ride the bus to school. I was driving my man's car and it was a Camaro. I was so happy! We were great together.

I was living in a beautiful dream, but then things began to change. We started hanging out with some of his old friends and they were headed nowhere. We stopped going out and hung out with them at their trailer. I was an outsider to the group and I would sit there and have to deal with the annoying people getting drunk. I hated their lifestyle. I hated the fact we were wasting time and wasting our lives. They would be laughing the entire time about nothing in particular while I sat there longing to leave. Of course, they weren't drunk twenty-four-seven and the times they weren't we had fun. My guy wasn't drunk all the time either and when he wasn't life was awesome. He doted on me and spoiled me with good conversation and meaningful gifts. He nurtured me by getting me food and water (sounds like prison, LOL) when I was hungry. He always made sure I was taken care of. I appreciated that about him and it was the main reason I stayed with him.

Even though other girls would dote on him, he chose to dote on me. Even still, I disliked the other girls. Why would they flirt with a guy that was taken? (Those types of girls are what I call a fleabag!) One of them was married and she acted trashy while openly flirting with my man. I felt bad for her husband. Another girl was single and a little overweight and she flirted as well. Luckily, neither of them made my guy blink-an-eye. To him, I was different. I was the girl still in school with a bright future, making good grades, playing sports, and was the only person in his life not doing drugs or drinking. I was his anomaly; his North Star. He let it be known that he hoped to get out of this mess and leave with me. We were planning our future together. We were going to make it. I just needed to get through the six-weeks of basic training and then we would run off to our happily-ever-after.

Our relationship deepened. We were constantly together, talking, laughing, and having fun. Then one day he came to my house and gave me a diamond ring. He gave me the ring as a plea for me to not forget him. He said he loved me and was scared I would break up with him. We cried and then laughed as I assured him I would not leave him. That same night we went out to celebrate and had a great dinner…that night was a fairytale every girl dreams of.

Everything was going great. I was kicking butt in track and had the hope of leaving the dreaded trailer park with my dream guy.

Shortly after the night he gave me the ring, he had to return to his offshore job. He was gone for two long weeks and when he returned I jumped into his arms. That night we went out, but I wasn't feeling very well. I was coming down with some sort of cold, running a fever, and I never got sick. But I was more concerned with spending time with my man so I got ready and went with him to his friend's trailer.

When we arrived, everyone decided to get high. Again I was left sitting alone on the couch. As I sat, I could see everyone huddled in the kitchen and hanging out with my guy were those two fleabags. He was spending more time with them than me. I know it was his first night home, but I grew jealous. Two chicks were openly flirting with my man right in front of me and I didn't have the energy to say anything. I was tired and sick. He didn't once come over to sit with me.

After about thirty minutes of watching this, my stomach began to ache and my fever started getting worse. My heart was breaking. I was confused. I didn't understand. Something in me snapped. I wasn't going to sit by and watch. I loved myself. I had a big heart and a huge future.

I wasn't going to allow it to be destroyed by a guy that didn't respect me.

I looked over one last time at the three of them (I can still close my eyes, remember it, and feel the pain), stood up and walked out the door. I couldn't bare it anymore and wasn't going to let him hurt me. I had worth. I had value and I mattered. After I left, I walked over to the convenience store and called step-dad #4 to come and get me. I stood in the store for fifteen minutes while trying to stay warm until step-dad showed up in his old beater car to take me home. Out of all the step-dads I had in my life, I liked him the most. His name was Pat. He had a big heart like me. He cooked dinner every night and treated me kindly. I digress, sorry.

When I got home I immediately went to bed. A few hours later I heard tapping on my bedroom window and knew it was my guy, but I didn't answer. Without budging I fell back asleep. I was sick, but not dumb. My boyfriend intentionally hurt me by choosing to disrespect me. I didn't deserve to be treated with such disregard. *I deserved better*. If I was giving 100%, he had to give it 100% also.

The next morning I woke up and felt better. It was the weekend so I went outside to help my family mow the grass. My guy showed up and I was covered in mud, grass, dirt, and sweat. I looked like a groundskeeper. He apologized profusely and begged me for forgiveness. I told him how I deserved better and reminded him how disrespectful he was. I told him I wouldn't put up with his disregard. If he didn't want to act like a gentleman, I didn't need him or want him. Solemnly, he said he would never do it again and asked for another chance. I was hesitant, but I gave it to him and for the next few months life was bliss again.

Before I knew it, the big day arrived. It was my very last night to spend in New Orleans before leaving for Air Force basic training. My guy brought me two dozen roses and we cried in each other's arms. I think we both knew it was over. I didn't know if he would stay true and he didn't know if I would break up with him for a better life. We stayed in each other's arms until I left for basic training the next morning.

This relationship taught me a great deal about my self-respect. Not only did it teach me how to gracefully say goodbye in the best way, but it also taught me about my self-worth. I found the courage to disavow a man who disrespected me. I stood up for what I wanted and what I believed in. I didn't allow someone to get away with treating me unjustly. I stood firm and spoke up. I didn't settle. I didn't tolerate my significant other having women flirt with him, especially right in front of me.

I would rather be alone than be with someone who openly disrespects who I am and our relationship. I learned a lot about myself and am thankful we happened. I wasn't the girl who begged for love from anyone. I loved myself enough to walk away. I was not and would not become a Doormat for anyone!

It's better to be alone than to be with someone that makes you feel alone even when you are together.

Moral of the Story – You have dignity! Never allow anyone to belittle or demean you! No one should take your value away! No one should undermine you! No one should stomp on you! No one should ever treat you as an option; instead you should be treated as a priority! No one should ever hurt your self-esteem so much that you become weak and worthless! No one should ever manipulate your mind or create intentional pain! And you shouldn't allow it! Know your worth!

When you give your love to someone who doesn't respect you or your time, you surrender pieces of your heart that you will never get back. There will be failed relationships, but losing someone who doesn't appreciate you is actually a gain.

Some people come into your life temporarily to simply teach you something. It's perfectly okay that they're not in your life anymore. You now have more time to focus on the relationships that truly matter. Your love for yourself is worth far more than any other person's any way.

Stand up for yourself because you're worth it! You are not a doormat to be walked on. I validate you. I validate your feelings and they matter. I validate your strength to speak up for what you feel. I validate you for not settling for less than you deserve!

Please don't ever be a doormat for the sake of being with someone. You are better than that! You deserve more.

Stop spending time with toads.

Spray kindness on fleabags.

Take yourself off the clearance rack and believe you are worth full price. Change your thinking, change your life.

Chapter 23 – You're Fat!

After I raised my right hand to enlist in the Air Force my recruiter said these words to me, "You need to lose weight before Basic Training and get healthy." What I heard was, "You're fat." Those words were the first glimpse I had of someone genuinely caring about my health.

I was never super-skinny nor was I ever the kid that weighed upwards of 200-lbs. I was the athletic kid with muscle, but also with love handles. I grew up on processed food, eating mostly at fast food chains, frozen dinners, hot dogs, canned goods, boxed sweets, soda, sweet tea, and potato chips. I didn't have the luxury of eating fruit, homemade meals, vegetables, or even drinking filtered water. My mother worked three jobs so everything was quickly prepared and cheap. My sister and I were the primary cooks and since we never learned the finer art of cooking, everything was popped into the oven or prepared out of a box or a can. This didn't benefit our waistlines or our hearts.

I was never obese because I played a lot of sports, but I was unhealthy. My recruiter got my attention when he told me I needed to lose weight. I looked at him like a deer in the headlights. I didn't know what he meant. I regularly looked at myself in the mirror and never thought of myself as being overweight, but according to military standards I was hovering around the "fat girl" line. My recruiter told me I needed to lose at least ten pounds and to eat better. He told me I needed to run more long distances and to drink water more often. He told me to get healthy if I wanted to pass Basic Training and that he would even help me.

The next day he came over to our trailer and explained the Food Pyramid to me. I was thinking to myself, who does this and why does this guy care so much? Was I just a new member to meet his monthly quota, did he have an ulterior motive, or did he actually care about me as a person? After explaining the Food Pyramid, he taught me about water consumption and why it was important for a healthy body. He then explained the difference between processed foods and real foods and the importance of eating fruits and vegetables. He also educated me on the techniques of running, push-ups, and sit-ups. After he finished, I was totally adept in how to become a future basic trainee success story. But in order to be successful, I had to immediately start applying what I learned.

I started running around the trailer park. I was already in track, but was a sprinter not a long-distance runner. One lap around the park was about one-half mile. As I began running around it to break myself in, the first lap had me gasping for air. I continued running every day and gradually increased my laps to two while also learning how to keep a pace. I eventually found my breathing rhythm and enjoyed the sound of my feet pounding the pavement. Over time I noticed my body taking on a slimmer form, my legs became muscular, and my thighs trimmed down. (I have tree stumps for legs.) I heeded my recruiter's suggestion to begin drinking more water, less sweet tea, and no soda. I cut back significantly on the processed foods and began eating as best I could. However, being poor made it challenging and not to mention I had no one at home to help me with clean eating.

As time went on I realized my recruiter did have a heart for me. He began taking me to Air Force functions so I could meet other members and future trainees. I think he could tell my home life was horrible and my eating habits were just as bad and seeing that no one really cared about me, he gave me attention. I kind of thought of him as an uncle. At the functions we attended, people treated me with respect, were courteous, asked me questions, and made me feel important. I learned when you're treated well, you feel good about yourself and take on a different mentality.

Then my first weigh-in happened. I was nervous. Even though I knew my body had changed, I had no idea how much I weighed since we didn't have a scale at home. I nervously got on the scale and to my surprise I had lost ten pounds. Running lap after lap in the trailer park paid off, but not as much as what I gained in terms of eating healthier. I understood physical fitness was important, but eating right was also very important. I learned whatever fuel I was burning came from the fuel I consumed. What you consume really does matter. It can be medicine or it can be cancer.

A balanced diet is important for our organs and tissues. They need proper nutrition to work effectively. Without good nutrition, our bodies are more prone to disease, infection, fatigue, and poor performance. Healthy eating helps us get the right balance of vitamins, minerals, and other nutrients. They help us to feel our best and provide an abundance of energy. They allow us to effectively handle stress. It's important to remember healthy eating shouldn't be construed as a temporary diet. It should be viewed as making a life change to our eating habits that we can adopt and enjoy for the rest of your lives. With diets, we relate to begrudgingly giving something up. By associating them with lost comfort foods we're apt to crave those foods and cave to the temptation of overeating them. Eventually our new viewpoint would reframe our thinking that eating a healthy and balanced variety of foods are far more satisfying than eating junk and processed foods. If we match it with increased physical activity, we can ultimately achieve a healthy bodyweight and stay there. Don't diet. Instead, adopt a healthy eating lifestyle and it will lead to an improved, more fulfilling life. Off my soapbox now. :)

Having all of this new knowledge was great and I was losing weight. I was toning my body and learning about healthy eating, but I had one massive problem--my mind. When I heard the words, "You're fat," my self-image dramatically changed. I was no longer the innocent minded teenager. I was tainted with the world's image of what I should look like. I was okay with getting healthy, but I wasn't okay with someone telling me I had to lose weight. In my mind, my body image was no longer appropriate. I believed I was fat so I became obsessed with being thin. Every time I looked into the mirror I cringed at what I saw even though I was healthy looking. I didn't want to see any fat on my legs or cellulite under my bottom. Most people would have killed for a body like mine, but I still only saw a fat girl.

Body image is how you see your physique when you look in the mirror or how you mentally picture yourself. It encompasses everything you believe about your own appearance, including memories, assumptions, and generalizations made by others. It affects how you feel about your body, including your height, shape, and weight. It makes you cognizant of how you control your body's movement and the way you feel inside. The way you perceive your body could be positive or negative and it plays a significant role in your overall mental health.

Positive body image is when we have a realistic perception of our bodies and we are satisfied with the way they are. Positive body image means understanding healthy bodies come in many shapes and sizes, and physical appearance says little about our character or value as a person. A healthy body image means our assessment of our bodies is kept separate from our sense of self-worth and it ensures we don't spend an unreasonable amount of time worrying about food, weight, and calories.

A negative body image leaves us with a distorted perception of normal size and shape, as well as an emotional sense of shame, awkwardness, and anxiety about ourselves. People with a negative body image tend to feel their size or shape is a sign of personal failure and it defines their self-worth. A poor body image has been linked to diminished mental performance, low self-esteem, anxiety, depression, sexual dysfunction, dieting, and eating disorders. It's so sad.

Our perceived body images have been morphed into something unrealistic due in large part to the media. The media is a powerful conduit that feeds and enforces our cultural beliefs and values. Although they may not be exclusively responsible for setting the standards for physical attractiveness, they make escaping the frequent exposure to these images and attitudes almost impossible. People see the same images displayed and start to believe they are reality. People begin to think if those bodies are ideal, than their own bodies are imperfect and they are failures because of it.

Now many years later after being sworn-in to the Air Force, I still suffer with my own body image at times. I'm being totally honest! I look at myself in the mirror sometimes and think I'm overweight even though I weigh 135 pounds and its muscle. Granted, I am very healthy in terms of diet and exercise, but my thoughts are unhealthy at times. What I see is very different from what others see. They see fit, but I see fit with flab. I don't know if I'll ever be able to truly overcome what I see in the mirror. But I've learned ways to combat my thoughts of a negative body image when I begin to feel a certain way. I fall in love with who I am wholeheartedly and remember that it's not about the numbers on the scale; it's about the person. I then stop comparing myself to the stick girls on the covers of magazines. I know it's not realistic, plus most them are enhanced by Photo-shop.

Lastly, I eat healthy and exercise frequently which gives me physical strength. I choose strong over skinny any day of the week. I love all of me, inside and out. That's how my thinking has changed gradually overtime. Even though those words from my recruiter negatively changed my thinking in some ways, overall he changed my life because I am healthy and enabled myself to live a longer, more prosperous life.

The question for you is how is your physical health? If you don't exercise, you should. If you don't eat healthy, you should. Also, how is your mental health in terms of what you see when looking at yourself in the mirror? Both aspects of health are crucial to your overall health and well-being.

Moral of the Story – When you're told something negative, it stops you in your tracks. It turns your life upside down and you change mentally. Sometimes for the better, sometimes for the worse.

Men and women are inherently different in terms of body image. A man looks in the mirror and sees Superman. A woman looks into the mirror and sees every single flaw.

Particularly for women, when we're told we're overweight, our body image mindset can steer us in an unhealthy direction. It can destroy us if we don't mentally change our body image perception from destructive thinking to constructive thinking.

The media conveys an unrealistic image of what beauty is and it's more than what they portray as stick thin. Being broad and muscular are one thing, while being overweight and unhealthy are another. It's not about numbers on the scale. It's about who you are as a person. However, if you can't walk up a flight of stairs without getting winded, you have some health concerns that need to be addressed. Being physically unfit can be a detriment to you and to your family.

Wanting to be healthy means you care about yourself. *Acting* on it means you care enough to change. It could prolong your life or even save it. As a friendly reminder, people who speak truth to you with love only want the best for you. They're taking time out of their schedules to help you. Even if you disagree with them, take heart to what they are saying. It may hurt to hear, but if their point is valid, it may be wise to consider.

Turn off the television and put down the ice cream, chips, or beverage. Put down the electronic gadgets and go outside to experience the beauty around you. If you want to get healthy, then get healthy. Stop making the poor choices or complaining about what you have the power to change.

Good health won't be handed to you. It takes discipline, making hard decisions, time and effort, self-control, and a determined mindset. Most people don't want to put in the hard work, which is why we have an obesity situation in the country. **Don't be like most people.** Instead, be the best version of yourself that you can possibly be.

Choose a healthy lifestyle because you only have one body to live in so you should take care of it the best you can.

Chapter 24 – Beautiful Disaster

What does every teenager want to do besides turn eighteen? They want to graduate high school and start their journey in life. Young adults want to leave home, be in charge of themselves, vote, and start living a life without parental control. My final high school days at the Maroon Tide were rapidly approaching and I was thrilled. (Note to pending graduates: This sounds exciting, but it is much harder than it seems.)

Before the big day occurred, our final week of school entailed daily events. We had spirit day, college day, sports day, test day, and an awards banquet to wrap it up. All of this was special because it was commemorating our final year of school celebrating everything coming to a close. It was our climactic moment, the highest of highs, where we could proclaim our lofty teenage accomplishments.

The day of the awards banquet was especially memorable for me because I received two athletic awards. I won Best Sprinter and Miss Maroon Tide for Softball. I still remember that night as I close my eyes. I walked up to receive my first award and someone whistled at me. No one ever seemed to take notice of me in school, but that night someone did. Not only did I win two awards, but I also got a whistle! Still to this day, I don't know the person behind the whistle, but I'd like to thank him because it still puts a smile on my face.

After all of the daily events of the week were over, the big day had finally arrived, high school graduation day. The day I had been dreaming of since I started at my new school. It was finally here. It was a real achievement some never experience. It was my chance to walk across the stage and receive a diploma. It was my ticket to leave home and never return. I was ecstatic. I was floating on cloud nine. My mother, step-dad #4, sister, and a few friends of the family came into town to join the grand affair. I styled my hair in curls, put on make-up, borrowed a dress from a friend, and looked cute. What made the event even more special was being able to hang out with my friends while my family sat in the stands. The ceremony was held outside on the school's football field and there wasn't a cloud in the sky. All of us who were graduating took our seats and the graduation ceremony began. The sun was on our shoulders to start; however, by the time all of us received our diplomas and tossed our caps in the sky the moon was high above. It didn't matter. It was finished and I had the biggest smile on my face. I did it.

After the ceremony I was given a dozen roses and smiles were plastered on my family's face, except my mother's. It was always like that. She could suck the life out of everyone. I'm still, to this day, not sure why she was sad. Either she was crying because she was finally getting rid of me or she knew that once I left I would never return. Given that our home life simply sucked, I think her tears were for the latter.

We eventually left the school, went back to the trailer, and sat down to have dinner together. It was nice being the center of attention for once, well, sort of. My mother was still crying so everyone was busy consoling her. Following dinner we had cake and afterwards I decided to leave and go hang out with my friends. My boyfriend was at his offshore job so I took his car to meet several of my friends at various places to celebrate. I was happy and needed time to let it all soak in. Once I was done visiting, I decided to call it a night and went home.

By the time I had arrived to the house everyone had left, but my mother and step-dad #4. My mother was no longer crying, which was a good thing, but something was off, way off. As soon as I walked in the door, my mother began yelling at me and saying, "Where is it?" I had no idea what she was talking about and responded, "Where is what?" She immediately lunged on top of me and I fell backwards. I started to say I don't know what you're talking about, "Where is what? I don't know anything. I just got home." By this point, she was screaming at me and asking me where the baby picture of my sister and me was. I had no idea where it was and told her so. She didn't believe me. She went into my room while pulling me by my hair and started opening my dresser drawers and throwing all of my belongings onto the floor.

She was in a crazy rage and I was scared. I didn't know what was going on. She then moved to my closet and did the same thing all while yelling at me. She called me a liar and other horrible names making me feel like the lowest person on earth. She then went to my daybed, picked up the mattress, and dumped it on the floor. For being a small woman, she was surprisingly strong. My entire room looked like a tornado had hit it. This was all because of a picture she was looking for, which she accused me of taking. And I didn't even do it. When she left, I sat in the middle of the chaos, by myself, crying. I was alone in my destroyed room knowing I didn't deserve this. I lost track of time sitting there and crying. My moments of pure joy I felt just hours before were instantly destroyed by my mother's blatantly insane destruction.

Have you ever had everything going so well and then something radically opposite happens? It makes you want to run away and never return? It makes you put up walls so you can never be hurt again? It makes you shut down? It makes you hate someone? It makes you hurt to the very being of your core? It makes you not want to trust anyone? Well, that was me and how I felt. I was hit by an 18-wheeler at full speed and I felt dazed.

It was at that moment that I knew resolutely I would be better off without my family. I didn't want their insanity to latch onto me and burden me while on my journey to a better life. I had roughly six weeks to go before I left for Basic Training and with leaving as my goal I knew I could endure anything.

I slowly began picking up my room. I don't know where my strength came from, maybe God, and the will to move forward. I was strong…a fighter. It took about three hours to put things back in the drawers, hang-up my clothes, put my bed back on the frame, and get the rest of my things back in order. The rest of the night I kept to myself. I never left my room and actually slept under my bed. I cried the entire night. I was used to being alone and feeling unwanted so this didn't feel any different.

When my mother left my room, she never even returned to check on me. I was a 17-year old girl that just suffered immense heartache for no reason because of her mother's irrational behavior. But I was strong and that's how I began to smile again the next morning.

As morning came, I left my room and saw my mother sitting on the sofa. She didn't say a word to me. Maybe it was because she was embarrassed. I'm not sure. She never apologized, didn't hug me, or even mention the picture again. Oh, the picture? It was in the place it always was, in her room on the television. I'm not sure how it came up missing in the first place, but miraculously it was found. In the interim of its search, I paid the price, the horrible price of being called names, getting my room destroyed, and having my joy crushed.

One person's actions and words can destroy another person's spirit, if they allow it. I knew my worth and knew I didn't deserve how my mother treated me, especially when I didn't deserve it. For you, don't let another person make you believe you're unworthy or make you feel despair. No one deserves to be treated in an abusive manner. I ask that you leave immediately from their abusive hold and get help if you need it. Help is available at all times.

Know what you allow will continue. You are the CEO of your life. You control what happens to you and how you respond.

Moral of the Story – When you're happy, enjoy it. Enjoy every single moment. Relish all that is good because one never knows when sorrow will arrive. Unexpected pain that destroys the soul, hurts the heart, and makes you cry like a baby. It breaks you. But, without pain one will not know what happiness feels like. Therefore, without one we can't really understand and appreciate the other.

Celebrate your moments of joy and soak them up so they will always be in your mind and heart. Celebrate the victories in your life. Take a moment to reflect. Take a moment to smile. Take a mental picture of the situation so you will always have something to cherish when tragedy strikes. We never know when pain will come, but we must always be ready for it no matter what.

If you are struggling with pain, hurt, sadness, please know you will overcome it…eventually. You are strong, capable of the struggles life throws your way and wise enough to know darkness will eventually turn into light. Be patient. Just like the sun shines in the morning, it's your sign of hope that you will rise and shine again. You can overcome whatever or whoever is holding you down.

If you're the victim of someone else's torment, I am very sorry. You don't deserve it. I ask that you love yourself enough to leave the toxic environment before it becomes a detriment to you. Your heartache will heal, but only if you get the guts to depart from the torment. No person on this Earth deserves abuse so don't tolerate or accept it from anyone.

Never settle when you can soar.

Chapter 25 – Goodbye

The day I left for Basic Training was a day of closure with my old self and a new beginning with the person I was meant to become. I was saying, "Goodbye" to the person I was and to an unhealthy living environment. I wasn't sure if a person could really change their life, but I was going to try. I no longer wanted to be the poor girl from the trailer park with the horrible, dysfunctional family. I wanted to be the smart girl with money in her pocket and a family that was stable. Darkness was no longer going to be the center of my life. A light living all around and within me was going to become my 'present' and my 'future.'

For seventeen years I lived in darkness. Sure there were specks of light, but darkness was the primary ominous shadow that encircled my life. My family was poor, didn't get along, unhappy, uneducated, deceitful, abusive, controlling, manipulative, hurtful, and just plain old mean. They would rather put each other down than pick one another up. Negativity was the nucleus of our lives and we couldn't see beyond its barriers. We didn't know how to be kind to one another. We just spent our lives trying to survive. Sometimes it was just us three, but most of the time it was four who lived amongst one another because we had to, not because we wanted to.

I'm not sure why, but there were many nights I slept under my bed afraid. I doubted myself even though I wore a smile. I didn't want people to know about my life so I hid behind a mask. I hid my real life from everyone. My mask of happiness was a facade and the only times I was really ever happy was when I was playing sports, hanging out with my friends, spending time with other families, or away from home. The beatings, verbal and emotional abuse, constant fighting, and feeling of being unloved was the horror that plagued my home life. There wasn't any joy. It was sadness, hardship, and unhappiness. These were the reasons why I so desperately wanted this chapter in my life to end. I wanted to become someone new.

The specks of light emanated from the kindness of others were a blessing to me, but I wanted the light to be constant. To me, the light was a feeling of hope that created the possibility of a life of significance, love, and overall goodness.

I needed to end my childhood and begin adulthood, but I was afraid. This would involve starting a brand new life…alone. Growing up in an unstable home was hard, but it provided a sense of security. Even though my family treated me horribly, they were still my family and the only people I had. In the end though, I had to reconcile with the truth and leave in order to begin a new life, fear and all.

While pondering the arduous journey ahead, I reflected on the moments that inspired me to make the jump into my unknown future of hope. When I was fifteen, a man I didn't know did something for me which left a speck of light that forever changed me. His name was Amos. Amos had his family to take care of, but he graciously took care of me too. He was well-off, but didn't live as the money-hoarding sort of guy, he paid it forward. One softball season I didn't have money to play ball at the local Friendship Park, but desperately wanted to so step-dad #4 reached out to Amos on my behalf and convinced him to sponsor me. It wasn't a lot of money, but it was the thought of him paying for me to play that made such an impact. Who would do that? Amos would. The memories I have from Friendship Park will stay with me forever. I developed solid friendships and was able to dramatically improve my softball skills. Plus, the time I spent at the park kept me off the streets and enabled me to work extra hours by keeping books so I could buy an occasional hamburger to eat. Additionally, I made the All-Star Team and helped lead my team to win the league championship. Amos' act of kindness for a kid he didn't even know was awe-inspiring for me. His kindness will remain with me for the rest of my life and has humbly inspired me to pay his generosity forward.

Other specks of light in my life occurred on Christmas and my birthdays. My mother didn't have extra money, but on those special days of the year she always tried her best to buy gifts. On my birthday, she would make me a cake and take me to buy my one gift. Every year the gift I chose would be new running shoes. They were expensive, but she always managed. On Christmas, mother would make a dinner feast and give gifts to my sister and me. To keep things fair, she would buy us the same gift to curtail any fighting. Christmas day was special because of getting presents, eating good food, and spending time together without fighting. Those moments are a treasure in my heart because it only happened twice a year. It wasn't so much about the food or the gifts, it was about spending time with one another without the heartache. I find you deeply relish those good memories when they are few and far between.

It's hard to recall the other specks of light I had in my life other than what I have written about in the first half of this book. In plain terms, my life sucked as a kid. I really didn't have a lot of moments that made me laugh. It was Groundhog Day at its finest. I was living life, surviving, and making the best of what I had so I could get through each day without tears. I've struggled with this chapter because it gave me a faint wisp of nostalgia with respect to the few good times I had as a child. I was closing a portion of my life and releasing the pain of what I felt as a kid. I was saying goodbye to the physical beatings of belts, cords, spatulas, hands, switches, and shoes and the verbal abuse of curse words and hateful talk.

In transition to creating my future, I decided to keep my personality because I loved my jovial spirit, my boldness to take on anything and anyone, my outgoing attitude while interacting with people, and my courage to leave everything behind and start over from scratch. Those were the attributes I possessed then and wanted to hold onto for the rest of my life. They gave me power, like a superhero's cape. I felt like I was flying into unchartered territory to conquer a new beginning, a new life.

Imagine starting completely over in life. It has been done before and any person that has done it would say the same thing - it's scary, very scary. Leaving home changed me as a person, empowered me as a human being, gave me strength to climb from rock bottom to reach greater heights, and to become what I was meant to be. No one told me how to do it or what to do and no one held me back or helped me leave. I did it alone. I started over. I made it happen. Just like all the other people that have been able to completely restart their lives. It is hard work, but worth it.

If you need a change, I implore you to find the courage to make the change. *You only have one life so make it count.*

Moral of the Story – When you're at rock bottom, the only way to go is up. If you're miserable, at some point in your life you must choose to make a change. You either can choose to stay where you are, thus remain unhappy or you can choose to change for something better. You can stay lost in the darkness with a few glimmers of light shining sporadically throughout your life; or you can believe in yourself, garner your strength and courage, and experience constant bouts of triumphant bravery while striving for change. You can leave the darkness completely behind and be engulfed in light always. That's called joy. It's okay to close the door on "who you are" right now and open the door to "who you're meant to become." The memories of who you were will positively blend into the person you are to become because those memories are the attributes that will direct you to where the light shines forever.

Every decision you make from this point on sets you up for your future. What you do or don't do today will determine what you will or will not become in the future. Your life is in your hands, no one else's. You can live in the "now" moments or prepare for the "future" possibilities. Most people don't plan for later, they want things now.

I challenge you to think about every day as a gift and your future as endless. You have the power to change. Every Saint was once a Sinner and every Sinner can become a Saint. It's up to you. Don't be afraid of doing it alone.

The best is yet to come. You must first take a leap of faith. You can cut the anchors in your life and soar to new heights. It begins with one small step, one foot in front of the other. You can do it, trust me.

Remember, **it's better to soar with eagles than to stay where you are and cluck with chickens.**

It doesn't matter how you start in life, it only matters how it ends. ~ Smile, Shine, Soar ~

Transition – Mess to Message

In my life, you can portray me as two people. One person was the first 25 Chapters of my life. The trailer park girl story has mostly come to an end. I closed the hurt, anger, sadness, insecurity, confusion, anxiety, and heartache. Like the colors black and white, I had no gray in the mix. I bid goodbye to that part of my life and rarely looked back.

Who I am today and have been for 20+ years are portrayed in the next 25 Chapters. What is often said is often true…the person who loves the most was often hurt the most. The person who gives the most knows what it's like to have nothing. The person with the kindest heart has had their heart shattered. That was me.

Who I am today is made from who I was before. Everything I went through has created me into who I am. Without the pain, sorrow, and sadness, I wouldn't know happiness, wholeness, and healing. My life is a beautiful disaster, and my childhood mess is now a real message of hope, perseverance, and transformation! I'm a girl full of love, joy, and kindness. I matter! I am here for a reason. I am loved. I am thankful for my childhood because it made me…me!

You will notice a vast difference in the coming chapters. The pain is mostly gone. Joy is now in the forefront. I've been learning to grow into my best possible self because it's the journey I choose to be on. I choose to look up and climb over whatever life throws my way. I choose to be the real me.

It's time to begin. Cheer with me, my Friend.

II. White House

Chapter 1 – Sink or Swim

Have you ever been thrown into the deep end of the pool and had to decide whether to sink or swim? That was me caught in a life or death dilemma and needed to decide which option to take. Would I take the easy way and give up or take the hard way and give it all I had? My childhood life was hard and it would have been easier to just give up then to push forward into a better adulthood, but that wasn't who I was. So, I chose to swim, because the possibility of happiness could become reality. I couldn't live in a trailer with dysfunctional people anymore and wanted a real future. I decided to fight for my life, get to safety, and escape the possibility of mediocrity, death, or prison, and to work towards a new beginning. I chose to swim and fight because my life future was at stake.

It was my first time on an airplane and I was scared. I had no idea what to expect, but a new life. I was flying into the unknown. People never know what they're capable of until they are out of their comfort zone. My time was now.

The plane landed safely and we were escorted to a nearby bus. Whoever said Basic Training was difficult had no idea what they were talking about. Everyone was nice. I sat on the bus by a really tall guy and we chit-chatted. The conversation was comforting even though it was 0100 hours in the morning. We arrived at Lackland Air Force Base (AFB) around 0200 and were shuffled into gender-based barracks lined with beds in four long rows. There were several people sleeping, but the Training Instructor (TI), a female who looked like a dude, turned on the lights, and started screaming. This was a feculent moment I will remember for the rest of my life.

The TI began screaming, "Remove valuables and put them in the locker!" I removed my watch and tried my best to hurry to put it in the locker, but I was having trouble because my hands were shaking. The TI was screaming as I struggled to unlock my locker with its key. Not to mention, it was a trick lock. The next thing I know, the TI was walking closer to me and I started fumbling even more. As she approached, I finally got the locker to open and hurried to stand. She looked at me and screamed, "Are you dumb? What's in your pockets?" I looked down and my pocket was bulging. I forgot that I had money. I hurried towards my locker and the stupid key wouldn't open the lock. The TI kept screaming at me, "You are stupid. You won't make it past the first day. How could you be so dumb for forgetting you had stuff in your pockets?" She kept shouting while I'm still fumbling to unlock the locker for the second time. I told myself I wasn't going to cry, but I was close. I finally got the locker open, threw the money in, and immediately stood up. The TI turned to walk away. I had a momentary sigh of relief until she turned back around and yelled, "You will be the first one to go, to get kicked back, and sent home because you can't even follow instructions." Finally, she relented with her tongue-lashing, told us all to get into bed, and left.

I cried that night. I cried my eyes out. It was tough, more tough than I expected. I didn't want to be sent home, but was doubting I could even last. I felt stupid for failing to follow simple directions. I finally fell asleep in my tears.

The next day we got up and headed for chow. Not one person stood next to me. No one wanted to be around the girl that would be sent home first. I was like the black plague, the disease everyone knew to avoid. After chow, we were taken to get clothes, shoes, and supplies, and the entire day no one talked to me other than the screams from the TI's. I was alone and felt dejected. That day of silence turned into three long days of sheer avoidance by my fellow Basic Trainees. Then it all changed.

On the fourth day, another TI made us stand in line and report in. We were instructed to knock on the door and repeat, "Basic Trainee (Insert your last name) reports as ordered." After being told to enter, we would stand at attention and answer questions. We would turn around, walk out, and proceed to our bunks. When it was my turn, I reported in, answered questions, and when leaving the door I did an about face movement and walked off. He screamed at me…"Where did you learn that?" I replied, "Sir, ROTC." Impressed, he decided to immediately make me Dorm Chief.

The Dorm Chief was commander of the dorm, in so many terms, and worked with four element leaders (assistants). I was seventeen years old. The women in the dorm ranged from 17-35 years of age and I was in charge of all of them. It was a big responsibility. Ironically, it helped remove the target from my back planted by the TI on the first day.

Over the next few days, it was a huge sigh of relief when the first five women were sent home and I wasn't one of them.

For being so young, the leadership skills I displayed even impressed me. I knew the basics of how to lead, but this was different. I did my job as best I could and resolved I wasn't going to allow the TI to break me or break us.

Dorm Chief duties included marching the dorm to chow, reporting in, and being screamed at. It was worth it because I had become friends with the four element leaders. We did everything together as a team and we built an awesome dorm together. In fact, we were winning physical fitness awards, test awards, and had no discrepancies. Our beds were kept within tight specs and we were coined the best of the best. Our shirts and clothes were 6x6, boots shiny, hair neatly kept, uniforms crisp, showers sparkled, and our personal areas were deemed exemplary. Sure, we had our bad days, but our TI said we were doing great.

The first week quickly turned into week three and before we knew it, we were on our sixth and final week. We were scared in the beginning, but had found our rhythm quickly, and sailed into graduation. We had done it. From what I remember, we started with 50 women and graduated around 40. The other women were either sent home, opted out, medically discharged, or recycled. Recycled meant they were going back to some phase of Basic Training with hopes to graduate after a second attempt.

Right before graduation I was assigned my job. Under the Delayed Enlistment Program, I was guaranteed a position in the medical field. I opened my letter and it said Public Health. What the heck was Public Health, I thought? The job description summarized food facility inspection, communicable diseases, occupational health, entomology, and epidemiology. I didn't even know what those things were! I was wondering what my life had turned into at that moment. I didn't know what to think. I solemnly came to terms with the fact that the Air Force owned me for the next four years so I decided I'd better suck-it-up and make the most of it.

It made things better when I was given my first paycheck, which amounted to $300. That was huge money. I saved it by putting it in my locker, which I didn't have a key problem any longer--pushing in the key and turning did the trick. I received a second paycheck and had a total of $600 to my name. I asked my mother to come to graduation, which she did. She was the only "family" I had, plus I wanted to show her that I made it. She said she would come, but she didn't have any money. I ended up giving her my $600 when she showed up. I figured there's a price to pay for everything.

It was time…I did it. I graduated. I had succeeded. I was off to the next chapter of my life. I no longer had to worry about where my next meal would come from nor did I have to worry about my mother anymore. My past was about to be behind me.

By leaving home, I was thrown into the unknown of life, the deep end of the unknown actually. This unknown would either change my life for the better or make me sink further into mediocrity and hardship. But all I knew was mediocrity at that stage of my life so I chose to swim out of it. It was then that I vowed to never sink to mediocrity or to anything else in life again! Excellence would be all I desire.

Moral of the Story – When you have nothing going for you and want things to be different, you have to make a drastic change. You must go into the unknown and leave your comfort zone. That's the only way to succeed. Commit to what you desperately need to change and do it. You may fail, but at least you have tried.

You have a better chance of succeeding when you try a new approach. The weak give up. The strong survive. A person will do anything--kick, scream, fight, turn, move, thrash, maybe even ingest a little dirt--to accomplish their dreams, if they want it bad enough. How bad do you want to change?

If you're a survivor, like me. Forget the easy way. Stop avoiding problems. Believe in yourself and your abilities. Stop being insecure. Stop blaming your childhood and parents for your current life situation. Take responsibility. Be accountable for the decisions you choose going forward. Evaluate your past mistakes and learn from them.

Stop playing the victim. Stop allowing people to treat you like a doormat by letting them walk all over you. Decide to make the change for what you *need* in your life, not what you *want*. Apply your decisions and turn them into actions. Those actions are your only hope of changing. You must do it to make it in the world because life is unavoidably hard. It's all or nothing!

Stop sitting idle and choose to do something about the beautiful legacy you could leave behind.

I challenge you to swim. Say goodbye to all the anchors in your life--people, places, and things. Cut the cord. Pull the Band-Aid. Start now!

If you want to experience change in your life, it starts with you. No more excuses, no more "I'll get to it" tomorrow.

Life change is now…sink or swim!

Chapter 2 – Managers Solve Problems…Leaders Change Lives

After graduating from Basic Training I went to Air Force Technical School to learn my career field, which was Public Health. This job specialty turned out to be a blessing. Public Health consisted of inspecting food and public facilities, preventing sexually transmitted diseases and other communicable diseases, trapping mosquitoes and other insects for entomology purposes, preventing occupational health related injuries and illnesses, tracking immunizations for military personnel, and all other public health concerns. When I discovered Public Health's mission was to keep military and civilian personnel healthy, I fell in love with my job.

After Technical School graduation, I was off to my first duty assignment, Reese Air Force Base (AFB), Texas. I really wanted to go to Keesler AFB in Mississippi, but going to Reese turned out to be another blessing.

Side note: Isn't it amazing how we want something, yet we get something else and it turns out to be a huge blessing that we would have never even dreamed of? Everything happens for a reason. Next time you want something, but get something else, don't complain. Embrace it instead.

I was amazed by my sponsor when I arrived at Reese. This person taught me what it was like to be a sponsor for new Airmen upon arrival. My dorm room was loaded with food, a candle, a made bed, vacuumed carpet, and a welcome card. All of this was done out of his generosity and kindness, which made me feel welcomed and greatly appreciated. Military personnel wouldn't normally do this unless it was a commander or high-ranking officer. I was stunned that my sponsor did it for me, a brand-new 18-year old. I was no longer uncertain, sad, and scared out of my wits. I will remember walking into that dorm room for the rest of my life with tears in my eyes and a smile on my face. The kind gesture will always be cherished. Pay kindness forward.

The next day I headed over to my work place to meet my supervisor, Technical Sergeant (TSgt) Browning. He immediately took me under his wing. TSgt Browning took me to in-process that morning and then sat me down at lunch to talk. He informed me that even though I was new to the Air Force, I was the future. The Air Force depended on me to live out its Core Values, on and off duty. He assured me if I didn't live out the Core Values, he would gently remind me of their meaning. From that day forward, I had a role model to look up to, along with a Nation and an Air Force that was depending on me.

TSgt Browning was the epitome of what a supervisor and a Non-Commissioned Officer (NCO) stood for in the Air Force. His job, life decisions, personality, demeanor, drive, interaction with others, and his entire being was demonstrated in excellence. I dedicated myself to become his mini-me. I wanted to be like TSgt Browning because he lived and breathed the Air Force Core Values! He backed up his words by his actions.

TSgt Browning cared for me like a dad. Many times I was going down the wrong path and he steered me back on course. When I was due to take my upgrade skills test for my career field specialty, I hadn't been studying. TSgt Browning found out and sat me down for weeks to study with me. He asked me questions until I got them all correct. I passed as a result!

One time I spontaneously decided to get married to my colleague's best friend. TSgt Browning was concerned, brought me to his house so he and his wife could educate me on marriage, and to convince me I was making a mistake. Who does that? Who cares enough about someone else's future to sit down and discuss the consequences of marriage and how it could affect their future? Only someone who cared!

There was another encounter when I was trying to lose weight. TSgt Browning came up to me and asked, "Shannon, how much do you think you weigh?" I said, "125-lbs." He said, "Come with me." I followed him to a scale and he asked me to step on it. I weighed 113-lbs. He looked at me and said, "You are tiny. You need to stop losing weight. You are perfect as you are and a number on a scale doesn't define you, so stop." That was an eye-opener. He changed my outlook on how to take better care of myself.

Another situation was when I wanted to learn more about my job so he enrolled me in classes. He made me take extra tests for certifications and motivated me to start going to college in pursuit of a degree. He made me want to become my best self and helped me to achieve it. He saw the potential in me even when I couldn't see it. He put me in for awards and I won them. It wasn't that I was awesome; it was more because he wrote awesome things about me.

TSgt Browning pushed me to play softball for our base team. I played so well that I went on to try out for the Air Force Women's Softball Team.

TSgt Browning was hard on me and I never appreciated this until much later in life. Sometimes I would ask him a question, "TSgt Browning, what does this mean?" He would respond by saying, "Shannon, that's a great question. Go find the answer and come back and tell me." I would then go (grudgingly) find the answer, return to tell him what I found, discuss everything I learned, and then he would add in what he knew. He never made it easy for me. He taught me to be independent and reliable. He assigned me to the hardest projects and programs and though I suffered through them, it enabled me to learn more than what was expected of me at my level.

TSgt Browning would take me to the gym. He told me mental aptitude was great, but physical exercise would release stress, anxiety, and it would help me think clearer. I spent hours-and-hours of jumping rope, cranking out sit-ups and push-ups, running, lifting weights, and playing sports. All of this exercise strengthened me and allowed me to forget about work. It gave me balance. It fostered my love for work and for play.

TSgt Browning taught me what it meant to care for others and to help people no matter what the circumstance. He taught me to be my best, give my best, and do my best. He made me better as a person, a fellow colleague, and a devoted Airman. He taught me to work hard and to have balance in life. He taught me to be self-reliant and to learn my trade. He helped me strive to be the best Subject Matter Expert (SME) in my field, to never allow myself or anyone else in my sphere of influence to settle, to never be mediocre or average or tolerate those who do, to call myself out and anyone else out when not living the core values, and to never give-in nor never give-up. According to TSgt Browning, <u>the sky was the limit and to always aim high.</u> I knew without a shadow-of-a-doubt that he cared about me as a person and because of that, I gave it my all. I owed it to him, the Air

Force, and my Country. This was the only way I knew how to thank him for believing in me and pushing me to become my best.

I wouldn't be the Airman I am today without TSgt Browning. Thank you for changing my life. I salute you and hope I made you proud.

Moral of the Story – It takes one person to change someone's life, either for the better or for the worse. Any person has the power to make an impact, a lasting impression. One person can change the course of another person's life forever! All a person has to do is show they care and take action. The world needs more genuinely caring people.

In my humble opinion, most people are not impacting others in a positive way; dreadfully it's just the opposite. We need to show we care by helping others become their best, do their best, and live out their best. We need to be life-changers; people of impact. If more of us acted in favor of the welfare of others, the world would become a better place.

One person can make a difference, be that one person! You never know how a chain reaction of goodness and life change could occur because of a selfless contribution you make to someone else's life. If you don't believe me, read the beautiful story about Kyle.

The Story of Kyle -
http://www.snopes.com/glurge/kyle.asp

One day when I was a freshman in high school, I saw a kid from my class walking home from school. His name was Kyle. It looked like he was carrying all of his books. I thought to myself, "Why would anyone bring home all his books on a Friday? He must really be a nerd." I had quite a weekend planned (parties and a football game with my friends), so I shrugged my shoulders and went on. As I was walking, I saw a bunch of kids running toward him. They ran at him, knocking all his books out of his arms and tripping him so he landed in the dirt. His glasses went flying, and I saw them land in the grass about ten feet from him. He looked up, and I saw this terrible sadness in his eyes. My heart went out to him. So I jogged over to him, and as he crawled around looking for his glasses, I saw a tear in his eye. As I handed him his glasses, I said, "Those guys are jerks. They really should get lives." He looked at me and said, "Hey thanks!" There was a big smile on his face. It was one of those smiles that showed real gratitude. I helped him pick up his books and asked him where he lived. As it turned out, he lived near me, so I asked him why I had never seen him before. He said he had gone to private school before now. I would have never hung out with a private school kid before, but we talked all the way home, and I carried his books. He turned out to be a pretty cool kid. I asked him if he wanted to play football on Saturday with me and my friends. He said yes. We hung out all weekend, and the more I got to know Kyle, the more I liked him. And my friends thought the same of him. Monday morning came, and there was Kyle with the huge stack of books again. I stopped him and said, "Boy, you are gonna really build some serious muscles with this pile of books every day!" He just laughed and handed me half the books. Over the next four years, Kyle and I became best friends. When we were seniors, we began to think about college. Kyle decided on Georgetown, and I was going to Duke. I knew that we would always be friends, that the miles would never be a problem.

He was going to be a doctor, and I was going for business on a football scholarship. Kyle was valedictorian of our class. I teased him all the time about being a nerd. He had to prepare a speech for graduation. I was so glad it wasn't me having to get up there and speak. On graduation day, I saw Kyle. He looked great. He was one of those guys that really found himself during high school. He filled out and actually looked good in glasses. He had more dates than me and all the girls loved him! Boy, sometimes I was jealous. Today was one of those days. I could see that he was nervous about his speech, so I smacked him on the back and said, "Hey, big guy, you'll be great!" He looked at me with one of those looks (the really grateful one) and smiled. "Thanks," he said. As he started his speech, he cleared his throat, and began. "Graduation is a time to thank those who helped you make it through those tough years. Your parents, your teachers, your siblings, maybe a coach — but mostly your friends. I am here to tell all of you that being a friend to someone is the best gift you can give them. I am going to tell you a story." I just looked at my friend with disbelief as he told the story of the first day we met. He had planned to kill himself over the weekend. He talked of how he had cleaned out his locker so his mom wouldn't have to do it later and was carrying his stuff home. He looked hard at me and gave me a little smile. "Thankfully, I was saved. My friend saved me from doing the unspeakable." I heard the gasp go through the crowd as this handsome, popular boy told us all about his weakest moment. I saw his mom and dad looking at me and smiling that same grateful smile. Not until that moment did I realize its depth. Never underestimate the power of your actions. With one small gesture, you can change a person's life.

Be a Life-Changer…Every Life Matters.

Chapter 3 – Three Times a Charm

Relationships are one area in my life where I've *always* used poor judgment. I'm not sure if it resulted in never seeing healthy relationships growing up or if I had the savior complex. Either way, it's been a struggle. Most people don't know this because I'm too ashamed to tell anyone how I was following in the footsteps of my mother, but I've been married three times.

I met #1 when I just turned 18-years old at my first duty location. He was my colleague's best friend. We had common interests and got along well, even though he was 6-years older. We enjoyed being off base, being able to cook, and relax without the dorm drama. One evening while walking, we jokingly agreed if we got married than we could have no drama all the time. The next day, we were playing basketball and he talked about marriage again. He said if we got married, it would be temporary until the base closed and then we would get divorced. You know my childhood, my mother married for money so I didn't really know any difference.

We decided to go down to the Justice of Peace to get married the following week. It was weird being in our Battle Dress Uniform (BDU) and committing our lives to each other (for the next year). We celebrated our honeymoon at Burger King with Whopper Combo's. I was 18-years old and married to a guy I didn't love, just to live off base, have a house, and get out of the dorms.

Right before the base closed, we had come to a turning point. He had fallen in love, but I had not. I wanted to keep the agreement and he wanted to stay married. When the base closed, we moved together to the next base and I filed for divorce. I would have never married #1 if I understood what marriage actually meant, but back then I did not.

 # 1 – Shame on us.

Out of nowhere, I met #2. We were sitting in a college class and were introducing ourselves when #2 mentioned he was from a small town in Mississippi. In response, I said, "Where?" He returned with "Picayune" and I exclaimed, "That's where I lived." We were inseparable since introductions, minus the arguments, and we disagreed a lot.

We dated for two years, but I knew I loved him instantly. The old saying, "when you know, you know" holds true and I will remember the moment I knew. We had returned from a road trip to Picayune and when he hugged me goodbye I felt it. I felt something that couldn't be explained. We later married, but it wasn't meant to be. We were young, scared, and didn't know how to compromise. Plus, selfishness, stupidity, lying, and insecurity led to our marital demise.

Here are a few examples:

a. We were slated to go to my mother's friend's house one evening. Everyone was waiting for us and we began the hour drive down. All of a sudden #2 started feeling sick so we turned around to bring him home and we decided I would go by myself. I dropped him home, made sure he was good, stopped to get gas, called my family, and was on my way. About 10-miles into the drive, I pass #2 in his truck. I was shocked and started telling him to roll down his window and answer his phone, but he didn't. He kept driving. I don't know where he went. I cried and went home. He never came home that night and I don't know where he went to this day. He wasn't honest and it hurt.

b. We were sitting with my Airman Leadership School classmates having a great time and enjoying conversation. One moment he was there, the next minute he was gone. He didn't say goodbye or tell me he was leaving. He always did that routine with me, but I never learned.

c. The day before my birthday I went out with a friend to get some ink engraved on my skin (my first and only tattoo). He didn't want me to go and was mad I went. I came home that evening, only 3 hours later, and had learned he moved out.

d. The next year on my birthday, he asked me to wait for him at home and let him play his weekly basketball game. He said he would take me to dinner, wine and dine me, and we'd have cake. I waited and waited, called him, and didn't hear anything from him till 0200 in the morning when he banged on our front door. He had driven drunk, wasted, and I never even got a happy birthday.

e. The third year on my birthday, his sister asked us to go to their house and have a celebration. I was excited because his sister didn't like me. We got there and she had a house full of people and immediately said happy birthday to me when we arrived. It was great. She got the cake and everyone started singing…to her friend, Chris, who had a birthday the next day. I was hurt, but then I saw a second cake. Well, the second cake was also for Chris because one was chocolate and the other vanilla. No one sang Happy Birthday to me. When #2 and I left, I cried while driving home and he took sides with his sister and told me I was overreacting. (My birthday's really sucked with him.)

f. I made more money than him so I would pay the mortgage and he would pay the utilities. He rarely pitched in or gave me extra money. I was the dumb Sugar Momma. I know what stupid women do for the desire to be loved. I lost who I was and gave him my all. What hurt most was knowing he never loved me.

g. I was going to become an Air Force Officer and was slated to go a base in Florida. We decided to go to FL during a Holiday weekend and invited some friends to go with us. Everyone knew I wanted to check out the area and look for a house, but it didn't go as planned. The entire 2-nights and 3-days we were there, #2 was drunk with friends so I ended up looking for places to live by myself. The people with us and #2 were making fun of me and calling me righteous and uptight because I didn't want to get drunk.

There were so many problems. From him legally changing his last name, making himself throw up after eating, gambling thousands of dollars, and verbal abuse. Not to mention the lies, flirtatious women, anger, drinking, disrespect, and heartache…I could go on, but let me tell you why we finally divorced.

On his deployment I caught wind of him spending a lot of time with a certain female. I saw a picture of a girl in a bikini on his desk and questioned him about it and he said it was his boss. I thought it was inappropriate and stated my concerns. The next picture I saw him without a wedding ring and he said he took it off because he was weightlifting. The next picture I saw was the same girl sitting on his lap in the pool. We fought and he called me insecure. I told him it was inappropriate behavior and to stop acting like he was single. About a week later, I told him to stop hanging out with the girl. He said, "No" and I said "either stop hanging out with the girl or don't call me until you get home." He said, "I'll see you when I get home." We didn't talk for months and I filed for divorce. I had enough of him…and his "Christian" sister. Ultimatums for toxic relationships do provide hope in the end, but you must be willing to accept the decision and not retract from your stance.

I was dumb and wholeheartedly loved him. I was vulnerable and have never been so open and honest with anyone. This was the first time in my entire life where I loved a man with every ounce of my being and my soul.

We tried making it work for a year until a 4th of July weekend when he suddenly canceled plans. Something didn't feel right, call it intuition. I found out a few days later he was with another girl. It crushed me…again.

I found strength to move away and bid farewell to the man who broke me more times than I should have allowed. But, the cycle continued. He called and begged forgiveness and we started talking again. He was in gambling debt and I gave him $10,000 to break free and start over. After talking for almost a year, he came to see me in Washington DC and we had dinner. He flirted and it was then when I finally understood.

It wasn't love for him. It was all a game.

2 – Shame on him

I vowed to never get married again, began counseling, and fell in love with me…strengths, weaknesses, and flaws. I was happy in life and then five years later a guy showed up at church. He was different. He was God-loving, kind, funny, athletic, and a typical Italian. He had the biggest smile and was full of energy. He glowed bright. We hit it off while serving in church. He courted me, was kind to me, surprised me with spontaneous things, and treated me like a true daughter for God. I had never been so happy in my entire life.

He surprised me by coming to see me at work, cheered for me at distance races, talked with me for hours, respected my boundaries, prayed with me, and was the kindest person I had ever met. The time he courted me was the best time of my life in terms of relationships. He gave me his heart, cooked awesome food, dreamed with me, loved to travel, volunteered, rode a motorcycle, and represented Jesus in the best way. I fell quickly. I knew I wanted to be with him and he wanted to be with me after our first date.

We took a Christmas trip to New York and he spoiled me rotten. He took me to see the Rockette's, the Broadway show Elf, and proposed to me on the middle of the Rockefeller ice skating rink in front of a crowd of people, in front of the Christmas tree. This was symbolic because I always called him Christmas morning. He was the best present in the world. We got engaged quickly, had our fair share of ups and downs, but we're going on 8-years.

He takes care of me and has taught me a lot about family and relationships. I never knew I needed someone to nurture me and that is what he does. I cannot imagine my life without the crazy Italian guy and am very thankful for him.

#3 – No Shame – I love him and he loves me.

Moral of the Story – Love is hard. You will fall in love and you will fall out of love. Life would be simple if we were alone, but we're not meant to be alone. We must interact with people and love one another, even our enemies. Relationships are many people's Achilles heel in life, I know it has been mine.

You will love and be hurt, people will love you and you will hurt them, you will lose yourself in love, and you can be saved by love. It's the best and worst in life and it makes you who you are. You may even lose someone you love, but you must never stop loving because when you do, you have nothing. And, if you say you have no one to love, my answer is to LOVE YOURSELF.

Love is being vulnerable. Love is getting hurt. Love is learning. Love is compromise. Love is forgiving. Love is selfless. Love is action. Love is the greatest gift to man.

No matter what happens, always love. Break down the walls of hurt and give someone a chance. It's better to love and be hurt multiple times than to never have loved at all.

Love teaches you something about yourself. Love is what makes the world worth living. Love is what saves us from death. A life without love is a life unimaginable.

Always choose love, even when it hurts. **Love never fails.**

1 Corinthians 13: 4-8

*And when you do get married, do it for love....**do it once!***

Chapter 4 – Rescued

Being married to #1 was drama-free and peaceful, and then I started getting sick.

I knew about sex and I knew you could get pregnant from having sex, but I didn't know the biological mechanics of pregnancy. As I explained in an earlier chapter when my sister got her period the whole family made a big deal, but my experience wasn't the same.

I was never educated about sex, birth control, or what a monthly visit from Aunt Flow and Uncle Cramps actually meant. I left home without grasping the concept of the birds and bees, nor did I understand ovulation so it shouldn't have been a surprise when I got pregnant. But, it was! I was very naïve.

I was happy with my drama-free life and the pending plan of divorce. Getting pregnant was something I never thought I wanted in my life. I wasn't attending church so I had no feeling of community support. Add to the equation my mother had previously hung up on me when I told her I got married and I hadn't spoken with her in months.

As a result, I was alone. I cried when I found out. I was scared. I didn't know how to be a mom. I had the worst mother in the world and I didn't want to carry on her legacy.

I began living in a daze. Going through the motions. Wanting to be loved. Wanting someone to hold me, someone to take care of me, and to take the fear away. The entire nine months I lived in despair and was constantly sick. It was like my body was rejecting the baby and making me miserable. I didn't come to terms with being a mom because emotionally I was still grieving my upbringing with my own mother.

I was pregnant and living with a man for all the wrong reasons. A man I didn't love. I was saddened by the fact I hadn't learned more about sex and its consequences. I was gaining weight, losing my hair, getting stretch marks, and clinging to the man that caused it all. I clung to him even though I hated him. I hated him because he fell in love and wanted this. I just wanted to live drama-free and move apart once the based closed. I was lost in my reality. I was 19-years old and about to have a baby when I was nothing more than a child myself.

Then it got real!

My doctor was leaving for vacation and I had to be induced early. The silver lining was being induced on Mother's Day. While on the delivery table I was throwing up. At 3:12 p.m. I started pushing. I pushed three times and at 3:17 p.m. a baby girl was born. I pushed so fast when she arrived she was turning blue and not crying. The doctor hung her upside down, pinched her butt, and then a huge cry erupted. The baby girl was alive and healthy at 20.5 inches and 6.8 pounds.

The doctor laid her on my stomach and she peed/pooped. I. Kid. You. Not. At least her vitals were working. I received a Happy Mother's Day gift…a big pile of poop and urine on my tummy. They placed her close to me and she cupped my face while looking in my eyes. It was at that very moment when I fell in love.

Fear was gone. My baby girl was here. I finally knew what love actually meant. It was at that moment when I was rescued from sadness, loneliness, and having no love for others.

My first priority was to breastfeed. It hurt when she latched on my breast for the first time to feed, but I didn't care. I wanted to feel the pain instead of her. I didn't want her to ever feel pain. It was strange not wanting to be a mother out of fear when, ironically, it turned out to be the first time when I felt safe and whole.

My baby girl changed me. I wanted to take care of her, be a better person for her, and make something of my life so she would be proud of me. I wanted to create a life for her that would bring her happiness. I would avoid making the same mistakes my mother had. I wanted to be there for her physically and emotionally. I was determined to be the mom that teaches her daughter how to act, what to expect in life, how to love, and how to make something of herself. I would do anything to protect her and show her how much I love her.

I grew up because of her. I had to for her sake. I didn't miss out experiencing the young life. I didn't go out, didn't drink, didn't smoke, didn't curse, and I started going to church again. I read to her every night. I was a mom first and foremost. My despair faded and I started going back to school. I did all of these things because of her. I was improving my life to make her life better. The only problem in this equation was #1. I didn't love him, but I did love my baby girl.

Eventually the base closed and all three of us moved together to our new base. Shortly after we arrived, we filed for divorce. I wanted my daughter's father in her life because I never had a dad in mine. I wanted her to grow up with a father figure, but the pain of staying married outweighed the pain of being a single mom.

The divorce was finalized. The most devastating part of the divorce was me losing primary custody of my daughter, the one person I felt genuine love for. That's what I got for being nice. I could have moved with her with full custody, but, again, I was naïve.

Her dad fought me for custody and ended up winning primary custodianship. We shared visitation rights, each getting two-month intervals until she was five-years old. After she turned five, I got to keep her for summers, special holidays, and one visit per month.

The only problem with my visitation rights each month was #1 getting out of the military and moving 12-hours away. I lost valuable time driving six-hours after work on a Friday, only getting to visit for a day and a half, and then driving 6-hours home. I didn't have a lot of money, but I did my best.

I struggled with the thought if I had stayed with her dad, I could have had her all of the time, but I needed to have real love and knew I wouldn't find it with him.

Feeling empty without my baby girl and sad, I decided to submerge myself in work. That was my life. It was all I had.

My daughter and I missed out on having a real relationship and it was my fault. She will never forgive me and I will never forgive myself. The one person in this entire world I vowed to never hurt or disappoint is the one person I did. I have to live with that pain forever.

As for parents, children grow up fast and they need you. Learn from my poor judgement because you'll never get the time back with them once they're older.

Moral of the Story – You may want certain things in life, but those things may change without your consent and put you on an entirely different path. And, you may fight it.

What I learned is the things we often fight the most are often our biggest rewards, most joyous moments, and greatest life changing events. Embrace moments of change instead of fighting them.

My daughter was a life changing event, something I never thought I wanted. I was wrong! She taught me what life was truly about. Even though she was no longer with me full-time, she was in my heart full-time.

She rescued me and is the first person in my life who I ever truly loved. I owe her everything I am today because she made me desire to become my best for her. She is the greatest legacy I can leave behind in this world. Thank you would never be enough to this angel on earth.

Please know some may never have a kid or can't have kids, and for those I kindly ask to find a child to spend time with. Consider volunteering at organizations because kids will change you, teach you, and make you better. They may even rescue you.

Children, they can be your greatest joy and also your greatest sorrow. No matter what, love them anyway even if it's at a distance.

A parent will not be perfect in their attempt to raise a child, but as long as they try their best, that's what matters.

I love you KB Toy Store.

Chapter 5 – My Person

In life, we meet people for a reason, season, or for a lifetime. Lifetime people are one in a million, a priceless treasure. That's what I found in a friend who became "My Person." Using My Person terminology is uncommon, but it became popular from the hit television show 'Grey's Anatomy' where Christina and Meredith stated, "They were each other's person." The husbands, boyfriends, and other friends were special, but these two people shared an emphatic connection that bonded them. A bond too rare to put into words other than…My Person.

If we ever find someone who fits the meaning, may we never do anything to break the rare bond.

I met My Person on my first day of military inprocessing back in 2000. She was full of energy and extremely helpful. She was six years older than me and one rank higher, but that didn't matter because we immediately connected. We shared similar goals, a passion for bettering ourselves, a disposition to help others, and were both striving to be personally and professionally successful. We were both married and just naturally happy people. We began eating lunch together on a frequent basis and laughed at the craziness going on in our lives. I had my first best friend since joining the military.

To help you understand some crazy moments we chuckled about, here are a few examples. My Person's car was old and when she brought it to a stop the engine would stall. One time she was giving me a ride back to work after lunch and when we arrived to my drop-off point instead of stopping the car completely, I jumped out to keep the engine from cutting off. It worked! We laughed about it for days. Another time

I was called into work on a Saturday to help with an unexpected crisis and it was raining outside. She came to hang out and we ended up sitting on a laundry cart for an hour in the rain until the work crisis was resolved. We turned the mundane into hilarity.

We would race to her house to watch Survivor, deal with our colleague's kid Night Terrors, wipe Spanish moss from our faces while locating a spot for a retirement ceremony, laugh until we cried, make the executive office staff laugh at onion jokes, experience every country at Disney World's Epcot, enjoy 7-11 coffee and cappuccino, and so many other adventures. We were referred to as "Two Peas in a Pod." We would turn the smallest things into the grandest, most enjoyable affairs.

We went to the bookstore for hours and would sit on the floor reading self-help books and articles to each other. We went to restaurants for hours to talk about goals, husbands, and life. We had almost everything in common and when we were together, we shined bright.

She was My Person.

Not only did we have similar interests, we also lived parallel lives. We both had problems with our families. When I was picked up for a high-level position at the Wing, she was picked up for a high-level position at the Group. She was a narrator for a ceremony, I was a narrator for a ceremony. I went to college with my husband and finished my Bachelor's. She went to college right after with her husband and finished her Bachelor's. I was picked up for Officer Training School and then she was picked up for Officer Training School.

When My Person started going to counseling, I saw how much it helped her so I started going to the same counselor. Reverend Haynes made us both reach the same conclusion: There are three things we have no control of in our lives, plus a bonus. 1.) You can't make anyone love you. 2.) You are only accountable for yourself. 3.) You are only in control of your own life. Bonus…Live by the Golden Rule. We shined even brighter with these rules and made them our compass in life. We wouldn't allow anything or anyone to keep us from becoming all we were meant to be.

After counseling ended, I left for Officer Training School and moved out of state. During this time, my husband didn't get selected for Officer Training School and neither did her husband. This is when things became rocky for both of us. My husband began feeling inferior and her husband began feeling something similar. Through it all, we helped each other navigate the rough times.

She was My Person.

Then it happened. Her husband cheated. I didn't find out the specifics until six-months after the incident occurred. It hurt me when I found out from someone else because I told her everything and never held back the truth. I poured out my heart and soul to her. However, when it was her turn, she remained guarded.

How I found out…an old secretary informed me of My Person testifying on her husband's behalf. The secretary asked me why I wasn't there to support my best friend. Talk about a gut punch! I called My Person immediately and let her know I was shocked and asked why she didn't tell me. She said she was embarrassed and didn't want anyone to know. Only one problem…I wasn't just anyone…I was her Person.

We made a promise right at that moment to always tell each other the truth and to always be there for each other.

I kept my word. She was my best friend, mentor, dreamer, encourager, and My Person. I didn't want anything to jeopardize our friendship and sisterhood.

My Person walked me down the aisle when I was remarried. I sent her wrapped gifts when she was deployed including her own embroidered Bible. I shared my heart with her. I trusted her with everything and never held back.

Then it happened…again! Everything came crashing down when My Person hurt me…again. When she was deployed, I reached out to her ex-husband to see if he would be willing to say Happy Birthday to her even though they were just recently divorced. She loved him and one needs all the love you can get when you're deployed. He had been a part of my life too because of her so I didn't think anything of it. When I reached out to him on Facebook, I saw a bunch of pictures of him and another woman I thought were inappropriate. I asked them both to remove the pictures while My Person was deployed. If I could find it so could she and she had a gun.

The woman in the pictures reached out to me. She began asking me questions about My Person and telling me some things I didn't want to know. I asked her to stop contacting me and to contact My Person directly when she got back to the United States. The ex-husband never responded.

For two months I suffered with the surprise news and knew it would hurt My Person. For two months I was sad, angry, and confused. It tore me up not being able to tell My Person about what I learned. I was certain I would be her comforter and to help her get through this. Not to mention this would be the second time her now recently ex-husband had hurt her. I wasn't there for her the first time (her fault), but I would be there this time.

When she arrived back to the U.S.A. we talked briefly and then had a heart-to-heart phone conversation a week later. I told her what I had done, all with a good intention, and what I had found out. Instead of seeing my sincerity, My Person got upset and told me it was none of my business. She said, "Unless she asked for help, don't help her. She is a capable adult and can help herself." Further she said, "She was sorry for me suffering those two months, but she already knew about them and it didn't matter anymore because they were divorced."

We soon got off the phone and I sat there stunned. I was shocked and upset. If My Person had known these horrible things and would had told me, I wouldn't have reached out to her ex-husband. Further, I wouldn't have been blindsided by what I had found out about her ex-husband and the other woman, which their relationship had been going on for five years! The ex-husband and this woman lived together, had a business, and loved each other….for five years!

My Person was living a double life the entire time…<u>for five years!</u> Who does that?!

I wouldn't have suffered for two grueling months waiting to talk to her if she had told me the truth…in those five years!

My Person withheld a huge part of her life from me. I came to the conclusion our friendship had run its course. Either she didn't trust me, didn't care, or only wanted to hear about my life trials and not share hers. I learned she was My Person, but I wasn't hers.

She hurt me more than anyone else has in this lifetime because of her dishonesty. I felt the integrity of our friendship was compromised, which I dearly hold as one of my core values. Integrity…a person has it or they don't. There is no in-between. *A person can't have integrity if they don't have honesty.*

Friendship cannot be one-sided. Both sides must trust one another explicitly and unconditionally. I deserved that and so do you.

Moral of the Story – In life we meet people for a season, reason, or a lifetime. Lifetime People are rare and known as a Best Friend, "My Person" or a Life-Giver. Shared interests, similarities, and parallels bind you together as "Two Peas in a Pod." That person is someone whom you need in good times and bad. Someone you can depend on and trust.

We all need a partner, a confidante, a mentor, or person to share our lives with and share our deepest most intimate details. Things we would never share with the public or just anyone close to us. This person must have our best interest and have our backs at all times.

A friendship thrives on trust and it cannot be one-sided. It is not a take-take or give-take, but a give-give reciprocal relationship. If we can keep that one person, "My Person" until we die than we are blessed.

Naturally, people change and relationships run their course because people grow apart. *Don't force a chapter to become a book.* It won't work!

A "My Person" will be tried and tested, help you shine brighter than the day before, and push you towards greatness. They will never hurt or betray you. They will always be honest even if it hurts you or them. My Person is your sounding board, your ying to your yang, and your very best friend.

Appreciate them every single day because one day they may be gone. If, as no fault of your own, the friendship should ever end, appreciate the time you had together, and wish them the best. Always try to be the better person.

To have a real friend, you must be a real friend.

6 – Lott of Lessons

I was blessed to work with some amazing people early in my career, which helped shape me into who I am today. These heavy-hitters, household names, and movie-star status individuals were 10+ years senior to me with a wealth of experience and knowledge. I didn't know the lessons I was learning at the time nor did I appreciate them, but being the sponge I am soaked up all I could. As a result, I am a better individual from their kindness and wisdom and graciously try to pass on their admirable traits to others.

The Senate Majority Leader from the great state of Mississippi and a Major General are two men I will never forget. They are two people I'm very thankful for because they educated a young and enthusiastic 23-year old while treating me with respect and teaching me the value of grace.

The Major General was a towering man who always seemed to be around when I messed up and never around when I did things rights. To add to the situation, most of the mistakes occurred while in the presence of the Senator. If I could screw it up, I did. And if I didn't know something, the towering kind man would teach me. He was a life-changing boss.

I can laugh now, but back then I wanted to crawl into a basement and hide a few times. Mississippi doesn't have basements or I would have been in one.

I met the Senator the first time while working an informal dinner at the Major General's home. Before the Senator arrived, the staff and I were preparing food, organizing nametags, setting up wine glasses, and ensuring everything was perfect. While setting up, my boss requested me to chill the wine. Determined not to let him down, I immediately went to work. I put all the wine into the coolers and everything was good to go. I think I even skipped afterwards with a big toothy smile.

The Senator arrived and was greeted with smiles, handshakes, and joy. The Major General asked me to get the Senator a glass of red wine so I jumped on the task and returned within minutes. I handed the Senator his glass of wine, but right after taking a sip he said, "The wine is really cold." The Major General took the wine and went to get him another glass. While walking with him, he asked me if I chilled the wine and I said, "Yes." He looked at me and said, "Only white wine is chilled, red wine is served at room temperature or just below." I was mortified. I was as red as the wine. I didn't know anything about wine.

The Major General looked at me, shook his head, and apologized to me. He said he should have known because I didn't drink. The fault was his because the communicator failed to deliver the proper message to the receiver. I learned two invaluable lessons that evening: 1.) Learn my trade by knowing all the event details and become the expert. 2.) The communicator is responsible for the message and must ensure the receiver understands what is expected or needed.

The second time I met the Senator was during a Retired Officers Association speaking engagement with him being the guest speaker. We used the Officer's Club for the venue. There was a stage, podium, 300 chairs, and a reception room with goodies following the event. As I walked around putting seating labels on chairs, the Major General asked, "Is everything in order?" I assured him it was. He said to follow him to the podium. He asked, "What would happen if the microphone lost battery power? Do you have a back-up battery or microphone for the Senator?" I didn't have one, but thought it was a 'great idea.' He then asked, "Where's the bottle of water to sit on the podium in case his throat gets scratchy?" I didn't have one, but thought it was a 'great idea.' He then asked, "Are you going to meet him at the car and escort him in?" and I said, "No, but thought it was a great idea." After this teaching moment ended, I planned to head out to the parking lot after I found a spare battery and a bottle of water. Little things make a big difference.

After greeting the Senator, my next step was to escort him through the side door so he wouldn't be swarmed by people. When he arrived, I led him to the side door and when I reached to open the door it was locked. Panicked, I knocked on the door for a few seconds, which felt like an eternity, but no one answered. The Senator stood there looking at me. I ended up having to walk him around through the main front entrance right into a massive crowd. While walking, I was on the verge of tears, but the Senator looked at me with reassurance and said, "Everything happens for a reason. Everything is okay. Don't beat yourself up." When we entered the front door, the other officers smiled and waved and luckily didn't stop him as we walked by. We made it to the pre-meeting room without a hitch, well sort of. Fortunately, the Major General never found out because neither the Senator nor I said anything. Looking back, checking to see if the side door was locked/unlocked would have been a 'great idea.'

During the Senator's Retired Officers Association speech the unthinkable happened. The microphone didn't fail, but the podium light did. The light bulb burned out and I didn't have a replacement. As a result, we had to disruptively turn on the overhead lights for the Senator to finish reading his speech. I ingratiated the entire audience with the unpleasant experience of full-powered ultraviolet fluorescent lighting, instead of the nice dim lighting. Checking the podium light bulb would have been a 'great idea' in hindsight. I learned another lesson: Expect the unexpected, which means no matter what tool, path, object, action, or scenario is used, always think ahead of what could possibly go wrong. Always have a plan for what you would do if things do go wrong. Thinking ahead for problems and solutions is nothing more than strategic planning.

The final time I met the Senator was during a Change of Command ceremony, which he was an invited guest. I didn't meet him upon arrival this time because I was ensuring the holding area was perfect. I checked all areas for security and had the military dogs sweep the room. I even set-up a few snacks for the guests.

When the Senator arrived, he walked in and went to the restroom to wash his hands. Moments later he walked out and straight up to me and said the towels and soap were really nice, but there was no running water. Confused, I looked at him with his soapy dry hands and asked if I could take him into the kitchen. I apologized and assured him he would be taken care of and then headed straight into the restroom. Sure enough, there was no running water. I quickly called Civil Engineering and they arrived within minutes. They had to walk through guests to get to the bathroom and eventually turned on the water. It was a flip-of-the switch type fix. It would have been a 'great idea' to check the faucet for running water. I learned an invaluable lesson that day: Have a checklist. Having a checklist would have ensured I checked every item in the room and if something needed to be fixed, I could have handled it prior to the event. A checklist ensures all basics are covered, people are not displaced, and one is prepared. This ensures a higher probability of success, which is essential in every aspect of our lives.

The Senator taught me many things even though I only interacted with him three times. The Major General taught me how to think and never made me feel incompetent. Over the course of eighteen months under his leadership, I slowly became an equipped employee and innovative thinker.

Each time I found myself in situations I would think to myself, 'What would the Major General do?' He taught me how to think three steps ahead and expect the unexpected. I am forever grateful to him for teaching me invaluable lessons I didn't know before I met him.

Bonus: The Major General's wife taught me how to be a lady and how a lady is supposed to look and act. Grace, internal beauty, modesty, poise, and strength do shine from one's core being. *If a woman has to tell people she's a lady than she's really not.* A lady is more than looks, she is class.

Moral of the Story – Some people enter our lives for brief moments to teach us life-changing lessons. These lessons could be based on a good or bad experience, but either way, they teach us something invaluable. The 'ah-ha' moments seldom teach us on the spot. Yet hours, days, weeks, even years later a lesson can emerge.

When the light bulb goes out, have a back-up.

In a lesson-teaching moment, even if you turn red, want to crawl under a desk and hide, or run away, don't. Be thankful for the lesson someone is teaching you. When people teach you something, it says they care about you because they are spending their time with you, which they'll never get back.

Everything in life teaches us something, but we must be open to the lesson.

Mistakes will happen! No one is perfect. Therefore, when someone makes a mistake let's show grace like the Major General did with me with the red wine incident. A legitimate mistake is exactly that, a mistake. It wasn't intentional. I bet the person making the mistake feels bad enough already. So please don't throw human error in their face. Instead, wash it away with love, patience, and kindness.

Remember, **the fool ignores the lesson, but the wise learn from it.**

Managers solve problems; Leaders change lives. Thank you to the Major General for being a genuine leader and changing my life for the better. You're a good person.

Let's all be a Major General in someone's life by taking time to grow and develop those we are blessed to lead.

The person that fails to plan will fail. Planning is key to achieving a higher success rate.

7 – I'm Not Good Enough

In the Air Force, there are Professional Military Education (PME) requirements for both enlisted and officers. Early in my career, I had my first taste of PME while attending Airman Leadership School (ALS). Every junior enlisted member is required to complete ALS in order to be eligible for their next mid-tier rank.

When I attended ALS, we were required to give three speeches, complete writing assignments, take tests, participate in one drill and ceremony competition between the two flights, perform several leadership exercises, and establish camaraderie. There were thirty enlisted members in a class divided into two flights with four instructors. The class was six weeks long.

On the first day of class I was nervous and full of self-doubt. It was the first time I had been to any formal training event since Technical School. I didn't know what to expect so I made sure my uniform was pressed and I smiled a lot. Thankfully, I have a cheerful demeanor so smiling came naturally and helped me fake it until I got comfortable.

The first speech was a typical 1-3 minute introduction speech. Introduce yourself, where you work, what you do, family, hobbies, and a fun fact about yourself. It was surprising how many people were nervous, bombed the speech, and turned red. I was one of them.

The second speech was 3-5 minutes and the topic educational. I spoke on the importance of hearing protection. Many people didn't do well and it became apparent why speeches were necessary. People must be able to effectively communicate with one another.

The final speech was on a controversial topic where we had to pick a side for-or-against and then defend it. All three speeches were entertaining and educational, and we recognized how important they were in becoming a better public speaker. Low ranking Airmen do little public speaking, depending on their career field, until they progress in rank so our introduction to public speaking was important.

The tests were based on standard military topics with some emphasis on leadership. The leadership exercises helped us identify our own strengths and weaknesses and demonstrated how no person was the same. We learned we must adapt to our audience in order to effectively communicate and lead.

The drill and ceremony competition was something I will never forget. As a Junior ROTC cadet in high school for two years, I was adept at drill competitions so I volunteered to be my flight's drill commander. The drill competition was a 36-count march with various commands. On the first day of marching, I thought I did very well, but several people kept messing up while marching. They either couldn't hear the commands, were making their own movements, or were driven in becoming the drill commander themselves.

The instructor got angry. He began switching people in-and-out as drill commander and everyone who tried did horribly. At that point, the instructor told everyone to pay attention and to suck it up. I was the best they had and to deal with it. He told us to learn the movements and clean out our ears so we could all hear.

We were expected to practice for two more weeks together, but I did more than required. After class ended each day, I would go to the drill pad and march the full 36-count movement for 1-hour. I lined myself up at the exact point where my flight would be each time and I gave a command. I knew the entire sequence by memory and marched it over and over. I then found out where our commander would stand and learned how to march the flight to be aligned with the Commander's center position. Each time in solo practice, I was improving the flight's imaginary movements and alignment. I brought the flight in a few times and marched them according to what I had practiced. It became seamless and the flight was beyond prepared. We lived an Air Force core value - Excellence in All We Do!

The day of the drill competition, the flight line area was packed with people from all over the base who had come to see the showdown. Both flights lined up and they flipped the coin to see who went first; it was my flight.

To start, I called my flight to attention and then began calling out the commands one-by-one. Thirty-six movements later, the show was over. Everything I practiced--the hours of extra memorization, the movements, the flight positioning--all of it went perfect. The next flight began their execution of the 36-count sequence and completed all of the commands, but their alignment was off-center from the Commander. Once the second flight completed their drill, the competition was over.

It was a tough competition. Both of the flights lined up parallel to the Commander and waited for what seemed to be twenty long minutes. Finally, the Commander carrying the big trophy in his hand began walking down the center path between the two flights. I was thinking, did we win, did we win, did we win? Will he turn towards me or the other drill commander? The moment when he was about to turn, he stopped. Then he turned towards the other drill commander and started walking. My heart sank, but then he did an about-face towards me, stopped, and said, "Congratulations. What an excellent show. Your alignment, vocals, and drill movements were perfect, the best I have seen." My flight won! We did it. We worked tirelessly together and accomplished our goal. The hours of extra practice paid off and was a memorable experience.

On graduation night, the class was gleaming with pride because of what we had accomplished. We completed our first big PME milestone and were ready to take the next step in our careers. Several people were recognized for displaying leadership, including myself.

In PME, awards were given to members for their overall achievement. One award is the Distinguished Graduate award. Another award for an enlisted member is the John Levitow award, which is the highest military honor an enlisted member can receive in PME. The award is named after a low-ranking enlisted Air Force member who earned the Medal of Honor. On that night, I was recognized as the recipient of the Levitow award. I gave a speech recognizing our entire class for this achievement. I knew one person couldn't achieve it by themselves. It was a team effort in every regard. That night was the highest-of-highs and our class celebrated into the night.

ALS changed me professionally and personally. In the professional realm, I was selected to work in the most visible jobs. I was 24-years old and working with full-bird colonels and general officers. I was being groomed to be a future leader. I wanted to continue growing so I took more classes to finish my college degree and started reading self-help and non-fiction books. I wanted to make myself better and wanted to make others better as well.

A short time later, I applied for Air Force Officer Training School (OTS). To my surprise, I was selected on my first board. I was going to become an Officer in the United States Air Force. At a little over 8-years of being an enlisted member and proudly wearing Staff Sergeant stripes, I left for OTS realizing my world was going to forever change.

On the first day, we had introductions and I wanted to quit. Mental sabotage started. I felt I wasn't as good or smart like my peers. I was in a flight with a Rocket Scientist (I kid you not), Engineers, Pilots, Research Analysts, and me, the prior enlisted Public Health technician. I felt underqualified. I was no longer the confident, take-charge person and became quiet and insecure.

By sheer determination, I didn't quit. I gradually befriended my flight and they no longer intimidated me. Sure they were super-smart, but my prior experience in the Air Force enabled me to become our Subject Matter Expert on various topics. I excelled in our leadership scenarios and even helped my other flight members excel. We all worked as a team and became a unit of one. We started with 15-members and graduated with 12. The 12-weeks of OTS training flew by and I was no longer an Officer Trainee (OT). I graduated as a Second Lieutenant.

OTS was one of the hardest things mentally I had ever done. I learned it wasn't about who the smartest person was in the room. It was about hard work and believing in yourself.

PME teaches you how to work with others, how to lead and follow, and most importantly, it takes you out of your comfort zone. In the beginning, you may want to give up and quit. You may begin second-guessing yourself and fighting your inner demons, but eventually, you find your way by pushing through and accomplishing what you set out to do. PME can be a beautiful blessing for all, but only some have the intention of benefiting from it.

Moral of the Story – There will be moments in your life where you will be tried and tested, and those are the times that will make or break you. Will you rise to the occasion or throw in the towel? Will you buy into the mental sabotage that you're not good enough and begin to doubt your self-worth? Will you work hard and put everything you have into succeeding? Will you only help yourself or will you help others as well? Will you roll up your sleeves and dig deep inside to work the task or will you do just enough to get by?

Who you are as a person is defined in the tough times, the times when you don't feel you're good enough, smart enough, worthy enough, strong enough, able enough, or talented enough. It's those moments in life that define you. The weary crumble, the strong stand.

What will you do when that life-changing moment appears? Will you face it head on, face it somewhat, or not face it at all? The unexpected blessings we cherish are usually those events we fight against the most. Many people choose the easy route in life, *and very few people choose the hard route.*

Overtime I learned when placed in new environments, a person must change their thinking to be successful. For instance, don't think you're not good enough. Instead, think how it's just something new. As a result, your nerves will eventually calm down while you figure things out. Enjoy the change and trust the process.

<u>Never give up because you're scared.</u> It's better to try and fail than to never try at all. **You could be the Levitow!**

8 – Jealousy

Have you ever had someone not like you just because of who you are? Maybe, you were a different race, opposite sex, too happy, too confident, too vocal, or maybe your strength was their weakness and you made them feel insecure? Whatever the case, the other person just didn't like you. Well, that's what happened to me with my boss lady.

When I arrived at my new job, I met my new boss lady and two colleagues. Unlike my colleagues, I entered the job with a wealth of knowledge and was considered a Subject Matter Expert (SME) in the field. Until I arrived, our boss lady was the go-to individual answering all questions and was very much needed.

Being a SME, I quickly jumped into my role and recognized areas needing improvements. These improvements would increase workload efficiency by reducing man-hours, enhance productivity, provide checks and balances, and were non-SME user friendly. The boss lady liked my ideas and implemented them into the organization, but never once said "Thank you."

During work hours, people would walk into the office asking questions and I would answer on-the-spot without having to look up instructions or guidelines. Whenever the boss lady was within earshot, she would come out of her office and begin adding her knowledge to the conversation. I was never quite sure why she did that. Was it because she didn't trust her people? Was it because she wanted to be all-knowing? Was she upset because I didn't need her like my colleagues did? Was it because I was wrong? Was it because she was jealous?

I concluded the boss lady was jealous. I knew my trade, which made her obsolete as the sole oracle-of-knowledge in our workplace. As a result, she viewed me as a threat. Unintentionally, I stole her spotlight. Hence the jealous conclusion. Then it got worse.

Due to a careless circumstance of one of my colleagues in another section, my colleague, the Deputy Officer in our office, was reassigned the detail of becoming the aide for the Head Boss. As a result, I became the highest-ranking officer in our office. This made me the Deputy by default. The front office, other divisions, and my fellow colleagues informally upgraded my duty title to Deputy according to protocol, but the boss lady refused to change my duty title officially. I did all the work, but never received the credit.

The boss lady was steadfast in her decision. I felt it was unfair, unwarranted, and unkind and to top it off the boss lady worked me like a dog. It was the first time in my career where I felt used, abused, and unappreciated. I knew in my heart she was wrong in how she treated me, but her actions were her own issue, not mine. Even though it was painful having to interact with her, I continued to work professionally and kept my chin up.

On many occasions, I was by-name requested to work events, conferences, and distinguished visitors trips. This added fuel to an already blazing fire. The boss lady kept adding more to my plate, but I excelled. I'm not sure if it was because I was stubborn or if I was naturally gifted in this specialty. Nonetheless, the flames grew brighter. Then the boss lady decided to stop talking to me on a personal level. She stopped inviting me to meetings and avoided me in any personal setting altogether. She was my boss and was supposed to make me a better Airman by training, educating, leading, and mentoring me. She was supposed to help me become my very best. Sadly, she didn't do any of these things. She left me to my own device and I didn't develop professionally or personally. How sad is it to work for someone and never get better due to their lack of leadership?

Jealousy destroys a person and hurts others. Its mental war-game doesn't belong to anyone and it shouldn't be allowed to leave victims in its path. People must rid themselves of the negative, sabotaging thoughts. Jealousy is not healthy, nor is it right.

Jealous people are dealing with internal conflict. It's an issue controlling them, which creates undue suffering. It may be a result of childhood trauma, fear, or low self-esteem. Whatever the cause, a person must work it out either alone or through counseling. When their insecurities start to impact you, that's when healthy boundaries between you and them must be created. Address their issues maturely by letting them know how their insecurities are impacting you. That's why the issue must be addressed honestly and quickly…because you're being impacted negatively!

If the problem has been addressed, but the insecure person continues, walk away. It's not healthy to endure their unhealthy behavior. **If you do, that's called insanity.**

Jealous people who want what others have should instead appreciate what they do have. They think the other person has something better or they themselves have something less. This thinking kills self-esteem and self-worth. It begins to deplete their joy and can lead to greediness, selfishness, and can even destroy good relationships. Jealous people are not happy and never will be, until they accept their reality.

You can't help jealous people. They must help themselves. Therefore, never change for anyone, unless you are going down a destructive path. There's only one of you in this world. You were made for a reason. Remember that! Don't let jealous people degrade your worth.

Remember: Healthy people don't try to steal the spotlight or deliberately try to make others feel inferior. Healthy people don't try to over magnify their strengths on purpose, especially the ones they're born with. Healthy people don't play on others weaknesses. Healthy people don't try to take anything away from others. A healthy person won't purposefully hurt others without just cause. Healthy people won't allow jealousy to control their lives.

The goal for all of us is to be a healthy person!

Moral of the Story – It's a fact, not everyone will like you. Shocker, I know!

I like who I am and don't want to change. I also realize that not everyone will like me. I don't see it as their fault; I accept it as reality. The same applies for you.

You could be the best person in the world and that could be the reason why someone doesn't like you. You may remind them of who they are not. Your strength may be their weakness. You might have something they want, but can never have. There are many reasons as to why someone might not like you, but remember it's their issue, not yours. They have the problem. They have an internal conflict they need to work on. Don't change who you are to appease them. Plus, it may not work anyway.

Don't try to get someone to like you, it shouldn't be a job. Accept the fact that people will not like you and it will give you a better outlook on life.

If you want to try and mend the relationship, ask the person if you have offended him or her. This provides an opportunity for them to give you feedback and help you better understand the situation. Plus, you could have been a jerk and never realized it. Be honest and let them know how they make you feel. This dialogue may help them realize what they are consciously or subconsciously doing. It may be a wake-up call for them, or for you if you were a jerk.

No matter what happens, remember your tribe of people because those in your court are the ones that truly matter. People come and go, especially jealous ones (thank goodness). Also, be thankful for those that celebrate you, these people are rare.

Comparison is corrosive. It eats away at your ability to be content and confident. Comparison is the thief of joy; and jealousy is often its partner in crime.

Jealousy doesn't do anyone any good. Jealousy doesn't allow people to be happy for others. Jealousy prevents others from reaching their best self because they are too busy comparing themselves and their lot in life to others.

If you want to take the higher road, actually pray for those jealous people. They are obviously lacking something. Prayer may be their answer.

A candle doesn't lose its light even if it lights another candle.

9 – Difficult is Remembered

For 6-weeks, hurricane season was at an all-time high with multiple storms rolling in and slamming the Florida panhandle. My job at the time was Chief, Readiness and Plans, which meant managing the Services Mini Command Center. It was a full-time operation 24 hours a day, 7 days a week for 6-weeks, and I sometimes ended up sleeping on my office floor.

Mother Nature is a powerful force and can turn in an instant, wreak havoc, produce deceptive calming effects, and then unleash her fury moments later. Tornadoes, hurricanes, and fires are not to be played with. Luckily, hurricanes provide fair warning so people can evacuate and prepare accordingly. In 2004, Hurricane Ivan was a storm that changed my outlook and taught me to punch fear in the face. It was one of the scariest times in my life.

Due to Hurricane Ivan's power, magnitude, and potentially devastating effects, the entire base was evacuated to ensure everyone's safety. Thousands of people left the panhandle of Florida driving to Tennessee, Kentucky, and Missouri, while 100 (roughly) Air Force members including myself stayed back. We were called the "Ride Out Team."

Two days prior to Hurricane Ivan reaching the base, we boarded doors, closed buildings, cut tree branches, stored anything that could become flying debris, fueled generators, parked vehicles in safe areas, built window protectors, and prepared the armory to house our "Ride Out Team" until the storm passed.

The reason for leaving a few of us behind was to provide base protection and have a clean-up crew ready for the storm's aftermath. Typically when a large storm passes, there's a higher probability of looting and civilians needing assistance. Some people either don't have the resources to evacuate or they think they can ride out the storm. The "Ride Out Team" is considered first-responders, base keepers, protectors of government property, assistants to the outside population, and helpers with crisis control. Once the storm passes, the base must be brought back up to normal operations as quickly as possible. Each member has a specific function to perform in order to expedite the base cleanup process, which ensures a timely return for the rest of the base personnel.

Back to Ivan, once we did all we could to minimize mass destruction, we hunkered down in the base armory building. We each found spaces where we could lay down our sleeping bags and establish a temporary shelter. I chose to be under a desk. Once settled, we waited for the storm to hit, glued ourselves to the news, and watched where the eye of the storm was heading and its current condition. We were prepared for the worst, hoping and praying the roof wouldn't blow off our shelter, and the armory would be able to withstand the massive hits from Ivan-the-Terrible.

Then the wind started.

I stopped watching the news and retreated to my personal makeshift shelter under the desk. I wrapped myself in my sleeping bag and laid there listening. As I could hear the wind speed picking up, it became loud and scary. I could hear the brutal snaps of tree branches, objects striking the building, rain pounding the roof, thunder, and constant unfamiliar terrifying noises for hours. It was hard to fall asleep. I kept thinking why did I stay, what was I doing, what would happen if the roof came off, and did I live a life that mattered and had purpose?

I nervously laid there for hours, and eventually dozed off. Then I awoke to a scream. I jerked awake, quickly tried to sit up, and struck my head on the desk, which I forgot I was sleeping under. Once I came to my senses, I realized what the scream was from. The lights had gone out. I heard someone telling people to stay put until the emergency power lights came on and they could manage to start the generators. There was nothing but silence, no one was moving, it was pitch dark, and all of us were holding our breath waiting for the sanctuary of the lights to return. I realized being in the dark makes a person appreciative of having vision, something we often take for granted. The buzzing sound of the generators came to life and a brief sigh of relief was heard across the entire building.

There were calm periods that occurred as the storm bands passed over. During those breaks, our boss and security staff went out to check on the base. They shortly returned and continued going out again and again and again with each trip lasting a little longer than the one before.

We were almost out of supplies and to make things worse, our water pressure dropped and were reduced to using toiletry disposal bags. Near our wits end from the relentless storm, the boss returned from his round of checks late on the second day and gave us the all clear to begin securing the base and cleaning up the aftermath.

My supervisor and I immediately went to our duty station to cook the perishable food we could use. Our goal was to feed the "Ride Out Team" a hot meal by midnight. We lit the burners and began cooking. I was a hot, sweaty mess from the heat and we had no air to cool us. I was cooking massive amounts of food and within four hours, we contacted the boss to tell him hot food was ready. It was our first hot meal in days because we were living on trail mix, Meals-Ready-to-Eat (MRE), and protein bars. I don't even remember what we made to eat, but it was hot and every person ate without complaint. We cleaned up, went back to our armory for the night to sleep, and did it again the next day. That day we served three hot meals, went to bed exhausted, and got up the next day to serve three more hot meals.

My supervisor and I continued to serve three hot meals until the base reopened because our goal was to keep personnel fed and keep morale high.

The week of the Ivan-the-Terrible storm taught me a lot about myself. I was afraid, but chose to punch fear in the face. As a result, I realized how strong I was.

I learned the meaning of what a true servant meant. I wasn't worried about my well-being after the doors to our weather-beaten ransacked base were opened. I shifted my concerns to the care and feeding of others.

I learned how to work with a team in a crisis situation, depend on them, and live with them in a confined space. I learned how to quickly react to life-and-death situations. I learned material things weren't important when human safety was on the line. When it came down to it, I chose to stay and defend the base rather than take my personal possessions and run.

I learned I was more capable physically, mentally, and emotionally than I ever gave myself credit for. During the storm, I learned how thankful I was for having my sight, which I never thought about before and took for granted. I've been thankful for my five senses ever since.

I learned I can quickly cook for a big group with limited supplies and make it taste good. I learned how to laugh during hard times and was thankful to have someone to laugh with. For instance, my supervisor and I were delivering a bassinet to a customer at 0200 in the morning and we were laughing hysterically about it. My sides hurt from laughing so hard. I have no idea why we were laughing like that, maybe lack of sleep, but I will remember that moment forever. Laughing is good medicine for the soul.

I learned I am a strong leader and a strong follower, especially in times of crisis.

I learned I am what I think I am so I better think good of myself.

I learned both effective and efficient communication are key.

I learned you can evacuate thousands of people in 12 hours, but it takes three-plus days to get them back home. I learned a lot and will always be thankful for Hurricane Ivan's lessons.

After a week of supporting the "Ride Out Team," I left the base to check on my house. I was worried I wouldn't have a home or would have damage like so many other people. To my surprise, living on a downward slope proved to be beneficial as I only had a few roof shingles missing. I was blessed with my house's good fortune as I had just lived through a massive hurricane and was alive to tell about it.

Looking back, I would do the same thing all over again.

Moral of the Story – You never know what you are capable of until you are faced with adversity. Real life and death circumstances change a person, for better or worse. You either make it or you don't. You rise or fall. You either look the situation in the eye, stand up tall with your shoulders back and feet squared, or cower and run.

In tough times, you realize material possessions are not worth as much as your vision or your other senses. You are thankful for things you once took for granted, like running water, a hot meal, a toilet with toilet paper, electricity, a strong building, the sound of laughter, a friend being with you in the darkest hour, and having loved ones.

When the majority of men and women run away from danger, there are some that run to it. Be thankful for the people risking their lives for you.

Every person should believe they are capable of being on the "Ride Out Team" because they can, yet very few choose to be. Most people will never know how strong they are physically, mentally, or emotionally because it's easier to live in comfort and be safe than it is to face fear and hard times. Don't be afraid of the hard times! Instead, embrace them.

Life without difficulty is tragic! The hard times teach you what you are capable of. Growth happens when things are hard, not when they are easy.

A diamond is made under pressure and becomes unbreakable, just like you!

You don't give yourself enough credit…you are so much more capable than you think. Hard times will come, some that you will never be truly ready for. In those times, remain steadfast with courage because you can overcome it by embracing the strength you never knew you had.

10 – Gunshot to the Chest - Suicide

I never witnessed death as a child. My one encounter happened when I attended a wake, but I never went up to the casket. I wish I had the courage, but I couldn't move my feet. I was fourteen years old standing there in a red outfit eager to leave the horrible feeling. It wasn't that I was afraid to see the body, I was afraid of death.

It changed when I was became a Mortuary Officer in the military. I had to attend Mortuary school for 1-week to learn Mortuary duties and to understand my role. In hindsight, I wish it had been longer. Mortuary Affairs school taught me how to properly handle a deceased member, understand roles and responsibilities of escorting officers, and learn required processes and regulations. Instead of being afraid of death as before, the school taught me to understand it.

Roughly 6-months after Mortuary school, I moved into the position of Assistant Wing Mortuary Officer. It was quiet for the first few months and then my first death occurred. My boss and I were called to the County Morgue because a military member had committed suicide. I will never forget that day.

We walked into the holding room, which was really cold and there lay a deceased man. I felt dizzy and had to sit down for a minute before I could turn back towards the body. The mortician informed us it was a gunshot to the chest. I watched the member's naked body appear as the mortician pulled off the sheet. Then I saw the hole. No words can describe what I saw and what I felt. I was sad, so incredibly sad. Holding my emotions in was all I could as we moved into job mode.

We confirmed the state of the deceased's body and identity of the Airman. It was tragic and heartbreaking. We informed the mortician a family member of the deceased was on their way from another State because the family requested an autopsy. The family felt suicide was not the cause of death.

Leaving the mortician to start the autopsy, my boss and I left for the deceased member's house. We conducted an inspection of the property as the Summary Courts Officer (SCO) arrived to inventory and pack the belongings to be sent to the family. This was required because the member was not married, had no children, and did not have a will.

I remember walking up the stairs to the bedroom where the body was found. As soon as I entered the room, I saw the blood stained mattress. It hurt my heart and I cried. I couldn't understand why he would shoot himself. Why didn't anyone see the signs? Why didn't he talk with anyone? Why did he think death was the only answer? I couldn't take the sight of the bloody mattress anymore because I was overwhelmed by the loss of a precious human life.

We returned to the morgue to conduct a post inspection of the body after it was autopsied. A Mortuary Officer must ensure the body was properly embalmed with no leaking embalming fluid. This was important because the member was being buried in a military uniform and we had to ensure nothing was out of order. To emphasize the importance of conducting the inspection, my boss and I surprisingly found a few areas where the body was not properly sealed and embalming fluid had been leaking. The mortician quickly fixed the problems.

We left the room so makeup could be applied and the uniform could be donned. While walking outside, we noticed the deceased's family member had arrived and was sitting on the sofa, crying. I sat down next to him. At a loss for words, I could only bring myself to say, "I'm very, very sorry." After a long time of sitting there in silence, we stood up and I began explaining what would take place. The military member's coffin would be transported with an escort to the place of burial and full military honors would commence.

My boss and I returned to the morgue holding room to ensure the uniform was correct and the member looked presentable. Within a week the member was buried and by month's end, his affairs and personal property were taken care of. More than a decade later, I am still haunted by the memories.

A hopeless soul hurting so deeply and not being able to see beyond darkness…a tragedy. Many people try to avoid the issue of suicide, yet many people contemplate it. More tragically, some go through with it. Instead of superficially talking about suicide, we need to get deeply involved in order to prevent it. **One life lost is too many.** People can hold deep pain so we should all be kind to everyone we come across.

My second death happened a few months later. A beautiful young girl who was a supervisor and her male subordinate were wedding-hopping all day and became wasted drunk. They finally had enough partying and got into the girl's car to head home. Neither one was sober enough to drive, but the subordinate was better off than the supervisor. He buckled in, but she did not. While driving, he veered off the road and struck a sand dune, which caused the car to stop abruptly. The girl not wearing any restraints was ejected through the car windshield. When the rescue vehicles arrived, they found the girl dead on arrival with several compound fractures and a broken neck. The subordinate was okay.

I was called at 0200 hours in the morning to head to the same morgue where my first death took place, but this time I was alone.

When I arrived, I met the mortician to examine the body. The young girl was gorgeous. She looked like a cover girl model, yet here she was on a metal table deceased. No autopsy was required so I began inspecting her body. I found my initial reluctance to being around a corpse turned into a high tolerance for being in the environment. I was able to bring myself to work with the mortician by helping him stop the embalming fluid from leaking out of the compound fractures of the girl's body. I was slowly overcoming my fear of death.

That next day, my boss met me at the morgue and we finished dressing the supervisor. Next, we left the morgue to go to her house. We finished the funeral plans and sat there pondering the life of that young girl. I will remember the supervisor on that metal table for the rest of my life and still wonder periodically what would have happened if she had worn her seatbelt. She was on the fast track to greatness and a day of bad decisions made under the influence of alcohol had ended it all. It was and still is devastatingly sad.

When most people think of death in the military, they think it's from combat related events not things like suicide or drinking-and-driving. Sadly, it happens more frequently than not. Senseless death that could have been avoided breaks my heart.

My next death-case is what most people think of. It was for five military members (four U.S. and one military member from another Country). The deaths were due to an explosion hitting their helicopter causing it to crash. Due to the violence of the accident, their individual remains couldn't be identified. The U.S. embassy worked with the other Country to request special permission for all five members to be buried together as a single unit in a National Cemetery. We received permission and had full military honors for the brave military members. During this time, we worked with the families back in the United States to ensure paperwork was processed correctly. I will remember it forever because it was my biggest death-case and one of the men that died was a big-hearted colleague of mine.

After the mass internment, I had a few more death cases, but nothing like my first three. The deaths changed me. They opened my eyes to reality. Suicide is real. People are hurting in the world and live in dark places with no hope or desire to live. Drinking and driving is real and could hurt or kill innocent people as well as destroy families. Combat is real. Lives are tragically lost. Death hurts by all accounts.

Death opened my eyes to the fact that we all die. The real question is, "How did we all live?"

Moral of the Story – Death is real. People die for a variety of reasons with some being intentional and some not. The in-between is life and it can be hard, which makes people choose to die on their own terms instead of trying to escape the looming darkness. People feel death is their only option because they allow the darkness to suffocate them. But, death is not the answer, life is. If you are down, please seek help. Your life is worth living.

Bad decisions can lead to death so we must strive to choose wisely. Drinking and driving is preventable. We must take the keys away, lock the doors, be strong enough to stop someone from driving, and prevent any type of unnecessary tragedy from occurring. One person standing up against bad decisions can save a life or many. A courageous or logically thinking person should intercede on another's behalf, but that person rarely does so. I encourage you to be that bold person because it could save a life.

Death changes people. Those impacted by the loss of a loved one must go on in life even though their pain seems unbearable. They have to pick up the pieces, carry on their loved one's name and legacy, and live with the hole in their heart that may never heal. I'm truly sorry for your loss.

Grief is real. I encourage you to seek counseling in order for you to learn some tools that will help you learn to live with the loss, as your life must go on. The loved one that you lost wouldn't want you to live the rest of your life in tears.

We will all die at some point so we must make the most of every single day we do have. Have a working Bucket List and live each day like it's your last. You only get one life and it goes by quickly. Make the most of it!

Live Full, Die Empty.

Final note: Please keep your head up and observe the people around you. Don't miss the signs. Suicide is real. It really is tragic because one life lost is too many.

11 – Pain is Real

Ironically, there was a time in my life where pain consumed me. I was sad, really sad. I wasn't involved in church, didn't have family around nor an outlet. Instead of turning to alcohol, food, or drugs as my escape, I turned to running. I never ran long distance before, but one day I just started to run. Running became the outlet I chose primarily because it was free.

I was hurting and didn't know how to deal with sadness, frustration, and anger. So I hit the pavement and hit it hard. My running distance was short because I was winded easily. I didn't stop though. My goal each day was to run a little longer than I had the day before. My speed never became anything to write home about, but the distance I ran made up for it. The longer I ran, the more pavement I hit. It gave me time to think about life and how to heal from heartache.

Running was the only time I could escape my feelings and didn't feel the emotional turmoil that loomed over me. I felt the physical pain, which was easier to handle than the pain of a broken heart. My endurance increased to running a few miles at a time. A feeling of accomplishment. The joy I experienced as I hit each new milestone began to overtake my sadness and I slowly began to heal.

I ran every day, even during the hottest part of the year on the flight line in Florida. The extreme heat radiating off the pavement made me sweat out tears instead of crying them. My days of running turned into months, my steps turned into miles, and my tears turned into smiles.

My love for running resulted in signing up for a half-marathon. In preparation, a friend began running with me. I was no longer alone in my thoughts, but was able to share something with someone. We ran the half-marathon and then did another one. My friend became my pacer and running partner. My tears subsided as running medals replaced them.

Next was the Marine Corps Marathon and our training began. I was a new person. My thoughts were no longer engulfed in darkness because my heart had found new light.

My friend and I ran a training plan for two months. During our first 18-mile training run, we both got sick from being overexposed to the sun. We were well hydrated and wore sunscreen, but the sun whipped us both. I remember laying on the shower floor needing to vomit, but nothing would come up. I was so hot. At that moment, I began to doubt my ability to run a marathon, but immediately stopped myself from thinking negatively. My mind was reprogrammed. I began to reflect on all I had been through and what I had overcome. I vowed to not let self-doubt take me out of the race.

The following week I had no problem with the 18-mile training run. In fact, I ran it with a smile. My own insecurities would not keep me from achieving my goal nor would I let them drag me back to the sidelines from where my journey originated. By readjusting my attitude, the mental barriers were wiped clear.

On the day of the marathon, everything was going as planned. The starting gun went off and my running partner and I worked our way from the back of the line all the way up to our race-pacer. We were doing awesome. I had never felt more alive! Being amongst the hundreds of people participating that day ignited energy and I was truly happy.

Then it happened. Around the 12-mile marker, my running partner said she was feeling good and felt she could beat her Marathon Performance Record. She decided to go for it and began accelerating ahead of me. I wanted to keep the pace I trained for and elected to stay back. She left me…and I was okay. This was my race!

The energy from the people around me motivated me and helped me maintain my running pace. Then at the 18-mile marker I hit 'The Wall.' I reached the part of the course that required running over a very long bridge. Traversing the bridge became a real struggle and I began thinking to myself, why was I running? Running was stupid!

I slowed to a walk, ate some energy Jelly Beans, and eventually made it over the horrible bridge. I began to slowly run again and made it to the 21-mile marker where I stopped to drink a Red Bull someone had given me. I asked them about my friend and they told me she had come and gone. This inspired me to keep up my original pace. My energy was renewed and I began running my pace again. I was now only five miles away from the biggest physical accomplishment of my life.

Those next five miles were loaded with determination. My legs carried me 21 miles, but my heart would carry me the rest. Around the 24-mile marker guess who I saw…my running partner. She was walking. I ran up to her and screamed, "DON'T STOP! YOU CAN DO IT!" and off I went. She was the one who taught me to always follow my training plan and not to veer off course, even if I felt good. She knew, as well as I, the feeling was temporary. With only two miles left to go, I pressed on and reached the finish line. I finished my race! Then several minutes later my running partner crossed the finish line.

Hitting-the-pavement healed me. It took two years to transition from one of my saddest moments to being completely healed. I haven't run another marathon since. It's hard on the knees, but I still like to run Halfs and 5Ks. Now when I look at the medals hanging, I smile and reflect on my ability to have turned raw pain into tangible joy.

Strangely enough the shower was another healing area for my life. It was my quiet place with no intrusions. Just my mind, body, and soul. My mind would drift and I would think about what I want to be, where I want to go, what I want to do, and why these things mattered to me. I figured out what I liked about myself and what I didn't. I thought about my strengths and analyzed my weaknesses. I thought about what made me happy and what made me sad. I thought about my relationships and what I did that led to their demise. I thought about retirement and how I needed to plan for it while in my younger years. I thought about my childhood family and the torment they caused me and then I would try to forgive them. I would talk to God and ask Him to teach me how to lift and encourage others and learn how to help people more than just helping myself. The water cleansed my mind, body, and soul. Sometimes, I would take showers twice a day to escape the busyness of life and focus on deepening my relationship with God. I was a new me.

Hitting the pavement and taking a shower were a sanctuary, my safe place, where I cried, prayed, and eventually healed.

What is your sanctuary in life? What is your outlet to heal?

Moral of the Story – Life is not perfect and there will be times the wind is knocked out of your sails. In those moments, you can choose to be self-destructive or self-constructive. Being self-destructive may numb your thoughts temporarily, but will permanently harm your mental, emotional, and physical health. Some people choose to cut, drink excessive amounts of alcohol, party, gamble, use drugs, or sleep around. Sadly, I've known people to choose one or more of these paths and it only ended up hurting them worse. Their sadness compounded into sadness with regrets.

I implore you to be the other type of person that chooses something constructive. There are many options to choose from. Find what makes you happy (to the core) and go there each day for a few minutes to get away from the demands of people, work, and life. This place could also help you heal if you're going through something difficult.

The reason why I felt compelled to write a chapter on having a sanctuary is because I feel our lives are too full. We are busier than ever before because of technology and our inability to say, "No" to the increased amount of commitments. We must take time for self-care. We give ourselves little time to stop. We need a pause in order to regroup. We need this in order to get through the hard times and heal. We need a place where we can be real, a place of comfort, a place to think, a place to forgive, and a place to escape life. We need this place so we can put our oxygen mask on first. A healthy us creates a healthy us for others.

Please don't rush into each day without taking time to reflect for a few moments. *Self-care is simply giving the same kindness to ourselves that we extend to others.* Create/define your sanctuary. You will be better for it.

An empty lantern provides no light. Self-care is the fuel that allows your light to shine brightly.

12 – Pentagon and Congress

I was in awe when I arrived at the five-sided building for the first time. I never imagined the largest government building in the world to be that big. I knew it would be large, but didn't grasp how massive it was until I saw it with my own eyes. I had arrived at the pinnacle of my career. I arrived at the Pentagon. My life was about to change forever.

I was nervous, excited, and ready to embark on a larger-than-life experience.

The Pentagon was a gigantic maze where any person can decipher the building once they learn the code. It's designed to help people not get lost, find the room and location they need, and assist newcomers and visitors needing help. I learned the code on my first day and can honestly say for the seven years I was there, I only got lost a few times.

People never have to leave the Pentagon if they don't want to. There's a post office, restaurants, fitness center with a pool, CVS Pharmacy, medical and dental facilities, optometry clinic, DMV, passport office, clothing sales, and so much more. It is a self-sustaining facility offering everything one could need. To boot, every wall displays historic pictures, quotes, information, and exhibitions that makes you stand in awe.

I would walk the halls looking at the different displays, stand in admiration in the Hall of Heroes, applaud the wounded warriors, watch tour guides walking backwards and never stumble and fall, explore the many different decorated walls, see security personnel trail behind Secretary of Defense, and sit in the courtyard with a book. It was magical.

Working in Protocol had its perks, which made up for the long work hours. I did things I never imagined or dreamed. I met famous people, high-ranking leaders, worked legendary events, and shared cherished memories with amazing friends. The outgoing Chief of Staff's Farewell Dinner left me in tears, the incoming Chief of Staff's Christmas Party left me laughing, meeting the 12 Outstanding Heroes left me in awe, working the Air Show left me exhausted, greeting and meeting political dignitaries left me puzzled, traveling to different countries on assignment left me thankful, and smiling at every single person while saying, "Hi" left me singled out.

Some people lacked a consistent smile because the work was hard, time consuming, stressful, and fast-paced. People were working to meet deadlines, trying to make the next promotion rank, and checking the box. My office was an absolute exception. We were a tight group and would laugh for hours, including Mama Leola, Dan-the-Man, Brenda, Sean, and Stromboley. We helped each other, learned from our mistakes, and ensured the team was set up for success.

Here's an example of laughter. I was sent to the House of Representatives and Senate for a variety of House of Armed Services Committee (HASC) and Senate Armed Services Committee (SASC) hearings. I was in awe when I arrived at the Senate Capitol Building. It was beautiful. As I sat in the first hearing, I looked up and saw a gigantic portrait and asked a colleague why Morgan Freeman was being displayed and they laughed out loud during the hearing. Apparently, it was a portrait of Associate Justice of the Supreme Court Judge Clarence Thomas. I know now they don't look alike, but in the picture they did. I was nervous. The remainder of the Hearing was interesting because everyone continued to chuckle while listening to the mundane hearing. The chuckling finally ended and we took a tour and ate a bowl of chili. We returned the next day for more hearings.

What I remember the most is how I personally felt during those two days. Many individuals were making decisions for the Armed Forces who had never worn a military uniform. It troubled me to have people making military decisions based on what they believed instead of what they knew first-hand. In my humble opinion, wearing a uniform is the only way to gain real experience and education in how the military functions. To boot, the majority of the House and Senate were acting cold to us even though we were the people wearing the uniforms. I didn't get a warm feeling from those elected officials who were making decisions on my behalf and our American military. It made me feel sad. I digress.

For almost seven years I worked in the Pentagon. I experienced life on the Headquarters Air Staff as a First Lieutenant, living the dream in Joint Staff as a Captain, and then moving onto the Secretary of the Air Force Space staff. I did things most people could never dream of. Not to mention cherished memories and wonderful adventures across the Globe.

One memory that stands out was when I did a cartwheel in the Chief of Staff's office. The office was in the middle of being remodeled and there was no furniture so I commandeered a cartwheel. It is probably the only cartwheel ever performed in the Chief's office. I also did 'The Worm' with another fellow officer in Vice's office. I'm shaking my head with our silliness. Work hard, play hard.

Another memory was when I was selected to go to an alternate site location. I was picked up at the Pentagon in a helicopter, which was my first time ever to fly in one. We lifted off the grassy front lawn area and flew away. We flew over Interstate 395, over the cars, fast and low. I have no idea who authorized our helicopter pilots to fly like that, but it was one of the coolest experiences I ever had. I have so many more memories, but not enough time to share. They'll forever be imprinted in my mind.

I would gladly go back to the Pentagon, but I would pass on Congress. If there is a next time for me to work at the Pentagon, I would have the same blessed mindset. I'll gently remind others we're there for a beautiful purpose and it's the ultimate honor to help our military brethren and Country. I will be the light that shines bright and try to make every person smile by encouraging them and having them remember their purpose too. The Pentagon's mission matters as it houses the defense of our Nation!

Anyone can make money, but you can't make memories if you never do anything. Memories are what you hold dear for the rest of your life. Friend, take the vacation that you've earned…the job will still be there when you return.

Moral of the Story – Things that seem bigger than life initially settle down after a while and become part of the norm. They seem bigger because they're new and different, but they do lose their gloss and appeal over time. Give yourself time to adjust and give change a chance.

What scares us the most usually changes us the most. I was initially scared to step into the Pentagon for fear of not being smart enough or good enough because I was a brand new First Lieutenant. Then I remembered I was in charge of my journey. As a result, I created life-long memories, explored history, and was mentored by many General Officers and leaders. The Pentagon was large and my role was small, but my role was important in the big scheme of things. Do what I did - punch fear in the face because you are stronger and more capable than you give yourself credit for.

Don't let something small hold you back from doing something big. Don't get a prideful head. Stay humble. Be a Servant Leader. Help your team succeed. Smile. Do the best you can. Take a chance and go for it. Take the helicopter ride. Explore what's around you. Appreciate every single day. Take a tour of the Pentagon. Remember it's not about you. Be kind to people. Get out of your comfort zone. Don't shrink yourself. Do a cartwheel. Be able to laugh at yourself. Don't be scared. Dream big and achiever bigger!

If you're ever given an opportunity to do something different, don't let fear dissuade you from doing it. You only have one life and if you do it right, one life is enough. YOLO.

Chase your dreams until they become reality.

Do well for yourself, for your family, for your team, and for your country…it's all that matters in the end.

When you love your job, you find that you will never work a day in your life. If you don't love your job, evaluate why you are still there because life is too short to work at a place that makes you miserable. You are spending 8-hrs a day at work, please make sure you are doing more than just collecting a paycheck. *Don't be a slave to job you dislike.* <u>You are worth more than that.</u>

13 – Courage

It's easy to stand with the crowd, but it takes courage to stand alone. On a heartbreaking day surrounded by a mass of a thousand I had the realization I was different.

Once a year in Washington DC, there's a festival that attracts hundreds of people, numerous rock bands, fair-booths and games, food, and alcohol. The day begins with laughter and usually ends with headache. I was fundamentally changed as a human being on this particular day.

The day began with droplets forming from the mist of rain falling while taking pictures with two of my best friends. My friends and I walked around absorbing the atmosphere. Bands were jamming, fists pumping in the air, people body surfing, dancing, and lots of smiles. It was starting out to be an interesting day.

We later met up with other friends including a guy who liked me. Most people were already drinking beer and it was still early in the morning. I don't like beer and was the sober one. Anyone who has ever been sober around drunk people should understand what I'm trying to convey.

The guy who liked me and I ventured out to get something to eat. Along the way we stumbled upon a large crowd of people, but we had no idea what they were doing. All we could determine was something was happening on the ground. I could see police officers. Some were watching the commotion and some were looking at the crowd. As I navigated my way to the front of the crowd, I saw what it was. It was a very large, young man who appeared to weigh almost 500-lbs lying on his stomach while several people were hitting him. Everyone stood there watching and cheering these monsters on who were attacking him. I became sick to my stomach.

I couldn't believe what I was seeing. No one was doing anything about it. What seemed like minutes passing was only a second when I decided to act. I ran over to the melee of monsters and screamed at them to stop. I screamed and screamed and screamed for people to "DO SOMETHING" to "STOP" and to "HELP HIM" while tears streamed down my face. The young man was trying to get up, but the savages kept him down with their relentless attack. I ran to the guy that liked me and said, "Please do something" and he finally did. He went over to the scene and then the cops moved in. The cops pulled the monsters off the young man on the ground and he just laid there. I've never felt so disgusted with what happened to this young man. He slowly began to get up, bloodied, and hurt. How could people do this to other people?

The crowd dispersed, but I sat with tears watching the guy slowly move. I had no idea how something like this could happen and couldn't understand why no one did anything about it, except me. Even though they weren't the ones beating him up, the spectators were just as responsible for not attempting to help in stopping this hate crime. Not even the cops reacted until I went over pleading for someone to help. The beaten man eventually regained his senses and slowly walked away. I will never forget the ruthless ordeal the young man suffered.

What would you have done?

I sometimes wonder how long it would have lasted if I had done nothing. I wonder how long the young man would have endured being hit. I wonder how people could watch and cheer on such a horrible act of inhumanity. Worse, people were taking video of the horrific scene.

A person was being beaten and no one did anything about it. It was like an episode of "What Would You Do?" and I now understood how real the show could be. If this resonates with you for any reason, I plead with you to not be the one who stands around and does nothing.

If a situation seems odd, then it probably is. If it looks and feels bad, then trust your instincts. When you decide it is bad, do something. If something in your past still upsets you because you didn't react, get over it. You can't change the past. If faced with a similar situation in the future, turn your previous failure into a second chance to do it right. Please never partake in allowing inhumane acts to take place.

I was shaky after the mob-attack incident and became quiet, which is not like me. I was analyzing my thoughts and feelings about what took place. Even though I lost my appetite, the guy that liked me and I continued on our walk to find food. In no time, a second episode occurred.

The guy that liked me bought me some French fries (one of my favorite foods) hoping to change my mood. As I begin to eat my fries, a drunk guy standing next to me nonchalantly puts his dirty, nasty hands in my basket of fries and took some. I said, "What are you doing!" The drunk guy then yelled at me telling me to share. The guy that liked me pulled me away and said, "He's drunk and to give him the fries." I gave my fries to the guy that liked me and walked away. I never looked back.

As I walked away, I came to the conclusion that this was not my scene, not now, not ever. I don't like situations where people are inhumane, drunk, and without manners. I don't like being one of the few sober individuals surrounded by negative chaos and conflict, physical or verbal. I don't like anyone touching my food with their hands without my permission. I don't like when people are acting disrespectful towards others.

This conclusion has helped me create a safe environment for my growth. I choose who I allow to be in my life. I choose the activities I want to participate in. I choose what I listen to, what I watch, what I read, and who I want adding into my life. I don't allow people to make me feel bad for choosing the things I choose. I don't allow negativity to take me away from the positive life I choose to live. A safe environment is necessary for the dreams I have, the life I choose to live, the goals I want to achieve, and the dreams I want to fulfill. I choose to limit my time with anything and anyone that counters what safe means to me. You should do the same.

The other conclusion I realized during my experience while at the festival is I have a backbone when most people don't. I'm a strong person. Not so much physically strong, but mentally and emotionally strong. On that day, I stood up twice for something I believed in. When's the last time you spoke up or stood up for what you believe?

A funny bone is nice to have, but a backbone is critical.

Moral of the Story – It's easy to stand with the crowd, but it takes courage to stand alone. Would you have been a spectator and watched a human life suffer or would you have acted? Would you have stepped up to help or stood back? Would you have followed the crowd and cheered on the travesty or jumped into the circle to try and stop the injustice?

On that day, no one stepped up to help a person in need. In this decade, we have people killing one another, cheating, lying, stealing, cops abusing their power, spectators recording people hurting others, discrimination, prejudice, leaders not acting like leaders, blackmail, verbal assault, physical pain, emotional trauma, spiritual deceit, and so much more. It's a tragedy. We need to step up for what's right, even if we're alone! At least you could look into the mirror at the end of the day and be proud of yourself for your noble actions.

Friend, don't look the other way when trouble shows up. Be willing to ask yourself what do you see, but choose to not respond to? I encourage you to not allow a bad situation to continue. Instead turn it into a good one. Help others. Standup for someone who can't standup for themselves. Be the brave person you are and if you aren't brave, you must find the courage to become brave. We need courageous people to stand up for good instead of giving way to evil. No one remembers those who are average, but everyone remembers the brave soul that stands up for what is right.

Having a safe environment is key. You should not be forced to do something that contradicts your values, morals, purpose, and thinking. If you don't want to do something, don't do it. You'll only regret it if you do. Your time is limited so don't spend time with activities or people not conducive to your well-being and life goals. **Create boundaries for your life** and hold yourself to them. It will only serve you well.

What you allow will continue until you decide to do something about it!

14 – White House

As a young girl I dreamt of becoming the first woman President, but never actually thinking I could do it because I was raised in a trailer park and on welfare. I didn't become President, but I did make it to the world's most powerful house working for the world's most powerful leader. A dream of its own. When I think back to my time at the White House, I pinch myself.

While working at the Pentagon I was fortunate to apply for a highly esteemed position in Washington D.C. The position was called White House Social Aide. White House Social Aides support and assist the President of the United States and First Lady during White House events and functions. Social Aides serve as an extension of the President and First Lady in their roles as official host and hostess of the United States. Social Aides elicit an exemplary performance that reflects great credit upon the President, First Lady, and the Office of the Presidency, thereby enhancing the reputation of the United States Government amongst its own citizens and the entire world.

How it began. I applied for the position and was selected to meet the first interview panel. The interview process was nerve-wracking because you were questioned by several high-ranking leaders and had to remain poised and be well-versed. We had to enter the room in a specific manner, state your name, report as ordered, and sit appropriately in a chair facing the board members, which was quite difficult while wearing a skirt. The questions were related to social etiquette and scenario-based. Meaning, we would describe how we would act in certain settings and confrontations.

The interview seemed like it was an hour long, but was actually less than ten minutes. I was nervous and when I finished the interview I had no idea of how I had done once I exited the room. It was a two-week waiting game before we were notified of the panel's decision. I think there were 25 people who interviewed in the first round and 10 were selected for the second round of interviews. I was blessed to be one of the 10.

In the next round, we were sent to the White House to be interviewed by the White House Military Office and First Lady's staff. This is when my stomach knotted up and I found myself having to go to the bathroom every few minutes due to nervous pee. I hope you know what that means! I was nervous about going to the White House being that it was my first time of something of this great magnitude. It was the office and home of the President of the United States of America.

On the day of my interview, I approached the White House, walked up to the security gate, gave my proper identification, and was allowed to enter. I made my way up to the second floor and sat there anxiously awaiting my interview. When it was my turn, I was asked to enter the room and staff members would begin the process of asking "What If" questions for about 30-minutes and then I was released. A few days later, I was notified I had made the second cut. By this point, they had whittled our number down to five candidates.

The next step of the process involved me going to the Old Executive Office Building (OEOB) in Washington D.C. for a security clearance interview. The interview lasted two hours and there were no unturned questions regarding my life. My finances were scrutinized, personal relationships discussed, and work history was analyzed. The results were in after a few weeks of waiting. Three of us were selected! I would become a White House Social Aide!

I achieved a milestone in my life I never even imagined possible. I was going to be associated with one of the most prestigious organizations in the world. I was going to work in the White House.

The celebration was short lived as the indoctrination process was just beginning. Upon acceptance into the program, the next task was to have my Top Secret security clearance request submitted. My clearance took six months to finish, but I was too busy to sit around and wait because I had to get special uniforms made, aiguillettes sown on to my military jacket, and learn the do's and don'ts of proper conduct and international etiquette. After many months of waiting I finally walked into the White House to conduct my first official duty as a Social Aide.

To understand better, White House Social Aides are selected from each military service and a certain number of Aides are utilized depending on the amount of support needed for an event. There could be several events in one day or over a week. The events range from visiting dignitaries, awardee and musical events, sports winners, military honorees, State of the Unions, press conferences, galas, delegations, Congress and Senator visits, holiday gatherings, and any type of event that requires a social gathering in the East Wing of the White House or in the President's private quarters. My first event was to shadow another Aide and from there my experience took off.

My time at the White House wasn't always perfect, but the experience I gained from it was memorable. During an

Easter Egg Roll, the Jonas Brothers were in attendance. While eating their food in the Blue Room, I was asked to not allow anyone to enter the room. I stood guard and didn't budge when a woman kept trying to enter. I said, "Ma'am, I cannot allow you to enter the room because the Jonas Brothers are eating and need rehearsal time before their performance." The woman looked at me and laughed and said, "I'm going to enter and it will be okay, promise. I'm their mom." I immediately sidestepped and allowed her to enter as my face turned beet red.

Another event was held on the South Lawn of the White House with the Vice President in attendance. As he sat down to eat, something happened to the picnic table and half of it collapsed, which caused the Vice President to fall to the ground. Secret Service quickly moved in to pick him up while other staff members hurriedly replaced the table with a new one. This all occurred within two minutes. It was astonishing to see the White House's impeccable precision and response time.

At another event, we had to step in because a crowd of guests were vying for the President's attention. We formed a security circle around him and he used my shoulder to balance himself while shaking hands with people. It was my birthday that day and the other aides laughed stating the President was pseudo hugging me as a birthday gift.

At another event in the State Room, I was in charge of seating. I ensured people sat in their appropriate positions based on Distinguished Personnel ranking. I would hold and release the rows of people as they entered and exited the venue. The President would go first and then the rest of the people would leave row-by-row. Well, it was supposed to work like that. On this particular day when the President was about to exit he stopped abruptly and held out his hand for Ms. Rice to exit with him. When he stopped I almost fell and accidentally hit Ms. Rice's bottom with my hand while trying to grab onto a chair. She didn't respond and continued walking out with the President while I stood there blushing. It was like I patted her bottom to tell her 'Good Job' just like athletes do.

During a Christmas party, the then Governor of California Arnold Schwarzenegger was there with his beautiful (now 'Ex') wife Maria Shriver and her mother Eunice Kennedy Shriver. During the event, Governor Schwarzenegger left to get something for Ms. Eunice because she wasn't feeling well. He stopped at the Social Aide podium to tell us, "**I'll be back**" in his famous voice. It was one of those historic cliché's that kept us White House Aides laughing for quite some time.

Another thing that happened during a Christmas party was getting the chance to compare abs with Denise Austin. We actually punched each other's stomachs. She was beautiful, thankful for the military, and polite. She even asked to take a picture with me.

An event that meant a lot to me was when the Louisiana State University football team came to the White House to be recognized as the National Champions. I was asked to be the liaison for Coach Les Miles because I was from New Orleans and they were my hometown Champs. Coach Miles, his wife, and I waited in the Palm Room for the President while we made small talk. He signed a football for the President, which I held and handed to the President when he entered the room. I escorted everyone out to the Lawn and witnessed loud cheers to the LSU football team. What was really memorable about this occasion was how the football players were so big, tall, and could eat gigantic amounts of food.

Speaking of eating, one of the best perks as a White House Social Aide was the food. After each event we were gratuitously given the pleasure to sample the leftovers. These leftovers were the crème de la crème. The White House Chefs were the best-of-the-best and their delicious treats were simply amazing.

As I reflect on my time as a Social Aide, I smile. I was a part of history and it was a rare opportunity to be an integral part of other people's memories, special days, and lifelong treasures. I was given the privilege to assist the President and First Lady and entrusted to represent the United States of America in a noble way. I made lifelong friends whom I was blessed to share such an esteemed honor with.

White House Social Aides play a unique role at the White House and never was a girl from a trailer park given such an honor until it was bestowed upon me. WHSA for Life!

Moral of the Story – I never thought I would work at the White House. I didn't think I was incapable, but it was more because I thought I would never get an opportunity. So for you, never doubt yourself or think you're incapable or unworthy of anything. You can accomplish anything and be anything if given the chance.

Strive for the biggest rewards and ensure you are ready to overcome any show-stopper. An opportune moment could arise with a relationship, finances, work issues, or even something on your wish list at any time. Being unprepared could preclude you from that opportunity. If presented with an opportunity, take it because you may never get that opportunity again.

Dream of unimaginable things, think outside the box, and live your life to the fullest. Cherish the memories you create. Never lose sight of all you have, what you can do, and what you could become. *Dream Big, my friend.* Do not let your past hold you back. If you shoot for the moon and don't make it, at least you'll land on the stars. Do not allow the past to define your future.

When you make a mistake, learn to not repeat it. No one is perfect so go easy on yourself. Every Saint was once a Sinner and every Sinner can become a Saint.

Last but not least, the President is a person just like us. They put their pants on one leg at a time. They are human. While the President's position is extremely important, please don't confuse a person with their position. Don't get me wrong. Respect and honor are due, but they're people. Once you understand that concept, you won't get awestruck and you will be able to talk to anyone.

Remember, **being a great person isn't defined to a duty title…it's just being a great person that matters.**

Never forget – It doesn't matter how you start in life, it's how you finish that matters.

You are White House material so don't discount yourself and your potential. *Don't put yourself on the clearance rack when you are full price!*

15 – Frenemy

As I grew older, I learned it's better to have a few quality friends than a large quantity of friends. Friendships are a gift and if you have one real friend, you're lucky. If you have two friends, you're blessed. If you have more than two friends, it means you're a good friend. To have real friends, you must first be one yourself.

I learned what a friend meant to me as different events took place in my life. I realized I had very few friends that I actually liked spending time with. It was sad, but true. I was a friend to everyone, but didn't have many people I could call a life-giving friend. Most people were really an acquaintance. I learned there was a vast difference in the meanings of acquaintance and friend.

When my last friendship caused me pain I decided to change my friend life. I searched within and set healthy boundaries around this one specific area. The boundaries became a road map for who I wanted to be, who I wanted to associate with, who I wanted to learn from, who would become my friend, and who would remain acquaintances. I was able to visualize the type of people I wanted as a friend and what types of people I didn't want to be friends with at all.

I wanted quality friends. Friends that made me a better person. Friends I could trust. Friends that would hold me accountable, encourage me, steer me back on the right path if I detoured, accept me and my idiosyncrasies, and people who lived with good moral character and integrity.

Boundary setting helped me identify characteristics of friends that I did not want in my life anymore. It resulted in me realizing I would rather be alone than to continue to invest my time with these certain types of people. These characteristics may not resonate with you, but they worked for me.

1. **Insecure** – Becomes a part-time job trying to make them feel better about themselves.

This bestie and I were inseparable. We held church classes together, went on international trips, she was a staple in my life while I was deployed, shared a good meal together once a week, hung out with the same social circle, created many memories, and even lived together for a month. We called each other 'lifelong friends' and were very close. I called her crying from Japan and she called me crying at Christmas. We were life-giving friends, but there were incompatibilities which made our friendship difficult. When we went out, she was on a mission to find a man and it became uncomfortable. She wanted to settle down and was constantly on the hunt. I'm not sure if it was pressure from her family or if it was her age that drove this desire, but she was hyper focused to the point that nothing else mattered. She required constant validation and it was exhausting. It became a part-time job keeping her as a happy friend. I began to lose myself in the effort and she didn't even notice. She hurt me and a few other people many times and finally one day I just had enough.

Her insecurities demonstrated how people with low self-esteem requires the constant need for someone else to complete them because they don't feel whole themselves. As much as I tried to value my friend, she needed to value herself. You may have the time, patience, and effort to stick with this type of friendship unlike I did. I wanted a friendship to be a give and take, not take-take. When she hurt me the last time and didn't think anything of it was when I finally had enough.

2. **Honest** – When you share your heart, but they don't share theirs.

I had a person in my life who I considered a soul-mate best friend. We were like two peas in a pod. But the relationship was one-sided. I shared personal details, but she did not. I was open, but she was closed. I was vulnerable, but she was guarded. She called me her best friend, but didn't treat me like one.

I was hurt when I learned something personal about her from an outsider. Things she never intended to share, yet I shared everything with her. However, when I confronted her with what I learned, she was caught off guard. She apologized and we made a pact right then to always be honest with each other. When it happened a second time, I realized she was not honest. It's not a friendship when honesty lacks.

Honesty is the foundation required for a genuine friendship to stand. A friendship doesn't work when one friend is being honest while the other friend is not. It can't be one-sided. This missing moral characteristic would give one person leverage over the other, which makes the friendship unrealistic, unequal, and uncommitted.

Honesty is a characteristic I hold dear. There will be no friendship if there is no honesty.

3. **One-up** – When they constantly compete with you instead of being happy for you.

Have you ever had a friend that has to one-up you? You know, if you received an A in class, they received an A+. If you were hit by a bus, they were hit by an airplane. If you did 100 push-ups, they did 101. If you went to 50 countries, they went to 51. It seemed like this person was always in competition rather than being happy for you and your accomplishments. A little competition is good as it keeps you on your toes, but not amongst friends. It's narcissistic.

If you have a friend like this, *please run*. If you stay, you will be made to feel inferior like this friend made me feel constantly.

<u>You aren't inferior!</u> Your accomplishments are meant to be celebrated at each and every milestone. Friends shouldn't compete with you, they should celebrate you. They should be happy for you, applaud you, and have your best interest. That's what a real friend does. No friend should be a building block to another friend's ego.

4. **Extended Chapter** – They come into your life for a reason.

There have been times when I needed a friend for comfort, to learn something specific, or for help. They weren't meant to be lifelong friends, but friends for a season or for a reason. I shared special moments with them for a time and then their chapter ended. What I learned is it doesn't work out well if you try to force the friendship to continue. I attempted to prolong a friendship several times and it only resulted in hurt feelings and resentment.

A seasonal friend should give reason to smile and not a reason to frown. Their involvement was invaluable to you at a time when you needed them most. The friendship ends and courtesy begins once the need was met. Forced friendships are not friendships.

Friendships also end because we change! Our interests and personalities simply are no longer compatible. It doesn't mean anything bad happened, it just means we are growing into who we are supposed to become. We must be honest with ourselves when this happens and not try to prolong a friendship out of kindness. We shouldn't feel guilty about it either because life is too short for pointless endeavors. I continued friendships with people I had nothing in common with for the sake of having a friend and it became miserable for both of us.

Appreciate the season you shared and then move on. We shouldn't force what's not meant to be. Don't force a chapter to become a book.

5. **The User** – They contact you when they need something or they show you off like a trophy.

Some friends only contact you when they need something, which is okay. But that is not a friendship. It's a business exchange. Some friends may consider you in high regard and try to benefit by knowing you. But these friends are not friends either.

It's nice to be thought of when people are in need, but not to the extent of only being called to help. Friends don't use friends. Friends are meant to be a part of your life, not just when they need something. I've had several people call me their friend because of where I worked. It was a false friendship. I was an acquaintance of convenience. I was a somebody in their eyes, which allowed them to namedrop. A name dropper is trying to signal a certain status by appearing to be important, which creates a false impression. A name dropper will drop you when you no longer serve their purpose.

When I set boundaries on what I wanted my friendships to look like is when I no longer tolerated people using me. I don't mind helping anyone, but helping people does not define friendship.

6. **Disrespect** – People who joke at your expense, give back-handed compliments, and gossip.

I've had many friends tear me down to make themselves feel better. They would joke at my expense, make passive-aggressive comments, gossip behind my back (people would tell me), and hurt my feelings and never apologize.

These friends weren't trying to be cruel. It was because they either didn't respect me or their personality differed from mine. A normal person would not cruelly joke at someone else's expense. They would not put other people down in order to feel better about themselves. They would not gossip. Instead, they would stick up for their friends if someone else slandered them. Friends respect friends, not hurt them.

Life got better when I decided I wasn't going to be walked on like a doormat anymore. I loved myself and knew I deserved respect as a person and as a friend. Being respectful is a characteristic I value in people. If someone was respectful to me, but not the waiter then that person wasn't a respectful person. I've never thought joking about someone in a negative manner was funny and decided to limit interactions with these types of people. Back-handed compliments are mean. The world is bad enough so why would I want to be around people who were insincere or sarcastic.

As much as people don't want to admit it, the company you keep does have an influence in your life. I didn't want to have that type of influence so I ended my disrespectful friendships.

7. **Drama** – This person is the star of their own soap opera.

These friends create unnecessary drama. Their lives are a soap opera and they are the lead stars. Everything in their lives is plagued with craziness, which becomes mentally unhealthy for you. People may run into situations of undue stress and worry, but not all the time.

For the most part, people live fairly normal lives and experience the occasional bump along the way. On the other hand, there are people who love drama, create division, cause heartache, push or step over other's boundaries, do not think about what they say or do, deal with consequences inappropriately, and act irrational. When you befriend a drama queen or diva boy, you're living precariously on the edge because you never know what they'll say or do next. This isn't the life you want or the friends you need.

Life is supposed to be balanced and manageable, not an emotional roller coaster ride. Drama might be initially fun, but it gets old fast. At a certain age you realize you're too old for drama and remove yourself from their scene just like I did and still do.

8. **Selfish** – It's all about them. Won't compromise, narcissistic, and entitled.

You probably know someone who only thinks of themselves and they also expect you to place them on a pedestal. By nature we are all selfish in some way. If you don't believe me, whose face do you look for first when you look at a group picture that you're in? Caught ya!

I had a friendship with someone who was self-consuming and didn't engage with anything or anyone unless it was to her benefit. When we shopped, it was for her. Where we ate was decided by what she wanted. What we did was determined by what she wanted to do. It wasn't fun. Further, she expected everyone to worship her and if you didn't comply then you were out. She was oblivious to the fact that friendship was a two-way street. There was never compromise with her.

Friendship like this may be heaven to one, but hell to the other. When I left my friend's presence I didn't feel good about the time I spent with her. She left me feeling empty and I wanted to have a full tank, or at least a half-tank of happiness.

I realized how fast life goes by. *Time was valuable and life was too short to be empty when I could be full with life-giving friends.* It is better to be alone than to be in the wrong company.

Moral of the Story – Those characteristics for friendships became the foundation for the friends I did and did not want in my life. I had enough of friends not being real friends. I craved more, I craved depth. I desired real friendships with quality people. I realized who was there for me and who was there for ulterior purposes. I realized how I no longer wanted to waste time surrounding myself with people who I didn't connect with.

There's something to be said about surrounding yourself with like-minded individuals. You feel at peace with them because they make you feel at home. They're your tribe. I was tired of the phony, superficial, destructive, selfish, and fake. These friendships were unrealistic and unsustainable. It was better for me to be alone than to be around people just to be around people.

Real friendships are a gift. A precious treasure that should be handled with care, love, and respect. Friendships take time to grow and nurture and only a second to destroy with ill intent. Be on guard to protect your friendships from harm. Friends do fight, but they will forgive and reconnect if their friendship is important.

If a friendship runs its course, let it go. Don't hold on to it thinking you'll never have anyone else to fill the void. You will meet a new friend. Friends come and go; it's life. Cherish the times you had with them once they're gone! And cherish the time you currently have with them because tomorrow isn't guaranteed. Friendships are hard to maintain as we age, but they must be kept a priority and nurtured.

Now, I can honestly say I have some amazing life-giving friends. Quality people living a life of good character, integrity, kindness, encouragement, and joyful consistency. When I set friendship boundaries, my life changed for the better. So could yours.

It's better to have four quarters than 100 pennies. Meaning, have all the acquaintances in the world, but be selective with your friends. **Quality matters.**

A small number of tested and true core friends are your tribe. Love your tribe and take care of them, and they will do the same in return.

16 – President and First Lady

Few people are bestowed the rare opportunity to experience life with a President and First Lady. It's a chance to witness their personal side in a more intimate setting. I was blessed to experience such an honor while serving The President and First Lady as a White House Social Aide.

I personally witnessed the President and First Lady entertain guests, interact with politicians, and hang-out with friends and family. What people see on television and news is the First Family's political face. Yet what the family does amongst family and friends is an entirely different story. They were genuine and kind-hearted people. Their consistent actions proved them to be good people to their core.

Let me start with the First Lady. She was caring and sincerely smiled at the aides. She asked our names, where we were from, and what we did in the military. She took interest in us as individuals. She would remember our names and say, "Hi, Shannon. How are you today?" It made me feel special, like I mattered. I never felt like an assistant or an aide. I felt like a person.

The First Lady was also the description of elegance and beauty. She was well dressed, make-up done perfectly, and a peaceful smile that put people at ease. One wouldn't know she had suffered something medically and had a scar from it until you were directly behind her. One day on the South Lawn I was assigned to her detail. Where she went, I went. If she needed something, I was there. At one point, someone got a little too close to her so I gracefully moved in behind her. Standing close to her was when I noticed a visible scar on the back of her neck. It was easy to see because she was wearing a dress. But I didn't see the scar defining her, I saw inner confidence, strength, and beauty.

I will remember that exact moment forever because it taught me something. Beauty isn't skin surface. It's internally deep and it radiates out from within.

We get beat up as we age and scars are a part our story. Scars remind us of our strength. It's a symbol of something we went through and overcame. Scars don't make us less beautiful, they make us more beautiful. Scars show us how we lived. Scars don't define us or limit us. Scars should be cherished because they made us who we are today.

As for the President, I smile when I think of this person. Ironically, the President was not liked very much by the media and by some people living in different parts of the Country. I think he got a bad rap. If people would have personally experienced his mannerisms, kindness, and personality, I think they would have thought of him differently. I observed a good man.

You can tell a lot about a person by their eyes. The President looked people directly in the eye when he spoke to them. He would pay close attention to people and sincerely listen to what someone had to say. Here was the most powerful man in the world taking time to listen without political bias. The President made you feel like you were the only person in the room when talking with him. He was genuinely interested in who we were and that says a lot about a person. I couldn't do anything for him, yet he treated me and all of the aides with genuine respect.

The President never complained. There were times when he would stand for hours to take pictures with guests, shake hundreds of hands, and be rushed from event to event. He did this with a smile. Christmas season included nightly events that would last up to 4-hours and sometimes there were two events a night. The events would span over the course of 14 days. As the night progressed, some Aides complained about not feeling their toes while the President persevered and continued to smile and chat with guests. I never saw him complain. In contrast, I did hear him say people were very important.

There was a family Christmas party each year which included the President and First Lady's closest friends. One year the aides were not able to gather the guests for dinner because it was loud from laughter. To help corral the guests into the Stateroom, one of the partiers let out a very loud whistle. It was the two fingers in the mouth type of whistle. That whistle came from the President himself. I will remember it forever. It was amazing. He was a down-to-earth good ole' guy. He was real.

The President doted on the First Lady and anyone could see the love he had for her. Sometimes you could see the President watching the First Lady out of the corner of his eye. He was her protector.

The President was considerate. One time the President walked around asking the aides if we had sampled any of the goodies. We said, "No" and smiled. A few minutes later, he brought us freshly baked cookies to eat. Who does that? A person with a good heart and someone who thinks of others. I never imagined the President of the United States of America doing that.

I saw the most powerful man in the world care about others. I saw a man treat people with respect and kindness. I saw a man who was real, down to earth, loving to his family, exercise with his bodyguards, and laugh out loud a lot. I saw a man who trusted me, trusted his staff, and treated all of us who worked there like an extension of his own family.

The President taught me that titles don't matter, people do. To treat everyone the same, no matter what position they hold. You can tell a lot about a person by how they treat other people who cannot do anything for them. The President treated me like a real person and that's something I will always remember.

Mr. President, I salute you. You have good character and a very good heart.

People will mostly not remember what you say, but they will always remember how you make them feel.

Moral of the Story – Never judge a book by its cover. Never judge a person by their appearance or what you hear secondhand. A physically beautiful person could have an ugly heart by how they treat others. A physically unattractive person may be the kindest person you'll ever meet. Beauty is in the eye of the beholder. Beauty comes from the heart.

Every person has a story. A story may be from the scar someone has because they risked their life trying to save someone else. A young pregnant girl may have been raped and her baby is her story. A person may have a unibrow because of their religious beliefs and that's their story. A person with one leg could have lost their leg in the war they fought in while protecting their country and its citizens. People are oftentimes judged by what they look like, their social status, or what they do for a living. It's not fair nor is it right.

We are all different in how we look, think, act, believe, and speak. We should get to know a person before we pass judgement on them. *A person who doesn't think for themselves is a person who doesn't think.*

Many people get caught up with people in positions of power and fame and often lose sight of the person. Please don't do that. Respect the position, but remember they are people too. More importantly, when you get to that level, please remember to stay humble, don't complain, treat everyone the same, be kind, and bring cookies to those around you. They'll be thankful.

Stay grounded so you don't fall trap to the Bathsheba Syndrome.

A job title doesn't define you. Character, how you treat others, and the words you speak do. You can tell more about a person with how they treat others who can do nothing for them than how they treat people that can do everything for them. A person who treats every person the same no matter their duty title and bank account number speaks volume of the person's character.

Friend, you only have your name so make sure when it's spoken, it's thought of reputably, honorably, and fairly.

The President and First Lady are positive role models for our country. In turn, we should strive to be the same type of role model for our home, friends, and community.

Let's stop the narcissism declining trend of our nation and start the movement for 'make the world kind' again. We are all people living in a hurting world just trying to make it another day. A duty title will change, but a kind heart never does.

17 – Love

Faith, Hope, and Love and the greatest of these is Love. Love is the most powerful force in the world. Every person wants to be loved. When you're loved, you feel strong. When you love, you feel full. Love is a feeling like no other. The best example of love I personally witnessed was when Vince and Amy arrived at the White House. I desire that type of love for all of us.

While at a White House Christmas Party, I remember seeing the stunning couple enter the door. She looked breathtaking beautiful in her gown and holding her hand was her handsome husband. They were stunning people, glowing, happy, and lively, but it wasn't their appearance that enchanted me. It was their act of love, which held my gaze the entire evening.

The gentleman held the small of her back when she entered the room, a beautiful gesture of chivalry. The small act is large in meaning. It tells a woman she is cared for, respected, and protected. He guided her into the room as they walked side by side. The way he looked at her when she spoke was something all women desire. His eyes were filled with adoration as he looked at her. His eyes were soft, but had depth. A depth of love that held no bounds. It was romantic. His eyes weren't that of puppy dog eyes, but of pure love. Eyes are considered to be the window to the soul and his soul said, "I love this woman." It was unexplainable, it had to be witnessed. It was beautiful.

When the lady excused herself to the ladies room, he watched her walk away. His eyes ensured she was safe. I saw him watch her from across the room even when she was talking with other people. I would see her smile and he would do the same in return. It was like two magnets being pulled together. One could try to put something in between them to stop them from connecting, but their love was not to be apart.

They rejoined after talking to people and he held her hand as she kissed his cheek. It was not in a sexual manner, but in an expression of love. Anyone in the White House at that moment could see their love was real, pure, and extraordinary.

While walking into the Stateroom for dinner, the band was playing a soft melody. The gentleman grabbed his lady's hand and they began dancing. Everyone in the room stopped to watch the romantic moment. As they swayed, he spun her around and then dipped her in his arms and leaned in for a kiss. I will never forget that moment. It was surreal. Beautiful. Majestic. It was like I was watching the climax in a romance movie when the two finally found each other again after a lifetime of searching. Then everyone clapped and then dinner was served.

I remember watching them and then looking at all the other people in the room. All the women desired for that kind of love as they reached for their partner's hand and their partners gently grabbed their hands in return. In a crowded room, it was like they were the only two people there. Everyone noticed the way they looked at each other, the way he held her, the way they danced, and the way she spoke and he smiled. Their eyes spoke of something so meaningful, profound, and rare. That night the two lovebirds reminded everyone what it meant to love and to be in love. It was a Christmas gift to us all.

The reason why this moment in time stayed with me is because that kind of love was what I had always dreamed of and desired for myself. It is a love like no other. A love that reminds me of the part in the Bible, "Love is patient, love is kind. It does not envy, it does not boast, it is not proud. It does not dishonor others, it is not self-seeking, it is not easily angered, it keeps no record of wrongs. Love does not delight in evil but rejoices with the truth. It always protects, always trusts, always hopes, always perseveres." 1 Corinthians 13:4-7. The reason it reminds me of this verse is because the way Vince and Amy looked at each other. Their eyes held nothing but love. No turmoil, no competition, no superior or inferior mindset, and no walls. Their eyes spoke of unity, trust, respect, commitment, understanding, and truth.

Their loving gestures brought me to think, "What is love?" It is one of the most difficult questions for mankind, yet tragically overused in a variety of expressions every single day. But, depending on its context, love can have a different meaning for each person, but the simple meaning is still the same...love!

The four levels of love that I have found to understand are:

Agápe: refers to a deeper sense of "true love" used to express unconditional love.

Éros: refers to passionate love, with sensual desire and longing. Eros can be interpreted as physical attraction, knowledge of beauty, and desire.

Philia: refers to friendship or affection, brotherly love. It includes friends, family, and community, and requires familiarity.

Storge: means a natural affection, like that felt by parents for offspring. It is also known to express mere acceptance or situations.

When we love, we love differently depending on the person and the situation. What I witnessed at the White House made me realize that Agape love is possible in relationships. It's rare. When you witness it, you feel like you are dreaming or watching a Nicholas Sparks movie.

Love is easily given, but often misunderstood. Many of us experience snippets of love, but rarely few of us experience real love. This chapter isn't about parents loving their children, or siblings loving each other, or people we love that have left special footprints in our heart. This chapter is about people in relationships of deep genuine love.

The love they shared is my wish for all of us to experience in life. I want every person to experience love in a way where our breath is paused, we get goosebumps, we have knots in our stomachs, we totally relax, we don't have to try, we give willingly and easily to the other person without taking, we want the best for the other person, they become our life jacket during storms, and our eyes speak of things words cannot express. We never stop looking for the other when a natural disaster occurs. We'd take a bullet for the other so they may live. We are dipped and kissed every single day. I desire that heart pumping kind of love for all. A love so meaningful that others witness it and remember it years later even if it were only witnessed for a few minutes. A love that holds life captive and gives it meaning.

When you are loved, it is a gift that has no price tag. It's priceless.

Love is complete acceptance when we allow someone to be exactly as they are without any reservation. Love is unconditional. If our love is dependent upon the other person acting and speaking the way we want, then this love is completely conditional. We often confuse this to be a part of unconditional love, but this is simply forcing the other person to be someone they're not. It's loving what a person says or does, not loving them.

Love is selfless. Love doesn't want anything in return because there is nothing else it needs. We love for the sake of love. When we love others, we don't look for them to fill our needs, love us back, or expect anything else in return.

Love may come and go so when you do find love, appreciate it and enclose yourself in the moment. The feeling will last you a lifetime.

It is better to love and to have lost than to have never loved at all.

Moral of the Story – The word "Love" is overused and has somewhat lost its value. The feeling of real love is a gift. It is a treasure in life that gives life its fullest meaning. The meaning of love can't be explained, it must be experienced.

Love can clearly be seen through the eyes of a loved one. It has no conditions and no expectations. Those two love birds at the White House taught me to wait for the one that would hold me that way, look at me in that way, and touch me in that way. I would not lower my standards or accept anything less. I would wait for that type of love forever. This goes for you as well.

Love is beautiful and precious. It's what I desire for all of us.

If you don't have it now, know real love is worth the wait. Don't settle.

If you and the person you're with are missing the type of beautiful love displayed that night at the White House then I implore you to ignite the flame and fall in love all over again. Have date night once a week so you have a better chance to remember why you fell in love in the first place.

If you have that type of love, stop reading this and go hug your loved one. Tell them how much they mean to you. Love them and never stop loving them. Always do your best to ensure their love tank is full.

Love matters.

18 – Air Force Kicked Me Out

Every office could hear me sobbing as I ran down the E-ring with several perplexed people following behind me. I was just given the worst, most unexpected news of my Air Force career. I was getting kicked out (Force Shaped) of the Air Force due to a manning reduction. Basically, the Air Force didn't retain me for Active Duty service and I had 6-months to leave the Air Force.

The separation notice shocked me! I couldn't breathe and felt dizzy. I didn't know how to do anything else. The Air Force was the only job I ever had as an adult. I never expected in a million years that I would be asked to leave military service. I had been serving our country on active duty for 12+ years. I never planned for anything of this magnitude. I hit rock bottom.

Let me explain. The Air Force was downsizing due to budget cuts and was given the task to remove a set number of personnel. The personnel would be from various career fields around the globe. Many of us would be let go within months. I was one of two Company Grade Officer's (CGO) assigned to Air Staff in the Pentagon e-ring to meet the board. By chance, both of us were working in the same office.

Working on Air Staff had its perks. Our supervisor was a colonel and our senior rater was the Assistant Vice Chief of Staff. When we learned of the upcoming board, our supervisor promptly requested us to write our retention packages. These packages would be submitted to the Force Shaping board for retention consideration. I wrote my package within three days and received glowing endorsements from the White House. Our supervisor blessed the package and the Assistant Vice Chief gladly endorsed it with only a few minor changes. I was relieved that my package was finished.

On the other hand, my fellow Captain was running into trouble. She submitted her package several times, but it kept being rejected. I realized she needed help and offered to assist her. She gladly accepted. I rewrote her package knowing I could be lessening my chance of being retained, but I knew in my heart it was the right thing to do. I lived by the Golden Rule.

When I finished rewriting her package, it was as strong as mine. She graciously thanked me and humbly stated if anyone should be let go, it should be her. She believed I was the better officer. Her unpretentious remarks were an eye opener to me. I realized when faced with life altering events, the best or worst of people comes out. In this case, it was both of our best.

Both of our packages were now approved, signed, and forwarded to the Board for consideration. Now we just had to wait.

A few months passed. Then one day a colleague stopped me in the hall and asked me what my plans would be if I were to be separated from the military. Somewhat dismayed, I said, "I didn't have any plans because I knew the Air Force wouldn't let me go. The Air Force was the only job I'd ever had and I love it more than anything." He shook his head and solemnly told me to begin thinking about my plans. Immediately, I went and told my colonel about the conversation and asked if he knew anything. He stated he didn't, but he thought the conversation was strange. There was one problem. That colleague worked in the Vice Chief's office and the Vice Chief had just received the results. I began to think, what if?

A few weeks later, my cohort Captain and I were each scheduled to meet separately with our senior rater to receive the retention board's results. I was scheduled first. I entered the room where my supervisor and senior rater were waiting for me. My senior rater asked me to have a seat and I will never forget that moment.

He looked at me and said, "Shannon, the Air Force has decided to let you go." I sat there, stunned, and silent. I couldn't process what he had just said. I couldn't breathe. I sat there staring right through him. He asked me if I was okay and if I had heard him. I nodded, got up, and walked out. As I exited the office, I collapsed. Next thing I remember is my supervisor picking me up off the floor while my other colleagues stood there looking at me. Then I lost it. I let out the loudest cry and ran to the bathroom.

I was still an officer in the Air Force and knew I needed to maintain my military bearing, but my tears wouldn't stop. Within a few minutes, the other CGO entered the bathroom and thanked me because the Air Force had decided to keep her. Irony at its best.

I walked out of the Pentagon that day feeling completely abandoned. I headed home in misery not knowing what my future held. I took leave for the next few days not knowing what to do nor wanting to face anyone. I felt like a total loser and was totally alone.

I had nothing. My daughter wasn't living with me. I didn't have any friends because I just moved to the DC area. I was no longer married and didn't have family. One would have considered me to be a prime candidate for suicide as I had just been given the worst news of my life. I had no one and no future. To add to the isolation, no one from work even checked on me. I was vocationally devastated, emotionally destroyed, and living in utter desolation.

Then I got angry. I wanted to know why!

I returned to work and began asking questions. I wanted to know why the Air Force let me go, but kept the other person. It didn't make any sense. Great officers were given the boot while mediocre officers remained. There were no common denominators. I was put on the chopping block without any tangible information. I was a number, a piece of paper. That's what it came down to in the end. I mattered, but not to the Air Force.

An Air Force Times reporter stopped at my desk one day and began asking me questions. I answered every question and the following week my interview was published. After the publication, my senior rater changed the policy on how the Air Force selected Airmen to meet future retention boards. At least, I had played a role in saving the careers of future personnel.

I had a little less than 5-months left in the Air Force and was determined to end my Air Force career on a high note. My boss assigned me to be the Air Force lead for the upcoming air show and I gave it my all. On the morning of the air show, I was positioning chairs in the Distinguished Visitor's tent when I met a Colonel who worked in the Air Force Reserves. I told her my story and the next thing I knew I was being interviewed for a position in the Reserves. Within a week, I was selected to become their Executive Officer.

Sadly, my active duty Air Force career was rapidly coming to a close. But, my senior rater arranged it to where I wouldn't lose one day of service. I bid a tearful goodbye to Active Duty on September 30th and gratefully embarked into the Air Force Reserves on October 1st. My dedicated service to our great country would continue.

It worked out in the end even though it wasn't the path I wanted nor ever expected. Complete devastation turned into hope. Tragedy turned into triumph. A mess became a message. My life didn't end, it was just beginning.

I am deeply thankful to the Colonel (now Lieutenant General) for helping me. I will always be grateful for her kindness. This leader didn't know me personally, but she took a chance on me. *In my darkest hours, she opened a door that gave me light again in my life.* I pray we all have someone take a chance on us like she did with me.

When one door closes, another door will open. If it doesn't open then it's not meant to be.

Moral of the Story – Have you ever wanted something so bad, but got the complete opposite? Have you had your dream ripped away? Have you ever been left with nothing? Have you ever hit rock bottom? I have! It's the toughest place to be and the worst feeling known to man.

I didn't give up and I beg you to never give up either. I beg you to get focused and fight back like I did. Look for a way out. Look for ways to overcome. Look for ways to create something better for yourself. Look for anything. Just don't give up.

It will be hard, but it will be worth it. The hardest moments in our lives provide the biggest outcomes. They can become life-changing moments for us. Stumbling blocks become our building blocks. The road that ends will take us on a new road to a better tomorrow, to a better us.

What we think may end our lives may actually better our lives. What was hurting us may actually help us. A bad ending may help us create a better beginning.

When something ends, it doesn't mean it is the end. When we think nothing is left is when we need to have hope that something is yet to come. We can't give up. We must fight for what we want. If we don't get it, then we need to find something else to fight for.

We must press forward in our toughest moment. That is what makes us who we are. It actually defines who we are. Falling down is easy, but only the strong get back up.

What are you made of? Are you a sufferer or a survivor? Are you a victim or a victor? Are you a healthy person or a hot mess? Are you a solution provider or a miserable complainer? Are you ready to throw in the towel when it gets hard or do you roll up your sleeves and rummage your way through? What are you made of when things get tough?

I encourage you to turn your ugly mess into a beautiful message that helps others overcome their troubles. We're all in this together! We will have heartache, but let's help each other heal when it happens. That way we can all be proud of the beautiful disaster we are and what we courageously have overcame.

Let's all try to be like the Colonel in someone's life who believes in others even when they don't. You are not a quitter...don't ever give up! Believe it and live it to your last breath! When you want something bad enough, you will find a way. If you don't, you will find an excuse.

19 – Who am I?

After my painful divorce I realized I had no idea who I really was. I needed to discover this before I would be truly happy with myself let alone anyone else. I had morphed into a marriage role immediately after I left home and never had any time to get to know the adult me. I had finally reached a point in my life where I needed to answer a very important question "Who am I?"

My search for meaning was prompted by the need to make a big decision. A decision that would change the course of my life forever. I needed time to think, face my relationship fears, and feel my heart smiling again. Leaving the United States and going to an isolated country by myself was what I needed to do. There were similar trips women had taken to find themselves and mine was no different. I was in search for meaning, healing, and understanding.

I was about to embark on a journey that would give me purpose, answers, and possibly a new future.

I decided to go to my namesake place of origin. I wanted to go where it all started even though I wasn't born there. It was a location of my given name. My name was important to me because it was all I had. I never really had anything or anyone to connect with, but I connected with my name. I packed my bag and went to Shannon, Ireland.

On the plane, I thought about who I was. For as long as I could remember I was a chameleon. I was trying to fit in with everyone just to be liked. I bit my tongue more than I spoke up. I settled when I should have soared. I ate the same foods as everyone else. I mostly followed the crowd. I didn't know what a good relationship consisted of because I never saw an example. I was always searching and never fulfilled.

It was time to get to the conclusion of "Who am I as an adult?" What was my purpose? What mattered to me? What made me smile or cry? What did I like and dislike? What caused me pain? What gave me joy? What was my favorite food? How did I like my eggs? Scrambled, sunny side up, or over easy? I didn't know. So many questions with so little answers.

I should have answered these questions a lot sooner because I was drifting through life, but I didn't think about that kind of stuff. If I had, my life would have been a lot better a lot sooner because I wouldn't have repeated the same stupid mistakes. This would have helped me in creating healthy relationships. For so many years I lost so much and was hurt by so many and it was mostly my fault. It was now time to put an end to the pain, isolation, and bad decision-making.

The question "Who am I" was prompted by meeting a man and deciding whether to start or not start a serious relationship. Before I could say "yes" to him, I first had to say "yes" to myself. I didn't know what I wanted in a partner because I didn't know what I wanted in life or who I was.

When I arrived at the airport in Shannon, Ireland in the early morning, I picked up my bag and headed to the hotel. I was tired from the trip, but didn't attempt to catch any sleep after I arrived. I immediately checked in, grabbed a cab, and headed to the Shannon River. I walked around the river for a while and took time to pause and reflect back on my life. Looking over the river's banks, I could see the river was strong, but mostly dry. The water was dark, but reflected light from the sun. Overhead, the weather was dismal, but a rainbow appeared through the clouds and gave the sky beauty. I was in awe of where I was at the moment and soaked it in. Nature reminded me to find comfort in my heart knowing that life would be hard at times. I learned the sun would shine again because it would eventually stop raining. Bad times would end and good times would begin. I knew I would suffer in the future, but I also knew it wouldn't last. Joy comes in the morning.

I vowed to reprogram my thinking…and then it would change my life.

After walking along the Shannon River, I came across a church. The image of the church profoundly represented a turning point in my life. It was at that movement when I thanked God for all I had been through and had overcome. I thanked Him for authentically making me. I accepted who I was, the good, the bad, the weirdness, and the ugly.

The next few days were spent walking green pastures, visiting castles and churches, seeing rainbows, and answering the many questions of "Who am I?"

I'll remember how life seemed to stand still as I sat for hours on the Cliffs of Moher where I let my feet dangle while listening to the wave's crash against the sides of the cliff. I'll cherish the moment when a beautiful rainbow appeared over the castle and how awestruck I was by the gift of life at that moment. A rainbow was God's promise to never flood the earth again. I promised to no longer live a life of pleasing others and losing myself in the process. I mattered!

The waves at Moher cleansed my soul, heart, and mind. What was crushing me before in terms of pain from my past relationships was no longer. The beating of waves against the cliffs symbolized the powerful strength I needed to find within myself. I withstood many beatings in my life, but I was still standing and stronger because of them.

The waves crashing against the wall represented the beating we can take and still stand strong. They were a symbol of life. They reflect how life can be hard, unexpected, knock you down, and even hurt you. But when you are strong, you have the power and courage to overcome the hard things in life and be able to get back up again. That was me. I was standing strong! **Fall down seven times and get up eight.**

After visiting the Cliffs, I saw a few more things along the western side of the country and then headed east. When I arrived, I immediately wanted to leave because it was crowded and busy. I went from the beauty of Ireland's open country to a city full of technology, tons of people, and no opportunities to self-reflect. I realized I wasn't a 'New Person' per se, but an 'Old Soul' who wanted the solitude of nature and the boundless, unadulterated pastures where less was more.

I hopped on a bus and headed south to explore and self-reflect. After arriving back to Ireland's glorious beauty, I stumbled into a beautiful church. The church had two pillars, which spoke to my soul. It was one of those feelings when you know everything is right and you are exactly where you are meant to be. If it ever happens to you, stay in that moment when you get there because it's life changing. It was at this moment when I knew the answer to my decision. I would say "yes." I was ready to try love again because it would be selfish not to. Just like the multitude of people who visited the Cliffs each day, I needed to allow real love to visit my life again just the same. I was ready to give myself to someone I loved and who loved me in return.

My solo trip turned out to be one of the greatest things I have ever done for myself. It made me think, self-reflect, and open my eyes and heart. It made me feel empowered, strong, and courageous. I explored a new place by myself. It made me believe and trust in myself even more. I got to learn new things about who I was and what I liked. The solitude I experienced and the inner connection I felt can't be explained. I had accomplished something I never thought I could and it made me feel more whole in the process. I finally was able to determine what my future held and to answer the question "Who am I?" I liked who I was. I liked scrambled eggs.

The trip also made me think about my failed relationships. I was like many people who was hurting and lonely. *I was settling for anyone just to have someone.* When one relationship ended, I quickly started another. I never took time to learn who I was and to analyze what went wrong. I passed on the opportunity to reflect. I lived a viscous, broken, and unhealthy cycle. Sadly, it all could have been eliminated by taking a moment to look inside oneself.

When I finally stopped is when life started. I learned how I don't need someone to be with me to complete me, I alone was enough.

Moral of the Story – Learning who you are is the best gift you can give yourself. It gives you a foundation of strength, purpose, awareness, acceptance, and stability. Knowing who you are will help you not lower your standards and give your life meaning.

We rarely take time out for ourselves because life gets busy and we're afraid to say, "No" to people. As a result, we go, give, move, take, do, schedule, and overextend ourselves.

This leaves little to no time for us. When we don't take time for ourselves, we don't know who we are. We must first answer the question of who we are before we can thrive in life, let alone make life-changing decisions.

To avoid making the wrong decision, we must take time to be alone and think. We need to dig deep inside so we don't settle, rush, or regret the decisions for our lives. We must take time, real time, to get away and think. Giving ourselves solo time is vital to being healthy and to making good decisions. **It's called self-care.** We must first care for ourselves before we can truly care for others.

If you leave a relationship, please give yourself time to recover before jumping into another one. It's okay to be alone. This special time is when your best thinking occurs and you get to discover the real you.

We are only given one life and if we do it right, one life is enough. Know who you are first and everything else will fall into place after.

This was the story of saying, "**Yes**" with confidence to **#3**, **my one true love**.

Chapter 20 – Less is More

I was living the high-life! I had a 6-figure salary, lived in the penthouse, drove a luxury car, cared about my duty title, earned multiple degrees, desired prestige, and was saving for retirement. I wanted success and liked feeling wealthy. I never wanted to be poor again and the idea of wealth and material things clouded my vision to what I thought mattered in life. I never had much growing up as a child and worked hard to never be poor again. I lived in the lap of luxury.

Then I got slapped with reality when I traveled across the ocean to Kuwait. It was there where I really learned the meaning of what being rich looked like. My eyes were opened. Let me explain.

After I left active duty military service, I joined a civilian company and was sent to Kuwait to work a special project. The special project was a new contract that required immediate assistance or it would be terminated. If the two other new hires and I didn't go to Kuwait then many jobs would be lost and people would suffer financially.

As the only female in the trio, I was asked what shift I wanted to work and I chose the nightshift. My decision was well calculated for many reasons. First, the nightshift was equivalent to day-time in the United States. Second, the average night temperature in Kuwait was 109 degrees and I couldn't imagine working in even higher temperatures during the day. Finally, there were less people walking around the compound at night. This would help my team perform our mission more effectively and not be bothered by interfering tasks.

My team consisted of third country nationals from Egypt, Pakistan, and India. I didn't speak their languages so I was assigned a translator. I was a work horse and I worked my translator equally hard. I didn't know anything about the project, but I knew what the goal was and I knew how to lead. Every night we would start by having a quick meeting before the shift began. Then during the shift my translator and I would get on the walkie-talkies and I'd have him running in every direction to translate instructions of what needed to be done. We only had so much time to turn the project around and eventually found ourselves working as a team in full stealth mode.

Unlike the other two new hires, I was working outside with my team every night. I didn't just direct them, I worked with them. I found myself lifting things considered too heavy for someone like me, driving forklifts, building boxes, and going full throttle. All of my guys wouldn't let a woman outdo them so they worked just as hard, if not harder. I discovered when you are working 12-hour shifts with a team, you get to know them even when you don't speak the same language.

Working side-by-side, I learned their mannerisms, learned they loved the United States, and learned they wanted to do good work. The problem was they didn't know how to do good work because they were never taught. I learned they didn't have much in life, but what little they did have was enough. I learned working for a woman was foreign to them and they were somewhat afraid of me. They had never seen another female like me before and didn't know what to think. I learned about them as human beings, their life, their countries, and families. Amazing men!

These guys worked 12-hours every day with only one day off for the entire month. They rode on a bus for one hour to and from work making their workday 14-hours long. They only had ten hours to spend at home to shower and rest before having to get up and start another day. They would eat their first meal on the bus driving to work and eat their second meal later in the evening. They had a 30-minute break to drink green tea in the early morning hour. This was their daily routine every single day.

They made very little money. Whatever they did make, they would send it back home to their families. This little bit of money would help their families eat and buy bare necessities for the entire month. These noble men sacrificed their lives and worked their butts off just to give away the little they did earn. It was the very definition of selflessness.

They were all different, but their differences created a dynamic team. The Egyptians were bigger guys and served as my work horses. They were strong and capable. The Pakistanis had longer faces with lighter skin and were my stability within every effort. The workers from India had rounder faces and darker skin. They were the backbone and kept everything running smoothly. Every person offered something special to the team. I was fortunate to be surrounded by greatness.

Sadly at times, they were treated by others as though they knew nothing. This was evident when I had my one-and-only day off in the month. One of the other new hires worked my shift. When I returned the next day, my nightshift team expressed how poorly they were treated. They weren't treated with professional or personal courtesy. My fellow new hire sat behind his desk while the team worked. The team was never acknowledged. They were reprimanded, told what to do, and spoken to in an unkind manner. It pissed me off. I exchanged words with my colleague.

The team worked hard and never complained. They had the same meal every day, lived the same routine, had little time to themselves, worked when exhausted, and sacrificed seeing their families so they could provide a better life for them. The team taught me what truly mattered and it wasn't themselves. These guys didn't think of themselves as being great, they thought of themselves as men being men doing what was necessary in life. They weren't born with a silver spoon in their mouth. They worked hard for everything they had and shared it with their loved ones. I no longer wanted to be the CEO or Vice President of a Fortune 500 company, instead I wanted to be kind, giving, and selfless like them. The team didn't learn from me during our time together. I learned from them. I learned the real meaning of what mattered in life.

I no longer desired the materialism that perpetually lingered in my heart. I wanted the happiness and appreciation they had for the little things. Experiencing the joy of sharing a cup of green tea with a friend meant more than spending $40K on a car. Breaking bread with someone that's hungry meant more than going out to eat and spending $200 on a meal. Going to the grocery store and getting a small bag of cereal was better than looking at the 100+ types of cereal on the supermarket shelves. I didn't want to be spoiled anymore. I like luxury, but I realized I had way too much in life. I could be happy with less stuff.

After our project was successfully completed, I wanted to do something special for these guys. They never had anything special done for them. The project boss and I created Certificates of Appreciation for every one of them. They had a piece of paper with their name on it. The boss and I bought pizza, soda, and cookies. It was a treat because they never had pizza. At the end of the feast, the boss called out every single person's name. We applauded each of them and then each one of them hugged me. I will never forget that day. A small certificate saying thank you was the first legitimate certificate they ever received with their name on it. A small piece of paper meant greatness in their eyes. You could see it in their faces. They felt special. I know my translator still has his to this day and I bet the rest of the guys do as well.

These guys tugged at my heart because they were the picture of what selfless, innocent, and kind look like. They are worth more than 7-figure bank accounts. I pray every person experiences the meaning of "less is more."

Moral of the Story – If you were lucky enough to be born in the United States, you are blessed. People in other countries would consider Americans spoiled. We make lots of money, have big houses, nice cars, outrageous salaries, and always want more because we are never satisfied. The meaning of life isn't to have wealth and a bunch of material possessions, but to help others in need. We're all trying to make it in life and it isn't about some having it all while the rest have hardly anything.

Having less can be more and having more can be less. Material things are nice distractions, but helping others without getting anything in return is priceless in its reward.

A person's character is revealed by how they treat others that can't give anything in return. We can all learn from each other. No one should ever be treated poorly just because of the position they hold. If you treat others poorly because you think they are beneath you then you're not a good person.

Never tell someone to do a job that you're not willing to do yourself. A real leader would never sit behind their desk while their team busts their humps. They would be out there with them!

If a person is working 12-hour days, every single day of the month, with only one day off and they are still living in poverty then the world's economy and fair wages need to be reevaluated.

Another thing I learned was the concept of interesting vs. interested. On the last day there, our boss brought the Americans into the room and told us to be *interested* in life. Confused, we asked for an explanation.

Interesting – A person who talks about themselves, doesn't try to get to know others, and they think the world revolves around them as they feel they are the most interesting person they know. No other person can even compare to their experiences and the life they lived. They are interesting.

Interested – This person asks others question in an effort to get to know the other person. They are interested in who the other person is, the experiences they've had, the life they've lived, what makes them happy and sad, and gets the other person to feel like they matter because they are truly interested in learning about other people.

Be *interested*!

Race, color, religious beliefs, gender, ethnicity, political preference…it doesn't matter. We are all in this together. It's time to be a team!

Chapter 21 – Not everyone is a Superstar

Due to a short notice cancellation by another military reservist, I was tasked to deploy to Kyrgyzstan for six months. With only a month to prepare, I finished the required military contingency actions, transferred my civilian job tasks to my boss (my civilian company allowed me to go and even supplemented my salary while deployed), and spent some much needed time with my precious daughter. It was a stressful period, but manageable. I was looking forward to finally serving our country on foreign soil.

Upon arrival in Kyrgyzstan, I immediately jumped into our mission. I had been performing this type of work for more than ten years, which enabled me to accomplish tasks easily, effectively, and efficiently. As I settled in, I began shadowing the outgoing Chief who I was slated to replace. It quickly became apparent that he wasn't performing the duties he was assigned. One of our colleagues in a different shop was actually performing the job duties. Once the outgoing Chief departed, I spoke to the colleague and informed him that my office would perform these tasks going forward. My colleague smiled and thanked me for actually wanting to do my job. I couldn't have slept at night knowing I was getting paid for work that someone else was doing.

Within a week, an enlisted member arrived and my office now was a two-person team. We were ready to execute the mission. Well, that was my dream. The enlisted member had never worked in this specific job function. As a result, he wasn't prepared to perform the assigned duties. The job required someone who expects the unexpected, thinks outside the box, reacts strategically, and executes seamlessly. The enlisted member had none of these qualities.

Due to our sensitive mission, I had to make a decision on how best to utilize him. After careful consideration I decided to give him the lodging mission. This was a huge undertaking because colonels and generals would stay in the Transit Center lodging so this made the enlisted member's job important. With this plan, our overall mission would be a success.

After a few months of working together the member asked me a difficult question about his future. He asked if he should continue working in this specific field when he returned home or should he stay in his current career field. I thought about it for a moment and answered honestly. I told him to stay in his current career field. I kindly alluded to his inability of not being able to react quickly enough, think outside-the-box, and how he lacked being detail-oriented. I told him this specific job wasn't for everyone. I tried to end on a good note, but my words came out wrong when I told him to stay working in the fitness center because he was a really good towel folder.

Due to my lack of political correctness and sugar coating, my response got the attention of our big boss. The big boss was the highest-ranking person on the installation. The boss called me and asked me to take a ride with him to the flight line. I knew I was in trouble. I will remember that day forever.

Upon arriving to the flight line the boss led me over to an aircraft. While walking around the aircraft he asked me about the conversation I had with my troop. I explained to him the conversation that took place and he looked at me and said these words, "Shannon, you can't always pick your team."

I looked at him and pondered as he began to elaborate. He made it clear to me there will be times in life when you are forced to work with people you don't like, who won't contribute as much as they should or you think they should, and are simply unsuited for the task at hand. <u>Bottom line is you can't always get perfection</u> and, in those times, *we must accept what we have to work with*. We must try our best to get along for the sake of the mission and help others in the process. "Not everyone is a Superstar" and a good leader would recognize this and then help them try to become one.

My boss asked me if I had helped the enlisted member learn the job or if I just set him aside? At that moment I realized how much I had failed my troop. I failed him as a leader not just in words, but also in my actions. I set him aside from the beginning because it was easier for me to do tasks than to train him repeatedly. I failed him as a person and as an Airman.

I relearned how everyone has something to offer. It's best to play off each other's strengths and weaknesses and work towards a common goal….together. When one person slips, the rest of the team is there to pick him or her up. By working together as a team, everyone would be a Superstar!

It took that gut-wrenching realization for me to make it my goal in life to begin helping everyone become a Superstar.

Then the day came, ironically, when *I was no longer a Superstar*. One evening I was celebrating my last month with some friends in the common area when a handsome young officer walked right up to me and kissed me. I was so shocked and taken aback that I didn't stop the kiss.

Immediately a fellow colleague came up to us and said, "What are you guys doing?" The next day I was called into the big boss's office and was being sent home a few weeks early because of it. While deployed, intimate relationships are prohibited and kissing in common areas was definitely not allowed.

For five and a half months I worked harder than anyone I knew in my circle. I was on top of my game and in one fleeting moment of not thinking clearly and not being able to react quickly enough cost me everything. I had just won "Officer of the Month" and was now witnessing my picture being removed from all of the walls. I was the "Officer of the Month" that didn't stop a kiss. I didn't get a medal for my service overseas and didn't deserve one. I was not a Superstar. Sure, I had bright moments, but every person has moments in which they shine.

As much good that I had accomplished, I had ultimately failed when I let down my troop, my boss, my colleagues, and myself.

It doesn't matter how you start, it's the journey and how you finish that matters.

Moral of the Story – There are times in our lives when we can't have or don't get the people we want. We are born into a family, forced to work with colleagues, and have to interact with other people on a daily basis. During these moments, we can't always pick who we want or who we think we should have. We must deal with what we have. Not everyone is a Superstar and we must accept what is, try our best to get along for the sake of peace and success, and help people become their very best in the process.

Every person will make mistakes. **How we pick ourselves back up is a testament to our character and strength.**

Trouble happens when we let pride fill our heads. When we think we're too big for our britches is when we will stumble and fall. Pride leads to destruction.

We must learn humility and practice it daily.

When my boss took me to the flightline to mentor me. He showed me how much he cared. He took time out of his busy day to teach me a new way of thinking. He helped me become a better individual. We should all care enough about others to do the same.

I realized later on in life that believing "Not everyone is a Superstar" is incorrect. Every person is a "Superstar" in his or her own way. They just have to find what they are good at and what their purpose in life is. They must know their purpose may change, but their gifts never do.

Being a Superstar is valuable, but helping others become a Superstar is priceless. It is costly in terms of time, sacrifice, and commitment, which is why so few people take time to make others better. However, the reward when others become their best self, a Superstar, because of your help is what your legacy will be known for. You made others better! That is selfless commitment!

When being a Superstar role model for others…**challenge mediocrity because our lives are too short to live a life of average when we are called to live a life of excellence.**

Chapter 22 – Biggest Winner

I went to church sporadically throughout my adult life, but never had a church home due to being in the military. As a result, I never had the chance to spiritually connect with people, let alone develop life-giving friendships. This changed when I began attending a church in Alexandria, Virginia.

One Sunday morning my friends and I walked into a movie theater and were warmly greeted by many happy faces. Everyone seemed genuinely kind when they spoke. All of them were cheerful and I could sense something different in their eyes. It felt like my heart was smiling in return to their smiling hearts. I wasn't accustomed to seeing so many people my age gleefully hugging others. They were normal people, but they were so happy and completely filled with joy. In my past experiences every church I attended had a few happy faces, but not every single person.

At the Alexandria church, people weren't pretentious in their appearance or attire. They were wearing jeans, shorts, and flip-flops. They were down to earth. I tend to dress like a tomgirl most of the time, but didn't feel underdressed in my jeans, t-shirt, and cute heels. I was captured by the environment and didn't feel outplaced. It was a different experience than I had ever had at church and this church was in a movie theater.

As my two friends and I sat down in the theater seating, we were shocked when the music began. Well, at least I was. The music was nothing like I had ever heard before. It was rock and roll, but with Christian lyrics. The music helped the attendees come alive while they danced in front of their seats. I only knew of a choir singing hymns in church, not a full rock band. The music had my blood pumping and I began singing along with the crowd, "Our God is greater, our God is stronger, God you are higher than any other." The band members were around our age and transformed my thinking of what church music should be like. In fact, that morning was when I fell in love with Christian Rock music. Now it's the only music I like to listen to.

The music ended and I sat down awaiting the Pastor to begin preaching. I was praying he would be good, but if he wasn't I decided to still come back to see the happy people and listen to the music. As the Pastor began preaching, I noticed how different he was from other Pastor's I had studied under. He was young, funny, relatable, and spoke about relevant issues. He showed genuine compassion for others and connected with me as well as the others in the audience. You could feel his love for God by his radiating warmth in his words and Biblical message. That morning changed my life forever.

I fell back into true love with God. In the past, I was lukewarm in my relationship with Him, but this time, a true, deep, unconditional love for my Father arose. God hooked me for real this time and did it through this up-and-coming church. This place would become my first Church home and the joyful people would become my Brothers and Sisters.

As I returned over the next few weeks, I began feeling something I hadn't felt since I was 14 years old. I felt peace, love, and stillness within my entire being. I felt God's presence. I soaked up everything the Pastor was preaching and immediately joined a community group with my two girlfriends. One of my friends was there for the guys, but my other friend and I were there for the Word. We were getting plugged in with good people and evolving into joyful people ourselves. Our weekly routine changed from Happy Hour Friday's to Christian Fellowship Sunday's, which eventually led to every day fellowship for me. I was becoming one of those people with a big smile, sparkling eyes, and a positive attitude.

After two years of attending, I decided to be baptized. Even though I was baptized when I was 14, I had an on-and-off relationship with God. The church helped me see who I really was and who He was. As I stood in line awaiting the baptism I began to cry. As I knelt down in the water the Pastor prayed over me as he immersed me. As the water washed over me, it was a cleansing feeling. A new beginning. I was God's as I resurfaced from the water. I had a clean slate and my past terrible mistakes had been washed away. The baptism was a new opportunity for me to portray what was in my heart for the whole world to see. From that moment, it was my desire that when people see me they see Him. I would be His bright light in this dark world.

I joined community groups and eventually started leading a few of my own. One group was co-led in my home for 8-weeks with one of my friends whom I started going to the church with. In this group, we laughed, cried, celebrated, prayed, sang, rejoiced, and connected on a deeper level. It became a profound experience with ten special ladies. My life was becoming something I had never dreamed of. It was becoming meaningful with a purpose.

Another community group that changed my life was when I started a fitness group called "**Biggest Winner**." I created it based on the show 'Biggest Loser' but changed the word 'Loser' to 'Winner' because everyone is a winner. *I don't know anyone that likes being called a loser.*

I led this group for two years. During that timeframe, I witnessed real triumph in the group's weight loss. I was their very own "Jillian" and drilled them with aerobic and anaerobic workouts. I also noticed something in each Winner that became instrumental in them gaining weight. A Winner struggling with finances was eating to escape their issue. A Winner struggling with mental abuse with their partner had used food to cope. A Winner who was emotionally scarred from years of anorexia allowed the emotional hardship to anchor her into food struggles. A Winner didn't know how to cook and was short on time because of her work constraints and was eating fast food for every meal. To help circumvent this problem, I brought in a nutritionist to teach each Winner how to cook large quantities of healthy food on Sunday's for the entire week.

Most of the Winners were dealing with hardships, which prohibited them from reaching success. I began acting more as a sounding board instead of a fitness trainer. It was then that I knew these Winners were off balance and were being weighed down emotionally as much as they were physically. They would need to come to terms with their real issues before they could treat their diet symptoms. The heaviness of the issues weighed my heart down and I just wanted to pray for them and their struggles, which prompted me to lead a prayer group.

My friend and I named our prayer group "Higher Ground" because we met at a local coffee shop. For eight weeks it was just us two because no one else joined. We were okay with it because my friend and I became accountability partners. We prayed with each other, shared our hearts, and got really close. God knew what He was doing when He brought us together. He knew we each needed a real friend and someone to hold the other accountable. There's nothing better than having someone like that in your life. An accountability partner makes you a better person, a stronger Christ follower, and a person being held to a higher standard in life.

The Alexandria church transformed me into a real walking and talking Believer. For the first time in my entire life I was deeply rooted in my faith. The church, friends, fellowship, community groups, sermons, devotions, and the living Word had me deeply planted in good soil for the first time in my adult life. I was flourishing and finally becoming who He always wanted me to be. I was no longer the superficial Christian. I was a true Christian that developed a relationship with God and felt pure joy. That's what I want for you…a real relationship with God.

Moral of the Story – One simple decision to go to church at a movie theater changed the course of my life forever. I grew into the person I was meant to be, found my identity and calling, helped people become their very best, made real life-giving friends, had an accountability partner to help me stay on the right track, and truly fell in love with God.

Going to a movie theater church was scary and it was complete change from what I knew. I learned that change was not bad. Sometimes it catapults us into an entirely different world and our life becomes more than we ever dreamed of. Sometimes it takes us to something else completely. No matter what, we must embrace the change. We are meant to evolve, try something new, and create a life worth remembering.

We should take a chance in life, have no regrets, and embrace whatever comes our way. I became the Biggest

Winner and got on Higher Ground because of a church change. Now imagine how your life could be with a change you need to make. Don't put off what needs to be done.

Change helped me understand that religion and a relationship with God are two totally different things. Religion won't save you, but a relationship with God will. You will radically change into a different person when you experience this fundamental change of Truth. My life changed for the better when I connected the knowledge in my head to the Truth in my heart. I pray you understand it one day.

I offer this Chapter as hope for you to get plugged in and experience what life can become when you have true joy. I desire for you to become a smiling, happy face all of the time. I want you to have those sparkling eyes.

Please find a church you connect with and get plugged in with. If that is too much for you, at least, get a Bible and begin reading it. If you need help finding a church or if you need a Bible, contact me and I will help.

Change is good.

Look up.

God loves you.

Amen.

Chapter 23 – Life Coach

Biggest Winner helped me understand how people choose to treat their symptoms instead of dealing with their real issues. This was my ah-ha realization! I began helping people understand the root cause of their problems had to be dealt with first or their weight issue would always be something they struggle with. Taking more stock in them as people rather than just their physical challenges proved to be their overall breakthrough and success.

Then one day a pastor told me I needed to become a Life Coach. I looked at him with a deer-in-the-headlights look and asked, "**What's a Life Coach**?" He answered with how I had already been acting as one. I was getting real with the Winners, asking relevant questions, and helping them seek solutions to their problems. These interactions got them back on track with their lives. This was in essence life coaching. The light bulb went off and my life purpose was discovered. I would become a Life Coach. I discovered it was my real passion and something very natural to me. Helping others uncover reasons why they were stuck, walking alongside them in their weakest hours, and working with them to get them to where they wanted to go. That's a Life Coach.

I began researching certification programs. Many programs had weekend certification classes and I knew I didn't want to spend a weekend learning a trade that I would be doing for a lifetime. So I continued to look. I researched programs that were not too costly, but still had relevance. I narrowed down my search to two different schools and set up interviews with both. After interviewing the founder of the first school I didn't even call the second school because I knew I had found what I wanted. I reserved a space and started the life coach program one month later.

The Life Coach program was not your typical school course. It required a weekly class session lasting two hours, reading a book along with completing mandatory assignments, developing marketing material, practicing coaching with two separate buddy sessions for a total of four sessions each, meeting with a Master Coach for four sessions, and coaching two clients four times each while being recorded. The program lasted for five months and I completed all of my assignments on the day class ended. The teacher said I was the only student to ever graduate with Honors. It was amazing to finally arrive at the destination and with honors. I was officially a Certified Life Coach.

A few weeks before graduation, I had to work with a buddy from my class to determine what our next steps would be. We began working on our coaching names for our respective companies. My buddy already had her vision and business name identified, but I didn't. We brainstormed many different names for me. Every name I liked, my buddy found a website that already existed. I needed a website that was available with a name I wanted. I was praying to God daily asking for a name, but nothing was coming to mind. Then one day everything fell into place. When I tell people what happened in finding the name, I don't think they believe me. It's the truth though.

It happened in Freedom 301 class in the Alexandria church. I was sitting there next to my friend, listening to worship music, praying hard to God about having a name for the business, and dedicating to Him whatever it would become. I was lost in the music and in prayer. My mind went quiet and these words were spoken to me "You Matter." I immediately opened my eyes and looked at my friend and said, "You Matter" and she *shushed* me.

The words came from God. I would have never been able to come up with something like that on my own. It came from Him. That night I looked for a website with You Matter Life Coach and it was available. I talked to my buddy the next day and ordered four website URL's with that name. I officially became You Matter Life Coach, LLC. I even own the Trademark.

I think the name hit me so hard because it spoke to my soul. My entire life I felt like I didn't matter. I felt like a person in a sea of people. I wasn't anything special, just someone passing through life. I was never meant to be anything, but ended up making something of myself. I only had people speaking death into me for so long, but now life was being spoken into me. It gave me a new beginning. I did matter. I mattered to myself, I mattered to God, and I mattered to others.

I believed there was a good chance that other people didn't feel like they mattered either. As a result, God and I would be on a mission together making people feel hopeful and no longer hopeless. God would use me to speak to other people and help them lose the victim mentality and become victorious. You Matter Life Coach would be a campaign to help people see the light, become the light, and spread their light to others. They would smile, shine, and soar into who they were destined to be. They would no longer settle for the valley, but look to the mountain and surpass its highest point. You Matter are two small words with a prolific meaning.

This is why I fell in love with becoming a Life Coach. Every single one of us can bloom and flourish. We may go through a whole lot of dirt to get there, but that's life. Life isn't all a bed of roses. There's many storms that take hold of us, but there is also much sunshine in the world. Helping people reach that sunshine is all I desire. Helping people believe in themselves is my core DNA.

Moral of the Story – Understanding how one issue leads to another was the eye opener that led me to become a Life Coach. This was a breakthrough. People struggling with finances, mental abuse, relationship issues, and family drama are off balance because they are focused on the issue itself more than its cause. As a result, they try to take their mind off of the issue by turning to food or other things to escape the pain, which leads to an entirely different set of problems. They are trying to fill the void, not fix it.

Most people don't know what a Life Coach is. They often have a deer-in-the-headlights look like I had. A Life Coach helps you get to where you want to go in any area of your life. Life Coaches are hired for many reasons. You've tried doing it on your own and it hasn't worked. You are overwhelmed by things that need to be done and don't have the energy to do it. You need to stop wasting time on meaningless details, but don't know how to create time management skills. You want more success at work and in your relationships, but don't know how to begin. You want to move up and perform better in your career. You want to lose weight, get fit, and feel better about your body. You need to get organized, become self-aware, learn how to balance a checkbook, finish or start a big project, or you need a plan and need help sticking to it. You've tried doing these things on your own - AND IT HASN'T WORKED!

A Life Coach has one purpose. To help you live a healthy and fulfilling life. You will thrive and no longer just survive with the assistance of a life coach. You will soar, not settle. You will live again and feel like you matter.

A Life Coach helps people get unstuck, assists them in making decisions, works with them to discover their purpose, holds them accountable, encourages them, actively listens to them while they walk through the issue at hand, asks thought provoking questions, and walks the journey with them, not for them.

When God gave me the name "You Matter," He did it because every person does matter! We need to know it and then live life like we believe it!

24 – Major Debacle

Many times in my military career I've been hurt, but the Major debacle was the most painful experience I've ever encountered while wearing the uniform. None of what occurred made sense, but I must live with it even though I will never understand it or truly get over it.

I was accepted into a new position in October, which had the potential of allowing me to be promoted early to the rank of Major. However, I was asked to continue working in my current Joint Staff position through the Christmas season because the Protocol Chief position was newly filled and my experience was greatly needed. I was assured that my new organization would be allowed to submit my Promotion Recommendation Form (PRF) if I stayed. It was worked out between the two organizations and all parties were on board with the arrangements. An award was even presented to me for the hard work and long hours I endured for staying with the Joint Staff up through the end of the year. I signed into my new organization in the beginning of January and life was good.

Immediately after signing into my new organization my new boss submitted my PRF as was agreed, but it was denied by the promotion board. The promotion board stated my PRF would not be accepted for promotion consideration because it was submitted late. We were all confused! In an attempt to rectify the problem, my boss began making phone calls to those involved with the decision and explained how I had been working for the Chairman and was granted permission to have my PRF submitted late. After talking with a personnel technician, my PRF was finally accepted. This meant I would meet the board. Life was good.

The day of the promotion board I was contacted along with my boss and informed that I would not be meeting the board. We were confused and upset again, but given hope because we were told I would meet a follow-on Subsequent Special Board (SSB). We were informed that due to the PRF being received late they didn't have enough time to pull my records. (What didn't make sense was how the Active Duty side was granted permission to submit a PRF up until the day prior to the board meeting.)

On the first day of the SSB, my organization was 'again' notified that I would not meet that board. This was due to me not being placed into a promotion vacancy billet at least 45 days before the initial board convened. My organization explained the extenuating circumstances and that I indeed had been selected for the position 60 days before the board met.

Even though they were presented with all of the appropriate details, the promotion board division wouldn't budge and I was told to appeal to the Board of Corrections for Military Records (BCMR). This was upsetting because a BCMR takes almost a year to process a request and I had already lost valuable time. I could have started the process almost 90 days earlier, but now was having to start the process, which caused me additional stress.

The BCMR was submitted along with letters explaining the unusual circumstances. To accompany the appeal, I had a signed letter from a Senior Executive Service (SES) (three-star general equivalent) and a letter from the Chairman's staff. The SES and Chairman's staff both requested I be allowed to meet a position vacancy promotion board because I had put my needs second and the Air Force's needs first; service before self.

As a result of the painful situation, both organizations requested to remain up-to-date on the status of my BCMR package in an effort to help me keep my spirits up. After almost a grueling year of waiting, the BCMR didn't acknowledge the letters or the appeal. I was denied the request to have my records be considered for early promotion because the PRF was submitted late and my inprocessing date was not within the 45-days even though it was backdated the 60-days I was selected/hired for the position.

Both organizations were disappointed with the system as was I. My new organization said they would support me by writing a promotion-proof PRF, which they did. Then I PCS'd (Permanent Change of Duty Station) to the exact location where the misinformation regarding promotion regulations occurred. I was slated to work in the promotion board building. I looked up to Heaven and said, "God, you have got to be kidding me."

After feeling like I had walked the Bataan Death March, the next year's promotion board met and I actually got to meet the board this time. I asked my boss back at the Pentagon if they would consider promoting me as soon as the results were released because I was eligible. My boss said, "No problem." He said, "We tried promoting you last year so this year shouldn't be an issue." When the results were released I received word that I was selected to be promoted to the rank of Major. It was a huge and humbling honor.

The big boss called me from the Pentagon and congratulated me and I asked him if he would consider promoting me early. To my amazement, he said I shouldn't have asked. He said he had to wait 7-years to pin on; therefore, so should I. I was confused and hurt because I could have been promoted the year before and now the big boss was telling me to wait. Originally, he said I was deserving of the early promotion and already acting as a Field Grade Officer, but now felt I needed to wait my turn just because he did. My boss was stuck and felt horrible about the situation regarding our big boss' stance.

As a result, my boss was leaving the organization because of the big boss so I decided to also start looking for a new job. We had enough of the horrible leadership and both wanted to go someplace where we would be celebrated for our strong work ethic and positive attitude. Another reason I decided to look for a new job was because of the timing issue with my promotion pin-on date. Promotion cycles are based on fiscal year, not calendar year. This means if one does not get promoted before the end of September then they would be pushed into the next year for promotion eligibility. Basically, this meant if I did not get promoted before the end of September, I would have to wait an additional year before being considered for promotion to Lieutenant Colonel. My December pin-on date would be too late and result in meeting the 2020 board instead of the 2019 board.

Note: If I had met the first board in which the misinformation debacle occurred, I would have met the position vacancy Lieutenant Colonel board in 2018 versus 2019. Sorry, I digress. Back to the current debacle.

To avoid this dilemma, I began looking for positions so I wouldn't have to return to the Jekyll and Hyde leadership I was experiencing at the Pentagon and possibly get promoted early. Within a month of searching for a new job, I was hired. Goodbye poor leadership. Hello possibility.

I spoke to my new boss and asked if he would consider me for an early position vacancy promotion so I could meet the critical September deadline. After a review of my records and a phone interview, he signed the letter requesting I be promoted early and I was officially promoted mid-August. I had a small ceremony, which included getting new Identification Cards (ID) cards for the family and me. I had a huge smile and life was good. I made it before the September deadline!

After a week of wearing the rank of Major, my boss received an email from the promotion board division stating the letter he signed for my promotion didn't qualify because it had to be an endorsement from an officer of Colonel rank or higher. My boss contacted the Colonel in our chain of command and afterwards told me everything was good to go. He told me the letter would be signed and sent in.

Randomly a few days later, I was contacted by my old boss that I worked for in the promotion building. He asked if I had "ordered" the administration clerks to illegally create my Promotion Order knowing the signed letter was incorrect. I strongly denied the accusation and was despondent to the fact that anyone would make such a claim. It wasn't true and I was being lied about because someone was trying to cover their mistake. Having to counter the false claim, I even explained how everyone was smiling and crying tears of joy with me for being promoted.

What an injustice I was dealing with. Everyone knew my character and knew I wouldn't make such a compromise to get promoted. I wasn't going to allow my good name to be defamed so I immediately requested an investigation. After being questioned as part of the investigation, my side of the story was corroborated. I don't even think the officer who made the false accusation about me got into trouble for the slander. This officer was also the same person that started my promotion order revocation. I quickly learned there will be envious people who try to bring others down, which is why we must always stay morally, legally, and ethically upright.

Back to the endorsement, after two weeks of waiting for my new Colonel to sign the letter for my early promotion, the Commander at the promotions division building said they couldn't wait any longer. The promotion division would officially revoke my promotion if the Colonel didn't sign by the end of the week. I called my Colonel to notify him of this issue and was informed the decision to promote me early was now going to our two-star general for approval. This was because early promotions were not allowed in our organization.

The end of the week came and there was still no word from our two star General with respect to my promotion. Tragically and without delay, the Air Force demoted me back to the rank of Captain. It was the most humiliating thing I had ever experienced. My family and I were utterly shocked and dismayed. I yelled, cursed, and cried out to God for comfort. I didn't understand!

Immediately after being demoted, I kept my wits about me and requested a decision on my early promotion before the end of September because there was still time. The deadline was getting close and I still had no answer. A week before the end of September deadline, I called our Colonel and requested the status of my package. The staff informed me it was sent back down the chain and never even sent to the General's inbox for approval or denial. Bewildered, I reached out to my mentor, another Brigadier General, who called the two-star General asking the two-star to take care of me because I was worth it. My mentor received no response. Overwhelmed by the total disregard for my welfare and suitable request, I had enough!

I contacted the Chief of Staff of the Air Force through outside channels. In turn, a three-star general reached out to my chain of command requesting promotion consideration. The two star General in my chain directed his staff to review my package and determine if I was worthy of an early promotion. The next day I was contacted by my leadership and informed the General would not consider me for the early promotion. My request to pin-on 80-days earlier than my mandatory pin-on date was not warranted because I didn't have enough acquisition experience.

I found this to be ironic because I was vectored as a High Potential Officer (HPO), placed on the Key Personnel List (KPL), and ranked in the top tier of my career field for the entire Air Force Reserve in the Acquisitions career field, which meant I was more than qualified. If the AF Reserve thought I was top-notch in the acquisitions career field than why didn't my active duty counterpart think that as well? If my new boss in my new organization and my old boss in my previous organization were willing to promote me than why wouldn't leadership in both organizations back them up?

The three star general contacted me via email and explained that sometimes active duty organizations do not understand the Reserve promotion process. It no longer mattered. I didn't care anymore. I would remain a "Captain" for another 80 days. I would meet the mandatory Lieutenant Colonel Promotion board in 2020 instead of 2019.

It pains me to this day. It hurts my heart. Both situations taught me about poor leadership. Why make someone wait who is more than deserving. It's like dangling a carrot in front of a horse when another carrot is already in the horse's mouth. I know the suicide rate in the military has gone up dramatically and I can only assume in my humble opinion it's because of the majority of managers, not leaders, we have in place. In both situations, I was told something, but their words didn't match their actions. Most managers talk a good game, but very few leaders actually follow through.

Managers are everywhere, <u>Leaders are rare.</u>

I vow to never be a poor leader who doesn't take care of deserving Airmen. *Proverbs 3:27.*

Moral of the Story – Sometimes we can pray, do our best, beg, cry, scream, and fight, but the answer is no. Or better yet, we could get a 'yes' and then it is immediately taken away. Life sucks in those instances. We may never understand why things happen the way they do, but we must accept them. It's okay to be hurt, angry, and sad and it's okay to cry. What's not okay is to stay in the pity party, remain angry, or become depressed for the rest of our lives.

Things will happen that we don't agree with. Things will happen when people say they will do something, but when the time comes they don't. It's during those times that we find out who we really are by how we respond and who we don't want to become.

Are we strong enough to stand back up after we've plummeted into despair? Are we able to forgive the ones that wronged us? Are we able to persevere and maintain our core values? Are we able to continue being the example for others even when we are dying inside? Moments of true despair define our character.

I will never understand those two years of hardship. I experienced pain to my deepest core, but in those two years I carried on. I made sure to uphold my character so I could be proud of the person I saw in the mirror. I chose to speak kindness to people that wronged me. I chose to pray for the ones that hurt me. I realized rank doesn't make a person, character does.

Character is one without the title. Character stands up for what is right, treats every person the same, and doesn't hold something over someone else's head. Character is something to be engrained. People either have character or they don't. It isn't a haphazard trait.

A message for leaders, help others who deserve it. Never withhold kindness and doing what is right because you were wronged. An eye for an eye is not just. Be better than how you were wronged.

A message for you, fight for what you believe in. Even if you lose, like I did, you can at least know you tried, which is more than most can say.

Friend, hardship will happen, be prepared. Sometimes you have to live with it for the rest of your life, but you will be stronger because of it. Promise to never hold your hardship, outcome, or hurt against someone else. Be the better person.

25 – Fear

I thought I'd end the book with one of my biggest driving forces and obstacles in life…fear. Fear sometimes holds me captive in life and has held me back (at times) as far back as I can remember. During those times, I try to punch fear in the face whenever it raises its ugly head during my insecure moments.

What is fear? Fear is an unpleasant emotion caused by the belief that someone or something is dangerous, likely to cause pain or is a threat. Fear can destroy us, but it can also protect us. Fear can block us from greatness, but also motivate us to achieve greatness. Fear causes us to stay quiet when we should speak up. Fear causes us to seek the easy decision rather than seeking the right one. Fear can keep us down in the valley instead of standing on the mountaintop, stop us from pursuing our life purpose, keep us in toxic and abusive relationships, make us think negatively about ourselves, and cause undeserving harm in our lives. In contrast, fear can cause the hairs on our neck to stand up when we're in danger, provide intuition that something isn't right, and protect us from harm. Fear can be good or bad, but either way having a good balance of fear is a must.

As a child, I was afraid of being left alone. When my mother left for work, I was left alone or left with my sister and she was mean most of the time. I had no choice in the matter and had to learn how to be comfortable with being by myself. After a while, I preferred being alone because everything was okay in my world. I didn't have anyone I was forced to argue with, discuss my routine, decide about dinner, or be obligated to converse with. It was always a happy place for me being alone. I eventually overcame my fear of being alone and an entire new world opened up as a result. Fear didn't stop me from living, it actually helped me live in peace.

I'm afraid of big dogs. I've been afraid of big dogs ever since my cousin was bit in the face when I was five-years old. Dogs are unstable to me because of the uncertainty of how they'll react. I've had a few small dogs in my life to help conquer my fear, but I am still very much afraid. I've yet to punch that fear completely in the face, but I'm trying to overcome it.

There are a few other fears I've yet to overcome and still hold me back from time to time. It's those insecure moments that hold me back from becoming my very best. For instance, I'm afraid to fail. Coming from where I came from I changed what I wanted for my future, which is why I work hard and am hard on myself when I make mistakes. I fear being poor or hungry again. Fear of those two things push me to knowing where my next meal would come from and not having to worry if it would come at all. Fear pushed me to work hard at my job so I could have money and never have to live on welfare and food stamps again.

Fear of failure helped me to get where I am. I've worked harder than anyone I know. When my friends were going to the clubs, I was doing homework. Instead of buying fine clothes, I shopped at lower end stores. I saved more money than I spent. I practiced routines for hours after everyone else went home. I desired to do everything to the best of my ability, not because I am a perfectionist, but because I didn't want to ever go back to where I came from. I was afraid to fail. I wanted to succeed so I pushed myself hard in everything I did and now, as a result, excellence is all I know. When I do something, I do it with all that I have, with all that I am. The task at hand deserves the best and I want to give my best. I think the fear of not doing my best has overshadowed my fear of failure because doing my best makes me happy.

I fear not being good enough, smart enough, or capable enough. This fear has held me back. When I was taking a class with an actual rocket scientist, several doctors, engineers, and a software programmer, I didn't speak for the first few weeks because I felt I wasn't smart enough or on their level. This wreaked havoc in my mind. I doubted my ability and myself. I did it again in a class with a few general officers. I even put myself down to my instructor saying, "I'm not that smart so I study really hard to compensate." It took time for me to realize I am smart and capable. I should never put myself down or make excuses for myself. I worked hard to get in the class and deserved to be there, and by the end of class I was the standout. I am my own person. I have my own experiences to offer just like other people. All of us are different and we can learn from everyone. I won't be afraid by thinking I'm not good enough or smart enough because the bottom line is…**I'm enough**.

A fear that strangles me sometimes is not having people like me. I fear rejection. As a result I do things I don't necessarily want to do. I say "yes" when I want to say "no." I commit to things that I didn't want to do and ended up regretting it rather enjoying the commitment. I don't say what's on my mind because I don't want to hurt anyone's feelings. I overanalyze when a friend doesn't text me back, forgets my birthday and doesn't send a card, or when I'm not included in an activity. I rarely confront someone on an issue unless I feel strongly about it. I am the peacemaker, not a troublemaker. I am getting better at dealing with this fear. Life is too short to not be real, honest, and upfront.

There's a way to be kind and constructive while being true to oneself. I've realized that not everyone will like me, and I'm okay with it. The right people will like me for who I am. With so much going on in today's society, we must be real and honest with others and ourselves. Let's take off the masks and say how we feel, think, want, and need in a way for people to understand and not take offense. Those that matter don't mind and those that mind don't matter.

We can't spend our lives people-pleasing or doing things we don't want to do for the sake of others. We need to compromise with others to prevent a dictatorship, but we don't need to be a doormat either. <u>Bottom line</u> - We need to be true to others while staying true to who we are.

I am working hard to overcome the small voice that pops in my head and tells me I'm not good enough. During those times is when I take a breath and recollect my thoughts. That's when I decide to punch fear in the face. Being afraid is not going to limit my life or stop me from truly living my purpose. Sure, I'm afraid at times, but I put on my big girl pants and move forward because that's my only option. The old phrase, "ready, set, go" sometimes misleads people and holds them back. One is never truly ready. One is never really set. One is never ready to just go.

When you plan, think, and prepare for too long, it gives fear a chance to creep in and hold you back. I've decided not to hold back. I will prep for the task, pray for everything, talk with my trusted advisors to get mentally prepared for the struggle, and then I'll go. Fear will not hold me back. Life is too short. It passes by too quickly for us to worry about the what if's. No one has time for the life preventing fear that continually lurks.

Fear has also saved my life. The basic instinct that pushes us to survive, known as a survival instinct is a subconscious thought process fueled by several factors. Its main component, believe it or not, is fear. It stopped me from going down a dark alley, from opening a door to a stranger, and reminded me to lock my car door while leaving a location when someone tried to open it. It possibly saved my life in Italy when my family and I were sitting in a small café and some kids kept coming up to us. My alert went up, thus adverting the situation because my Situational Awareness (SA) senses kicked in. A good amount of fear is good to have because it keeps you aware.

Channeling which fear to live with will be a blessing to living a healthy life. Say no to the bad and yes to the good.

Moral of the Story – There is healthy fear and unhealthy fear. Healthy fear can direct you to make wise decisions in a difficult situation, like the fear of breaking the law or the fear of perishing in a car crash because you didn't wear your seatbelt. Unhealthy fear may cause you to make stupid choices, like the fear of upsetting your friends because of the influence of peer pressure or staying in a job you hate because you don't think you can make it doing what you love. Understanding fear is beneficial as it keeps you in a state of balanced situational awareness, which protects you.

Don't let bad FEAR hold you back....it is False Evidence Appearing Real. Bad fear needs to be dealt with head-on so you don't lose out in life.

Let's make a vow together to punch bad fear in the face when it arises and attempts to hold us back in life's most opportune moments. *Ain't nobody got time for false fear*!

Closing – Not done yet

In the last two+ decades of my life, I've grown more than I had ever dreamed I was capable of. I took all of the stumbling blocks from my childhood and turned them into the building blocks for my future. I worked hard to remove the damaged emotional mentality of my past and relabeled myself as a mosaic masterpiece. I stopped playing the victim role and began proclaiming victory. I finally understood the good, bad, and ugly I experienced shaped me into the person I am today.

I honestly wouldn't say I am fully over all I have been through in my early years, but I have accepted it. I have forgiven the naysayers, abusive family members, and hurtful people that spoke death into my life. Though I have forgiven them, I don't have relationships with them. I chose not to because I get hurt when I allow these types of people in my life. They bring me down and are a detriment to my emotional health. In truth, I've grown, but they haven't so I limit my exposure. The old saying, "You are who you associate with" is very true. You gradually begin to mirror their mannerisms, personality, and attitude for the bad and the good….and I don't know about you, but I want great!

This isn't to say I believe I am perfect in any way. I mess up a lot. I don't think before I speak. I tend to shy away from people when I feel I have nothing in common with them. I have a critical nature and must mentally focus in order to not speak my thoughts. I don't mean to mess up, but I'm human. My flesh overtakes my brain and emotions. It bothers me when it happens and then I tend to harp on it for days, if not months. I'm hard on myself.

Here are some things I've harped on. When my daughter accidentally messed up, I yelled at her horribly. I can be naggy to my husband. I've cursed out loud when I was mad. I want to tell people they suck sometimes. I suck sometimes. One time while working an event at the Chairman of the Joint Chiefs of Staff's house, a man walked up to my table. I assumed he was looking at the nametags and I asked him if I could help him. He looked at me with a funny look and chuckled saying, "Hi, this is my house. I don't need a nametag and proceeded to introduce himself to me." It was the actual Chairman. Everyone was laughing at my expense and I turned red like a tomato. I am a work in progress…I mess up. I still think about those mistakes to this day.

I want to do and be better, learn from my mistakes, ask for forgiveness, and try to never let the same mistake happen twice. However, I tend to be a repeat offender with some things. Plus, if I do things I know aren't right, but do them anyway, it's no longer a mistake, it's a choice. Choices matter. I aim for perfection, but always fall short. I'm human! My heart gets the best of me at times.

Overall, as I reflect on who I was and who I am, I feel that I have grown into a respectable person. My growth will not stop though. I desire to make less mistakes, interact with life-changing people, help others become their very best, give back more, learn something new every single day, learn from different walks of life and diversity, become courageous enough to tell others my true thoughts and feelings, appreciate the gift each day brings, have others see Jesus in me, fulfill my life purpose and destiny, truly overcome the pain I endured and only use it as a compass for helping others, be more vulnerable, eat really well, laugh out loud, read at least 50 books a year, floss daily, be a better leader, change lives and not just solve problems, look into a mirror and learn to love my imperfections by embracing them, be able to call a person out in love for being selfish and not feel bad about it, teach people how their words have significant power and can really hurt someone, and be able to write more. Random thoughts I know, but so many things on my mind for growing into the person I was born to be.

My ultimate goal is to be a life-changer. I want us all to soar in life, not settle. I want us all to thrive, not just survive each day. I want to shine bright so that people in the dark may see. I want to be the hope for others because if I can make it, they can too. I want to build a forest of hope, not just plant a tree. I want to be an example of how hard work pays off. I want people to know they can accomplish their dreams and exceed all of their expectations if they just have faith, remove themselves from the people tearing them down, have courage to step out and speak up, and live out their dreams. Anything is possible in life, but we must be willing to do our part. Nothing is handed to us without the obligation to do something with it. Don't take the easy route because it won't mean as much in the end. Take the route you will be proud to accomplish because you earned it. Believe in yourself even if others don't.

Greatness can come out of a great mess and that's what my life used to be. I want to be great because I am called to greatness and so are you. I want to grow and I also want you to grow because life isn't meant to be lived average. I want to continue working on my life and shortcomings. I don't want my life to pass by and live with regrets and not be able to smile. I want to smile. I want to make the most of my life. We all are born and we all will die, but only some of us make the most out of the middle portion, which is our life. I want our lives to be all they can be, which is where our ability to thrive with greatness plays a role. I want all of this for you too.

My life is far from over and so is yours, God willing. So I ask you, "What's next? What needs to be changed, eliminated, added, created, or settled? What makes up your greatness? What is your plan to achieve it? What makes you happy, sad, motivated, and deflated? What is your story?"

It doesn't matter how your life started, it only matters how it will end. What will your legacy be like when you take your last breath? Were you known to be honorable or a hot mess? How will the world know you were even here? What will your obituary say? Did you help people more than yourself? Are you living a life you're proud of? Did you remove the person or problem anchoring you down or did you live with it, which ultimately blocked you from becoming all you could have been?

I'm not done yet and, dear friend, neither are you! The best is yet to come! **Anything is possible, just believe!**

And remember...
You must try, always try.
You must never give up.
You must believe in yourself.
You must be bold and courageous.
You must never doubt yourself if you know what you hold to be true.
You must get rid of naysayers, gossip-mongers, energy vampires, haters, doubters, and complainers in your life.
You must never settle for average when you can have great.
You must learn to trust people...within reason.
You must love yourself and love your enemies.
You must stop and smell the roses.

You must smile through the pain….even if you have to fake it till you make it.
You must accept getting mad and then learn to get over it.
You must do things right, but more importantly, you must do the right thing.
You must praise in public, punish in private.
You must accept taking credit sometimes, but never take credit from someone else.
You must appreciate life…it goes by fast!
You must travel and explore…life isn't meant to be Groundhog Day.
You must dream…and do your part in making it come true.
You must be a kind person even when others aren't.
You must not waste time with people or things that leave you empty.
You must take that chance even if you're afraid.
You must floss daily.
You must exercise even if you don't want to because you only have one body to live in and it's asking you to care of it.
You must be an example of what honor and integrity look like.
You must forgive those who have wronged you.
You must constantly educate yourself so you can grow.
You must earn your life so you can appreciate it more.

You must know 'You Matter' in this world because there is only one of you…believe it wholeheartedly!

~ **Smile, Shine, Soar** ~

Love,
Coach Shannon

www.ingramcontent.com/pod-product-compliance
Lightning Source LLC
LaVergne TN
LVHW051544070426
835507LV00021B/2392